Patterns of Language

INDIANA UNIVERSITY STUDIES
IN THE
HISTORY AND THEORY OF LINGUISTICS

Patterns of Language

Papers in General, Descriptive and Applied Linguistics

Angus McIntosh
Forbes Professor of English Language
University of Edinburgh

M. A. K. Halliday
Professor of General Linguistics
University of London

 Indiana University Press
Bloomington and London

Preface

In A.D. 535 the Chinese linguist Shen Yüeh wrote an address to the imperial throne putting forward his theory that Chinese was a tone language. Each syllable, he said, consisted of three elements: an initial (consonant), a final (vowel or vowel plus consonant) and one out of four possible tones, an inherent pitch movement which was as much part of its essential structure as were the vowels and consonants themselves. He illustrated this with a short sentence, containing four monosyllabic words, one of each tone, and meaning 'The Son of Heaven is holy and wise'.

If Shen Yüeh had been propounding such an important contribution to linguistics today, he might have offered it in the form of a paper to a scientific society or journal, or perhaps in a letter to *Nature*. Alternatively he might have presented his findings to a seminar and then distributed a note in mimeographed form to his colleagues and any others who came to hear about it. They would then have referred to it in their own footnotes, and before long the facts, or some of them, would have come to be generally known, by which time the original paper would probably have become unobtainable.

Meanwhile students of linguistics, teachers of languages and members of the general public interested in the subject, would have been demanding, very reasonably, some access to the new developments. And Shen Yüeh would have pointed out, equally reasonably, that he was too busy attending committees, writing letters, teaching and running a department to have time to write up his findings for general publication.

The present volume does not contain any momentous discoveries or contributions comparable to the work of Shen Yüeh. It contains eleven

short essays, some already published in journals, the rest being previously unpublished papers which the authors have at one time or another
during the past few years prepared for lectures or seminars and then
consigned to a drawer in the hope of one day taking them a stage further.
On this occasion, in response to pressure from their publishers, they
have refurbished them for inclusion in this volume.

We hope that these hitherto unpublished papers, together with those
others which are here reprinted (with supplementary notes and references) from various journals, will usefully contribute to the somewhat
limited stock of serious but not too highly technical discussions of
language at present readily available. We have in mind the possible
interests of a variety of people who are concerned to study language and
to gain insight into its functioning. It is our hope that the book may have
some value not only for students of linguistics but also for language
teachers, for scholars working on literature and in other fields of study
related to linguistics, and for interested laymen.

The theme which links these essays is that of pattern, and we try to
illustrate how in one way or another this runs through all the complexity and variety of human speech and writing.

A.M.
M.A.K.H.

Contents

Acknowledgments

We are grateful to the following for permission to reproduce copyright material:

Oxford University Press for material from *Gerard Manley Hopkins— A Critical Essay Towards the Understanding of his Poetry* by Father W. A. M. Peters, and Mr. M. B. Yeats, Macmillan & Co. Ltd and The Macmillan Company of New York for 'Leda and the Swan' by W. B. Yeats from *Collected Poems of W. B. Yeats*, Copyright 1928 by The Macmillan Company, renewed 1956 by Georgie Yeats.

Contributions by Angus McIntosh

PAPER TWO
'Linguistics and English studies' was delivered as a lecture to the Cambridge Linguistic Society on the occasion of its inaugural meeting on 7 May 1959.

PAPER FOUR
'"As You Like It": a grammatical clue to character' appeared in *A Review of English Literature* 4 (ii), April 1963, pp. 68–81.

PAPER FIVE
'Some thoughts on style' was delivered as a lecture at University College London on 16 February 1962.

PAPER SIX
'"Graphology" and meaning' was delivered as a lecture to the St. Andrews Linguistic Society in January 1961 and subsequently appeared in *Archivum Linguisticum* 13 (ii), 1961, pp. 107–120.

PAPER NINE
'A four-letter word in "Lady Chatterley's Lover"' was written in first draft in 1960 and is presented here for the first time.

PAPER ELEVEN
'Patterns and ranges' appeared in *Language* 37 (iii), July–September 1961, pp. 325–337.

Angus McIntosh is Forbes Professor of English Language in the University of Edinburgh.

Contributions by M. A. K. Halliday

PAPER ONE
'General linguistics and its application to language teaching' was first delivered as a series of four lectures to the Summer Vacation Course for Teachers of French at the University of Besançon in August 1960. It was subsequently published as 'Linguistique générale et linguistique appliquée à l'enseignement des langues' in *Études de linguistique appliquée* (Paris: Didier, for Centre of Applied Linguistics, University of Besançon), 1, 1961, pp. 5–42. The present version is translated and freely adapted by R. D. Huddleston and the author.

PAPER THREE
'Descriptive linguistics in literary studies' was delivered as a lecture at the Fifth Triennial Conference of the International Association of University Professors of English, Edinburgh, August 1962, and subsequently appeared in *English Studies Today, Third Series*, ed. G. I. Duthie (Edinburgh: University Press, 1964) pp. 25–39.

PAPER SEVEN
'Intonation systems in English' was delivered as a lecture to the Philological Society, London, on 13 May 1963. It embodies material from two published papers: 'The tones of English', in *Archivum Linguisticum*, 15 (i), 1963, pp. 1–28, and 'Intonation in English grammar', in *Transactions of the Philological Society*, 1963, pp. 143–169.

PAPER EIGHT
'Linguistics and machine translation' was delivered as a lecture to the Cybernetics Group, University of Glasgow, in November 1960, and a version of it subsequently appeared in *Zeitschrift für Phonetik, Sprachwissenschaft und Kommunikationsforschung*, 15 (i/ii), 1962, pp. 145–158.

PAPER TEN
'Typology and the exotic' is a combination of two lectures, one delivered at the Linguistics Association Conference, Hull, in May 1959, the other to the St. Andrews Linguistic Society, in May 1960.

M. A. K. Halliday is Professor of General Linguistics in the University of London.

Patterns of
Language

One

General linguistics and its application to language teaching (1960)

There are already so many definitions of language that it seems a pity to add to their number still further. Rather than attempting to define language, we can adopt an alternative approach and begin by specifying those properties of language which are relevant to the subject under discussion. Our starting point here, then, could be the observation that language is organized noise.

Linguistics and phonetics are the two disciplines whose purpose it is to account for language. Phonetics studies the noise, linguistics the organization. This explains both the similarity and the difference between the theories and methods of these two disciplines: they study different aspects of the same observable phenomenon. Various other disciplines also take account of language in one way or another; what distinguishes linguistics and phonetics from the rest is that the former study language in order to throw light on language, whereas other subjects such as literary criticism, psychology, logic and anthropology study language in order to throw light on something else. Linguistics and phonetics can thus be appropriately called 'the linguistic sciences'.

Both these subjects have their various subdivisions or branches. In linguistics what is usually recognized to be the primary division is that into descriptive (or synchronic) linguistics and historical (or diachronic) linguistics. In descriptive linguistics we are interested in the operation of language: how does a given language work? In historical linguistics, clearly, we are interested in the history of language: how does a given language come to be what it is? The main branches of phonetics, on the other hand, are concerned with the different stages in the speech event: production by the speaker, transmission through the air and perception by the hearer. To these correspond articulatory phonetics, acoustic phonetics and perceptual phonetics; the first and last are physiological studies, or physiological and psychological, while the second is physical.

These and the many other branches and divisions of each subject are united and controlled by the overall theories known as 'general linguistics' and 'general phonetics'. Since these two are in turn closely inter-linked they are often subsumed under the single name 'general linguistics'. In this paper I shall use the term 'general linguistics' to refer to the whole body of theory, linguistic and phonetic, that lies behind the study of language. Since the branch of linguistics that is most relevant to language teaching is descriptive linguistics, I shall be concerned with that area of general linguistic theory which bears on the description of languages. Here both phonetics and linguistics play an essential part: neither will suffice without the other. But their roles are different, and need separate discussion; in what follows I shall concentrate mainly on the role of linguistics. In other words I shall be dealing with the linguistics side of that part of general linguistic theory which enables us to describe effectively how a language works.

'General linguistics' implies a general theory of language, and this in turn implies that we can identify the properties that are common to all languages and distinguish these from the features that are specific to a given language. Many features often assumed to be universal, in the sense of 'common to all languages', are not in fact universals at all: concepts like *verb*, *phrase* and *syllable* are not linguistic constants and must to a certain extent be redefined for each language. The syllable in French, for example, has a very different status from the syllable in English; in some languages we do not find anything which we should want to call a 'verb' because there is nothing which displays enough of the properties of what are called 'verbs' in the languages to which this term was first applied. To find what is common to all languages we must invoke more abstract concepts than these. It is rather as if we said that all human beings must drink, and therefore all societies have some means of drinking; but not all societies use cups, and sometimes we are doubtful whether a particular vessel should be called a 'cup' or not.

The understanding of what are the inherent properties of language as such is extremely important, since it provides a framework of categories for a powerful and accurate description of any language. We will not find a *verb* in every language, so 'verb' will have no place in a general theory; but we shall find the category of which verb is a special instance, namely the category of *class*. All languages have classes, and the 'class', appropriately defined, does have a place in a general theory of language.

General linguistics is necessary if we seek to explain how language works. In fact all description of languages, however elementary, pre-supposes some theory or other; but the more adequate the theory, the simpler, more comprehensive and more exact the description will be.

Descriptive linguistics has other applications besides language teaching, although language teaching is certainly one of the most important. In all such applications the first essential is a good description of the language or languages concerned. For language teaching purposes we also need to compare languages; the methods are those of comparative descriptive linguistics, sometimes known also as 'contrastive linguistics'. The principal contribution of general linguistics to language teaching is thus that it makes possible the provision of adequate descriptions and comparisons of languages. A secondary but still important contribution is that it shows how a description may take different forms according to the aim that is in view.

1 The description of a language

The basic principle of description is to analyse the language according to its various kinds of patterning: to break it down into what we call 'levels'. Language, as said above, can be thought of as *organized noise*. To this we can add: 'used in situations', actual social situations. Organized noise used in social situations, or in other words 'contextualized systematic sounds'. I shall be concerned here mainly with spoken language; not that I wish to suggest that written language is unimportant, but merely so as to avoid complicating some of the formulations.[1] With this as a starting-point I should like to consider in outline one possible approach to the description of a language.

Language, whether spoken or written, has a substance: this is the material aspect of language. The substance may be phonic or graphic, but for the moment we will consider only the phonic. The noise, then, is the substance. Language also has a form: this is the organization. In language, therefore, we can recognize a level of *substance* and a level of *form*. Now the organization of language, its form, is meaningful: that is, linguistic activity participates in situations alongside man's other creative activities. Thus for a complete description of language one has to account for the form, the substance and the relationship between the form and the situation. The study of this relationship could be called the

[1] See Paper 6 of this volume, pp. 99 ff.

semantic level; but since it involves an approach to meaning rather different from that normally implied by 'semantics' we may refer to this as the 'contextual' level, the 'context' here being the non-linguistic environment.

There is thus a resemblance between 'context' as used here and 'meaning' in its non-technical sense. But what is generally understood by 'meaning' is perhaps too limited to be adequate for linguistics, being confined almost entirely to referents or concepts. For the linguist any consideration and any description of language, be it formal or contextual, is concerned with meaning: this is inevitable, for language is meaningful activity. It is often said that 'structural linguistics' represented an attempt to describe a language without reference to its meaning; whether or not this is so, we would rather insist that the aim of a description is to elucidate linguistic meaning at its various levels. At the same time it should be stressed that we are concerned here with linguistics and not philosophy. What 'meaning' means to a philosopher may be a rather different question.

The domain of the linguistic sciences, as far as the description of language is concerned, can be illustrated as follows:

LINGUISTIC SCIENCES				
Phonetics – – – – – – –				
	Linguistics – – – – – – – – –			
SUBSTANCE		FORM		SITUATION (environment)
phonic	phonology	$\begin{Bmatrix} grammar \\ lexis \end{Bmatrix}$	context	extra-textual features.

Language, by its nature as contextualized systematic sound, presupposes substance (phonic substance), form and situation, the last being the associated non-linguistic factors. Under 'form', however, we must make a further distinction between *grammar* and *lexis* (vocabulary), a distinction likewise made necessary by the nature of language. In every language the formal patterns are of two kinds, merging into one another in the middle but distinct enough at the extremes: those of grammar and those of vocabulary (or, to use a technical term, of lexis). I shall come back later to the criteria on which the distinction between grammar and lexis depends.

The link between form and phonic substance is provided by phonology: this is the meaningful distribution of speech sounds. It is here that phonetics and linguistics overlap. Phonetics covers the study of phonic substance and also of phonology from the standpoint of phonic substance. Linguistics covers the study of form and also of phonology from the standpoint of form. Linguistics also extends to the right of the diagram so far as to take in the study, not of the non-linguistic features themselves, but of the relation between these non-linguistic features and linguistic form: that is what we are here calling the study of context.

These then are what we call the 'levels of analysis' of descriptive linguistics: phonic, phonological, grammatical, lexical and contextual. For the written language, matters are a little more complicated: one cannot simply replace 'phonological' and 'phonic' by 'graphological' and 'graphic', for in most languages the orthography represents the linguistic forms not directly but via the phonology: we must therefore add the study of the relations between the two.

The levels of analysis are derived in the first place by a process of abstraction from our observations of the language material. We observe, to start with, the linguistic events we call 'utterances', in which we find regular patterns of partial likeness between events. Then we generalize from these observations, grouping elements together according to the likenesses. Afterwards we make abstractions: we set up categories of language and so construct a theory, with hypotheses depending on the theory, to explain the facts observed. Finally we present our description, made in terms of the categories so established.

Observation, generalization, theory, presentation: this, one might perhaps say, is the scientific method of description. The facts of language are such that we must proceed by a set of abstractions at several levels at once, all constantly interrelated but each level having its own categories. These categories enable us to arrange systematically the mass of events constituting a language.

2 Grammar

What do we mean by grammar? The most fruitful criterion seems to be this: when we are dealing with a *closed system* we are concerned with grammar. A *closed system* is a series of terms with the following characteristics:

    1. The list of terms is exhaustive—it contains (say) *a*, *b*, *c* and no more;

2. each term excludes all the others—if *a*, then not *b* and not *c*;
3. one cannot create new terms—if *a*, *b*, *c* then one cannot add a *d*.
To be more exact, as one can always imagine the creation of new terms and their integration into a grammatical system, the third condition should rather be formulated thus: (3) if a new term is added, at least one of the previous terms undergoes a change of meaning, so that in effect a new system replaces the old.

To take an example: the cases of the noun substantive in Latin form a closed system. No speaker of Latin could borrow a new case from another language or create one himself. The Latin case system is a flexional system: the exponents of the cases are bound morphemes (as distinct from free morphemes), which have not themselves the status of words. But one can also have a closed system whose members are free morphemes, for example the definite article in French. Let us suppose—however improbably—that French were to borrow the nominal category 'dual' from Samoyedic as a third term in the number system of the definite article; this would change the meaning of the word *les*: instead of as at present 'two or more' it would become 'three or more'. This change would be both formal and contextual. There would also be a change in the formal, but not the contextual, meaning of *le* and *la*, since *le/la* would be opposed not to one term in the sytem but to two, and this would lead to a redistribution of information. Thus 'information', in the sense it has in information theory, is in linguistics the *formal* meaning of an item or category.

Let us take by way of contrast a series of lexical items: the names of various means of locomotion, for example *train, car, bus, taxi, motorcycle, bicycle*. One day a new kind of vehicle appears: the *monorail*, let us say. This word is absorbed into the vehicular series without any change of meaning in any of the other words. My bicycle is still a bicycle. In this case we are in the domain of lexis, not of grammar. We readily accept that there are grammars on the one hand and dictionaries on the other, but often without asking ourselves where the difference between them lies. It is sometimes stated as follows: a dictionary deals with words, a grammar with the construction of words in sentences (one should add at least 'and of morphemes in words'). But this is not enough to distinguish grammar from lexis: does the classification of words, for instance, belong to grammar or to lexis? The real difference consists in the relations between the items. The dictionary—or rather lexicology, since there are other ways of describing lexis than by writing a dictionary—lexicology is concerned with *open relations*, whereas grammar studies *closed rela-*

tions. In other words where, in linguistic form, there is a choice among a fixed number of possibilities, this is the realm of grammar.

Grammatical relations are not, of course, confined to flexions (bound morphemes), nor even to relations below the rank of the word (morphemes in general). It is a characteristic of language that patterns occur over stretches of varying extent. In discussing a grammatical item or category one may thus ask at what *unit* it is operating: where in the language is this particular choice made? The stretches that carry the grammatical patterns are what I am calling 'units'. The unit is the first of the general grammatical categories that I should like to discuss, and it is a technical term in the description. In this sense every language will have at least two grammatical units: indeed this is perhaps one universal feature of languages. We might go so far as to say this: 'All languages have at least two grammatical units: a larger one which is the unit of contextual meaning, the one with which the language operates in situations, and this we call the *sentence*; and a smaller one which is the unit that also mainly enters into lexical relations, and this we call the *word*.' For our purposes it is enough to take it as established that the sentence and the word are two universal units of grammar.

It is doubtful whether any language operates solely with these two units. There are other units in between the sentence and the word, and in many cases there is also one below the word. Those between the sentence and the word are in many cases complex and often lend themselves to very confused interpretations. English grammar needs two such: the clause and the group. Textbooks generally treat these at length, giving a great many negative rules (what one must not say or write), but they rarely explain what a clause or group is. Obviously one does not expect definitions of these terms such as are found in dictionaries: scientific technical terms cannot be defined in this way, for each category is defined by its relations to all the others. It is only when the whole grammar of the language has been described that you can know what a clause is, and at the same time you will know what a sentence, a group, a word and a morpheme are. But in most textbooks such information is difficult to extract when one needs it.

In general the units of a language are related to each other in a hierarchy based on the notion of constituency; each is composed of one or of several members of the unit next below. The term *rank* is used for the position of the unit in the hierarchy. In English, for example, there are five grammatical units: sentence, clause, group, word, morpheme. A sentence is thus one complete clause or several complete clauses.

A clause is made up of one or more than one complete group; and so on. It may of course happen that a given sentence consists of one clause consisting of one group consisting of one word consisting of one morpheme, for example the sentence 'Yes.' or 'Pardon.' or 'Run.' French grammar in this respect is similar to English; in describing French it is most convenient to operate with these same five units. For example, the sentence *le concert commence très tard* is a sentence consisting of one clause (a 'simple' sentence); the clause consists of three groups which are made up of two, one and two words respectively. Unit boundaries may be indicated as follows:

|||		between sentences
||	,,	clauses
		,,	groups
(space)	,,	words
+	,,	morphemes

Each boundary of course implies a boundary at all lower ranks. Thus:

||| le concert | commence | très tard |||

The substitution of *commencera* for *commence* would give a compound instead of a simple word, the rest remaining unaltered:

||| le concert | commenc+er+a | très tard |||

If we substitute *a commencé*, we have:

||| le concert | a commenc+é | très tard |||

This time it is a compound group that has been substituted for the simple one. The clause in each instance consists of three groups.

The formulation used above was that 'it is most convenient' to operate with five units, and not 'one must'. It should be stressed that linguistic descriptions are not, so to speak, monovalent. A description is not simply 'right' or 'wrong' in itself (it may be wrong, of course, if it does not conform to the facts); it is better thought of as more useful or less. Some facts are quite evident and not open to question: we do not need very advanced general linguistics to tell us that French nouns are either masculine or feminine. But there are many linguistic facts which are much less simple. For example, the analysis of English compound ('phrasal') verbs: the differences in their patterning are extraordinarily complex, and it is difficult to decide whether they form one class or twenty or a hundred classes. The various pronouns and pronominal adjectives in French are likewise extremely complicated. The distinction between 'in French there are . . .' and 'in describing French it is useful to recognize . . .' is a very delicate one. One should beware of statements such as 'in French there are thirty-six phonemes'. The phoneme is a phonological abstraction (I shall return to it later) and there are several ways of regarding it. There might be no question of there being ten or ninety phonemes in a given language, but different analyses yielding twenty or thirty or forty might all be possible. The aim is to find the simplest description that will account for all the facts, and one often has to have described a considerable area of the language before being able to judge which of two possibilities is the simpler.

Each unit, then, is made up out of combinations of the unit next below it in rank. In this respect orthography serves as a model for grammar. In the construction of a written text each paragraph consists of (ortho-graphic) sentences which consist of sub-sentences which consist of (orthographic) words which consist of letters; and we may have a one-to-one relation all the way, as when 'I.' occurs, in answer to a question, as a complete paragraph in English. We do not say that the paragraph consists of one letter, in any meaningful sense, because it would be absurd to analyse the structure of a paragraph as a sequence of letters; nor do we deny that *I* is a word merely because it consists of one letter, or that it is a sentence because it consists of only one word. Grammatically, sentences in English do not consist of words in this strict sense; they consist of clauses, which in turn consist of groups, and these groups consist of words. To analyse a sentence grammatically as a string of words or morphemes is like trying to describe the patterns of a written paragraph by treating it as a string of letters.

In grammar however there are two complications to this relation of rank. In the first place, the boundaries between units are by no means always clearcut. Sometimes they are, with one item, say a group, begin-ning just where the previous one ends. Sometimes however they may be discontinuous, with for example one clause in the middle of another; or they may be fused, as when for example a word is made up of two morphemes but not in such a way that it can be split into two segments. An example of the latter is the English word *took*, which we can regard as consisting of two morphemes *take* and 'past tense'; unlike *walked*, it cannot be split into two segments, and indeed the morpheme 'past tense' has no recognizable item corresponding to it at all: nevertheless this morpheme is present in the word *took*. The French word *commence* above could (here is an instance of a choice in description) be analysed as two morphemes, *commence* plus '(third person) singular'; we might then write it *commenc + e*, but this would be merely a notational device and there would be no separate item corresponding to the morpheme 'singular'. All inflexional paradigms provide instances of fused morphemes.

The second complication is the phenomenon known as *rankshift* (or *downgrading*). Here an item of one rank is as it were shifted down the scale of rank to form part of an item either of lower rank than itself or of equal rank to itself: a clause within a group, for example, or a group within a group. English 'the man who came to dinner' has a rankshifted clause *who came to dinner* inside the group *the man who came to dinner*; 'the railway company's property' has the group *railway company's* inside the group *the railway company's property*. Many, if not all, languages display this phenomenon of rankshift in their grammar.

This then is the relation among the grammatical units of a language: for each given unit, every item of that rank is made up of one or more items (or perhaps rather *instances*, since in the case of fusion the 'items' may be pure abstractions) which will be either of the rank immediately below or, with rankshift, of equal or higher rank. But, as is readily observable, there are restrictions on the ways in which such items may operate, both alone and in combination, to form an item of next higher rank: it is not true, for example, that any group can go anywhere and play any part in any clause. In other words, each unit displays a limited set of possible *structures*.

Structure is the second of the general categories of grammar. It is an abstract category, of course, like the others: in the clause 'the old man is sitting in the garden' the elements of structure are not *the, old, man, is* and so on, nor even *the old man, is sitting* and so on. The structural elements of the clause are abstract functions established to enable us to give a precise account of what can be said or written at the rank of the clause. In English clause structure four primary elements are needed: subject, predicator, complement and adjunct. English grammarians normally distinguish between complement and object; this distinction is borrowed from Latin, but in English it belongs rather to a different stage of the analysis, as also in French. If we confine ourselves to these four elements, this means that all clauses in English are made up of combinations of them. Using the capital letters S P C A to symbolize them, we allow for SPC, SAPA, ASP and so forth, specifying that every item operating in every clause is an exponent of S, P, C or A.

Here two observations are called for. First, elements like subject are not best defined in conceptual terms such as these: 'the subject is the person or thing that performs a given action or is in a given state'; 'the object is the person or thing that undergoes the action'; 'the infinitive is the form of the verb that expresses the idea of the verb and nothing else'. Definitions of this kind are neither precise nor practical. In 'my son likes potatoes' (SPC: || my son | like+s | potato+es ||) what is the state my son is in or the action he is performing? What action do the potatoes undergo? The conceptual or notional categories of traditional grammars are not incorrect but irrelevant at this point. It is because of its value in the structure of the clause that 'my son' has the status of subject.

Secondly, it should be noted that sequence is sometimes a structural feature, sometimes not. Or, to put it in other terms, it sometimes happens in a language that to change the sequence of the constituents destroys (or changes) the structure; in other cases a change of sequence has no effect on the primary structure. In French, sequence generally has structural value. 'Le bateau a quitté le quai' cannot be replaced (at least in modern French) by 'a quitté le bateau le quai', which would not be understood, nor by 'le quai a quitté le bateau', which is possible but differs as to which of the formal items of the original fill which places in the structure. The description should show whether or not the sequence is, wholly or partly, determined by the structure, indicating here that it is an essential feature of this structure that the elements occur in a fixed sequence. This condition is very rare in Latin and Russian, where sequence carries more delicate distinctions (still structural, but not determining primary categories like 'subject'); frequent but by no means universal in English and French; normal, though still not without exception, in Chinese and Vietnamese. The French 'il y a des fraises dans le jardin' can be changed into 'dans le jardin il y a des fraises'; it is only the sequence of 'il y a' and 'des fraises' that is fixed, and this restriction has no contrastive function since the items are not interchangeable. I would not suggest that there is no difference between the two versions of the French clause: almost every linguistic variation is meaningful, so that where there is a formal distinction there is almost always contextual differentiation. But this distinction represents a more delicate structural difference: the primary grammatical relations between the elements of structure are the same.

We need now to consider the status of the forms which function in the structure of each unit. These are not unrelated items, considered as words or sequences of sounds, but rather sets of possible items that have the status of the unit below: in the structure of the clause, for example, the components are groups. It is clear that the choice of group, that is the possibility of choosing a given group, depends on the structure of the clause: in the clause 'the old man is sitting in the garden', the group 'the old man' could be replaced by 'the stationmaster' but not by 'will go'. Similarly, the choice of word depends on the structure of the group, and so on. Thus we can classify the items, and the important point here is that we do so according to their function in the structure of the unit above. This gives us *classes*: clause, group, word and morpheme classes. The third of the general categories of grammar is, then, the class. If we consider once more the group in French, there seem to be three main classes: the verbal group (which operates as predicator), the nominal group (subject and complement) and the adverbial group (adjunct). These have their more delicate subdivisions: active verbal group, passive verbal group, and so on; here it should be stressed in passing that it is the verbal *group* that is active or passive and not the verb, which is a class of word.

The class then is a grouping of the members of a given unit that have the same potentiality of occurrence. Moreover each class is assignable to one unit: different units may have different classes. The class is that set of items which operate in the same way, playing the same role in the structure of the unit next above. There will of course be classes and subclasses and sub-sub-classes, each more delicately differentiated according as one takes into account more and more delicate distinctions of structure. For example, at the first degree of 'delicacy' 'the old man is sitting in the garden' and 'the old man is served by the gardener' have the same structure SPA: subject, predicator, adjunct. Analysing more delicately, we distinguish the structures of the two clauses, so that 'is sitting' and 'is served' belong to different sub-classes of the verbal group, 'in the garden' and 'by the gardener' to different sub-classes of the adverbial group. We first display the likeness between them, and then the unlikeness.

Before passing to the fourth of the general categories, it may be helpful to consider the way classes are established. The class, it was suggested, is determined according to function in the structure of the unit above; that is, the unit immediately above. The relation is thus one of *downward* determination: it is the unit above that provides the basis for classes of the unit below. Upward analysis, giving groupings derived from below (that is, sets of items alike in their own structure), does not by itself produce classes—not, that is, unless the two groupings coincide.

There are of course many cases where the criteria of downward analysis and those of upward analysis do agree: so much the better. But when they do not, as is frequently the case, it is the criterion of downward analysis that is decisive. Consider the words *venait, venons, venant, venu*. In their own structure, they are parallel: the same bound lexical morpheme *ven* together with a grammatical morpheme which is related to it in structure, and which is also bound. These words form a paradigm in the same way as *vieux-vieille* or *cheval-chevaux*: they should, it might seem, belong to the same class. But *venait* and *venons* represent in themselves finite verbal groups: for example in 'nous autres venons plus tard'. On the other hand, *venant* and *venu* can never be the only element of a finite verbal group: *venu* requires *suis, est* ('je suis venu') whereas *venant* never functions in the predicator of an independent clause. *Venait, venons, venant, venu* are members of the same *paradigm*, 'paradigm' being the name of the grouping determined by upward analysis; they will however (at some stage) be assigned to different classes.

There are two technical terms which in their traditional sense have insufficient generality, and which we can thus generalize to refer respectively to downward and upward analysis: namely 'syntax' and 'morphology'. In the traditional meaning of these terms, at least in English, syntax is concerned with units larger than the word, morphology with units smaller. What is the origin of this distinction? It was recognized that the classical languages, Latin and Greek, tended to display one type of structural relation above the word, in the combination of words in higher units; and a structural relation of a different type below the word. The difference is between *free* forms and *bound* forms, which is a useful opposition in the classification of linguistic elements. A bound form is one that cannot be an exponent of the unit above (a morpheme that cannot stand alone as a word, and so on), whereas a free form is one that is able to operate at the rank of the unit above. In general, items below the word (morphemes) in Latin are all bound, while higher elements tend to be free. Hence the distinction between *morphology*, the formation of words out of bound forms, and *syntax*, the formation of clauses and sentences out of free forms.

A distinction on these lines is a feature of certain languages only, and there is no need to take it into account in describing other languages than these. To say of Chinese or English that the distinction 'does not exist' there is not the point, which is rather that there is a misplacing of emphasis if the distinction is drawn in this way. The same considerations apply also to French. We can however use the terms 'syntax' and 'morphology' to refer to an important and in fact closely related, but more general, distinction that is of methodological value. It seems reasonable to use 'syntax' to refer to downward analysis, from sentence down to morpheme, and 'morphology' for upward analysis, from morpheme to sentence. Hence one could say: the class is determined by syntactical and not by morphological considerations; in a word, classes are syntactical.

Finally we come to the fourth and last of the general grammatical categories, which we have already mentioned in discussing the criteria for determining what grammar is: this is the *system*. Consider the verbal group *ont été choisis* in 'les délégués ont été choisis'. In the selection of this as opposed to other possible verbal groups, various choices have been made. In voice, it is passive; it could have been active: *ont choisi*. In tense, it is past in present; it could have been simple present, simple future, past in future, present in past or past in present in past: *sont choisis, seront choisis, auront été choisis, étaient choisis* or *avaient été choisis*. In polarity, it is positive; it could have been negative: *n'ont (pas) été choisis*. All these choices are closed; there are no possibilities other than those listed. Wherever, at a particular place in structure (in this example, at P in the clause), we face a choice among a closed set of possibilities, we have a system: for example the system of 'polarity', whose terms are 'positive' and 'negative'.

If however we consider the set of items from which *choisir* was chosen, we find that it is uncircumscribable. It includes all the members of a large sub-class of the class of 'verb' in the French language, a class that moreover is constantly having new items added to it. We can never say that *choisir* can be defined by excluding all the other possible items, as positive can be defined by excluding negative. *Choisir*, then, is not a term in any system: it is a member of an open grammatical class. Similarly in 'celui du général', *celui* represents a closed choice (*ceux, celle, celles*), *général* an open one; in 'elle me regarde', *me* represents a closed choice (*te le la se nous vous les*), *regarde* an open one.

The system, then, is the last of our postulated general categories of grammar. At every place in the structure of every unit, one or more choices are made. When the choice is closed, we have a system. When the choice is open, we are dealing with a lexical selection, not a grammatical one. All that can be said about the choice of *choisir* is that there must here be some word belonging to a sub-class of the class 'verb'; the choice from among the members of this sub-class is a purely lexical matter. Where there is a system, the choice among the terms of the system is strictly grammatical, and the distinctions belong not to the dictionary but to the grammar. In such cases we can always define each term in the choice negatively as well as positively: in the finite verb 'not first or second person' gives exactly the same information as 'third person'. There is no way, on the other hand, of describing a lexical item negatively.

There are, of course, borderline cases: we are not always certain whether we are dealing with a closed system or not. But this does not affect the principle: it is merely one more illustration of the complexity of language. An example of a borderline case is to be found in the personal pronouns of several languages, including French. The question, basically, is this: do they constitute a whole class in themselves or do they form part of a larger class, the class of substantives, for example, or of an intermediate sub-class? The French conjunct personal pronouns, together with *y* and *en*, form a distinct class: they enter into the structure of the verbal group and may be considered as 'verbal pronouns'; this is a completely grammatical system. As for the disjunct pronouns, the nominal pronouns, it is difficult to decide whether they form a system or not. In fact, considered as a sub-class of the nominal group, they do make up a system; but this sub-class is fairly delicate and has certain features in common with the sub-class of personal names. From a syntactic point of view, there is some resemblance between *moi* and *Pierre*.

These four categories—unit, structure, class and system—provide the framework for the grammatical description. They are bound up with the general linguistic theory. One does not arrive at them inductively from an examination of the facts. They are established as primitive categories of the theory and retained because they enable us to give a fairly simple account of all the facts, as simple as we could expect considering that we are dealing with such complex material as language.

Let me not give the impression that such a view of the description of languages is revolutionary. There is no need to be revolutionary, to cast away all the work of our precursors. Linguistics, with mathematics and astronomy, is one of the oldest of sciences. It flourished in ancient China, in India, Greece and Rome. Twenty-five centuries ago, Indian grammarians were making extremely elegant descriptions of Sanskrit: rigorous, integrated and exact to a degree never surpassed before the twentieth century. It is this tradition, perhaps more than that of the last four centuries in Europe, that modern descriptive linguistics has inherited. Unfortunately for the modern language teacher many descriptions of languages written in recent years, and still current today, are not sufficiently rigorous, integrated or exact. In many cases they do not show the difference—nor, therefore, the connection—between formal and contextual relations; nor do they distinguish between particular description (looking at each language in its own light) and transfer description (looking at one language in the light of another).

How did these confusions, between form and context, and between one-language description and inter-language comparison, come about? The Greek and Latin grammarians studied and described their own languages; indeed for them other languages had no reason to be thought worthy of study. They took their languages as given. The Greeks naturally had no preconceived idea of an ideal language; they set about discovering the categories of Greek such as they really were, and then described them. Except perhaps for assumptions about language and logic—the belief that relations in language derived from those of some external logic—their theory and practice were exemplary. The Romans based their grammars on those of Greek; this could have been disastrous, but as it happens the structure of Latin is very like that of Greek: they were able to superimpose the categories of Greek on to the Latin ones, and by chance this worked fairly well. However, when the national languages of modern Europe came to be studied from the sixteenth century onwards, the grammars of Greek and Latin were used as models, and this time it *was* disastrous. It was assumed that all languages were like Latin; or, if they were not, they should be. As a result particular description tended to be replaced by comparative description of the type known as 'transfer'. Grammarians were saying, as it were, not so much 'this is what happens in French', but rather 'this is how we can make French what it should be: a reflection, albeit imperfect, of Latin'. Fortunately we no longer find extreme examples of this attitude, such as the imputation of a category of case to the noun in French or English. But the attitude is still reflected in many grammars, including those used for teaching English abroad. For example, one sees the subjunctive in English treated as though it were a general category of the verb used in contrast to the indicative, whereas in fact it is a largely non-contrastive variant, mainly limited to the verb 'to be' and to certain specific structures.

How did language come to be looked upon in such a way, almost as a form of behaviour ruled by the canons of good manners—manners, moreover, measured by the standards of another language and another civilization? To understand this, we must come back to the first of the distinctions mentioned above, that between linguistic form and context. This can be illustrated by an example. The noun substantive in Latin has a declension, the cases being formally distinct: the difference between the nominative and the accusative can, in general, be heard (or seen). Thus, in order to identify the elements of structure of the Latin clause, the subject and object are defined as follows: the subject is the noun which is in the nominative case, the object is that which is in the accusative. (There are of course complications of detail, but these do not affect the reasoning.) Now the noun in English and French does not show case, and to arrive at a definition of subject and object other criteria must be found. But instead of asking what in fact happens in these languages, what true linguistic difference there is between subject and object, grammarians abandoned the formal linguistic criteria and replaced them by conceptual criteria such as those quoted above. The subject, for example, became 'a noun or pronoun indicating what person or thing performs the action or is in the state expressed by the verb'. Definitions of this kind were, originally, attempts to explain the *contextual* meaning of what had been *identified* on *formal* criteria, and as such they were not unsuitable: at least there *were* facts to be explained. But the use of such concepts as criteria for defining linguistic categories is doomed to failure from the start. When one looks at or hears a Latin noun, one often knows whether it is nominative: the case is directly identifiable, by its *exponent* or manifestation in substance. It is impossible to tell by looking at a French or English substantive whether the noun is 'performing an action' or is 'in a state'.

The same thing happened with word classes, or what are termed 'parts of speech'. The Greeks knew what a noun was: it was something that could be inflected for case and number but not for gender. As a secondary statement, to explain its contextual meaning, they added that a noun was the name of a person or thing. How should one describe it in French? From a linguistic point of view, the noun substantive in French is the class of words having a certain value, filling a certain place, in the structure of the nominal group, which in turn has a certain value in the structure of the clause. But the noun substantive is clearly marked: admittedly it has no declension, but it has, at least in the written language, distinct forms for the singular and plural and it may be accompanied by the definite article. This is not a definition, for every class is defined syntactically; it is however a most useful formal indication, very much more useful than saying that 'nouns are the names of persons and things'. How can one expect a schoolchild to know that the word *soustraction* is the name of a person or thing whereas the word *celui* is not?

It is a principle of general linguistics that defining criteria should be formal and particular. 'Formal' implies first stating the linguistic relations and the items acting as terms in these relations; one then tries to state the contextual meanings, which however are never given as principal criteria. 'Particular' implies that categories are derived first from the language to be described: we can then go on to compare this with another language if this is useful to our purpose. Formal meaning is necessary to an understanding of contextual meaning, because the first is internal to language while the second concerns its external relations.[2] One of the most insufficient of the very many definitions of language is that according to which language is the expression of thought. This is significant for the psychologist, who is concerned with thought processes. But in linguistics, whether 'general' or 'applied', it is difficult to operate with a thought, which can be neither seen nor heard, nor systematically related to another thought. The linguist operates with *language* and *text*, the latter referring to all linguistic material, spoken or written, which we observe in order to study language. The linguist's object of study is the language and his object of observation is the text: he describes language, and relates it to the situations in which it is operating. Thoughts do not figure in the process, since we cannot describe them.

3 Lexis

Many of the same principles apply to lexicology as to grammar. The relation between lexis and grammar might be put as follows: if one analyses the grammatical units of a language, one will find that there is one unit, below the sentence, many of whose members enter into a different sort of relation with each other in addition to their relations in grammar. It is this unit we call the *word*. The word is a grammatical unit like all the others, with its own classes and structures; but it is distinguished from the other grammatical units in that, after it has been treated exhaustively in the grammar, there always remains much to be said about it. A grammar can state that the word *train* is a noun. A more 'delicate' grammar might add that it is a noun of sub-class, say, F.22. But even this will not distinguish it from *car*, *bus*, *bicycle* or *taxi*. Grammar has no way of distinguishing them, because they do not form

2 Cf. Paper 6 of this volume, especially p. 104 (and footnote 11).

a closed system. They are part of an open lexical set, and it is the task of lexicology to account for them.

Traditionally, lexicology is approached via lexicography: that is, the making of dictionaries. For the particular description of a language, a monolingual dictionary is normally prepared in which each article is composed of two main parts: definition and citation. In most dictionaries there are also of course additional pieces of information: word class (grammar), etymology (historical linguistics), pronunciation (phonetics or phonology, according to the dictionary); but these are as it were extraneous, not part of lexicology proper. The definition is the contextual description, the citation the formal description. In lexis as in grammar, the items have a contextual and a formal meaning: the definition aims at relating the lexical item, which is a linguistic item, to extralinguistic phenomena. For this it is necessary to use other words: all sciences use words, but the special problem of linguistics is that it is, as has been said, language turned back on itself. However, just as in mathematics one can define the number five as 'four plus one' but not 'one times five' (the concept *five* may not be used in the definition of five), so the word *x* must not occur in the definition of the word *x*. This sometimes results in strange definitions, when a word of high frequency is defined by means of a string of words some of which are much rarer, rather as though one were to define *five* as 'one hundred and thirty-two minus one hundred and twenty-seven'. For example, the definition of *cut* in the Shorter Oxford Dictionary reads 'to penetrate so as to sever the continuity of with an edged instrument; to make incision in; to gash, slash'. This is not much help to the student. Such definitions represent an important attempt to generalize about the function of the item in the language; the technique of definition has, however, clear limitations as a practical measure.

On the other hand, the citations are purely formal: they describe a word in relation to its linguistic environment. This relation between one word (or rather 'lexical item', since a lexical item is often more than one grammatical word, as for example *pomme de terre*) and another with which it is associated is called *collocation*.[3] The collocation of words is the basic formal relation in lexis. It is extremely important for the study of the language of poetry, since poets, and writers in general, draw their effects in part from the interaction of familiar with new collocations; and the creation of new collocations, interacting with other linguistic features,

[3] See Paper 11 of this volume, especially pp. 186 ff.

is a highly effective stylistic device. Collocation is outside grammar: it has no connection with the classes of the word. It is the lexical item, without reference to grammar, that enters into collocations. We can say 'open the window', or 'an open window', or 'the opening of the window'; it is in each case the same collocation of the item *window* with the item *open*.

The relation of collocation enables us to group items into *lexical sets*. The lexical set is formally defined as a grouping of words having approximately the same range of collocations. *Train, car, taxi* and so on frequently collocate with *take, drive, passenger, engine* and others. Contextually, the set is a grouping of words having the same contextual range, functioning in the same situation types. In a similar way the criterion of *disponibilité*, or 'availability', has a formal and contextual aspect: 'having a wide range of collocations' and 'operating in a wide range of situations'. In general formal and contextual criteria yield the same groupings; but the two are distinct from a methodological point of view, since they represent different ways of approaching the facts.

The dictionary provides of course an excellent framework for presenting the items of the lexis, especially when it gives citations. It is, however, not the only possible means. Note that in a dictionary the order of the lemmata, or articles, is, from a linguistic point of view, almost irrelevant to their meaning. Alphabetical order is an indexing device, by which each word has its place where it can be found without difficulty; but this place has no linguistic value and tells us nothing of the word's meaning. There is another method in which, this time, the order of words is meaningful: the place of each word is part of the description of the word. This is the *thesaurus*, a number of which have been produced such as Roget's *Thesaurus* for English and the Duden volumes for French and certain other languages. For the foreign language student, the thesaurus can be very useful, and would be more so if it included citations.

The principle underlying the way words are grouped in a thesaurus is basically that of the lexical set. Brought together in one place are all the items that can be used under similar formal or contextual conditions. The lexical set is thus the closest analogy to the grammatical system. The latter is in effect a set of possible terms available for choice under the same grammatical conditions: this means that where any one term in the system may be chosen, so may all the others, and it is this fact that gives its meaning to the one that is in fact chosen. In grammar the choice is limited: the *a* of *il y a* may be replaced by *avait, aura, aurait* and a few compound forms, but that is all. In lexis the choice is not limited: there are words that are more or less probable, which gives a continuous scale of probabilities. For example, the names of fruits, such as *apple*, *orange*, *pear*, *peach*, form a lexical set. They frequently collocate with *dessert*, *eat*, *sweet*, *fruit* and so on. In a large number of utterances containing the word *orange*, the word *apple* could occur in its place: 'I don't like oranges when they're too sweet', for example. The probability of the word *apple* (that is, the probability of its being able to replace *orange* in a given utterance) is higher than that of the word *coffee*; but *coffee* is by no means impossible: instead of *orange-coloured* I could say *coffee-coloured*. *Orange* and *coffee* both collocate with the item *colour*. Words like *disagreeableness* or *carburettor* are extremely improbable in such environments, but not altogether impossible. Nothing is wholly impossible in lexis, and one could construct ad hoc contexts to substantiate this. The thesaurus would therefore list the words *orange*, *apple*, *pear* in the same set and give citations for them: examples of sentences in which all the words of the set could operate.

Here it might perhaps be appropriate to say a word about the categories of 'idiom' and 'cliché'. These give a great deal of trouble to language teachers and even more to students. They should be considered, I feel, from the point of view of formal relations, especially those of lexis. It is often assumed that with the idiom one gives up all attempts at explanation, telling the pupil that it is 'an expression' and has to be learnt by heart as such. And it must be admitted that linguists too have often given up, saying in effect 'we don't know what an idiom is', or perhaps 'an idiom in the language being described is anything for which no equivalent is found in the mother tongue'. The teacher is doubtless right: it has to be learnt by heart. But at the same time he has the right to ask for a definition to enable him to recognize and classify phenomena of this kind. It may at least be possible here to observe and classify the facts. The question of naming the appropriate categories is secondary, although it is still important—it is said that linguists pay too little attention to matters of terminology. First, there are 'fixed' collocations of lexical items, which are of high probability and without grammatical restrictions, for example *danger de mort* and *danger mortel*; there are several examples of this type where one of the words thus collocated is never found except in association with the second, giving a unique collocation like the English *in the nick of time*. Is the word *zeste*, for example, ever used other than in the group *zeste de citron* or *gousse* other than in *gousse d'ail*? Fixed collocations of this kind, including unique collocations, could be called 'clichés'.

Secondly there may be one or more lexical items which are always tied to a particular grammatical structure; for example the French expressions *le cas écheant* or *en (avoir) plein le dos*, or the English *let the cat out of the bag*. You cannot say *le cas échoit, est échu* or *the cat is in the bag*. This category may be called 'idioms'.

Thirdly there are the so-called 'compound words', which I would prefer to call 'compound lexical items': items like *pomme de terre* and *pèse-lettres* (letter balance) which collocate as single units. The list of probable collocations of *pomme de terre* is different from that of *pomme* or of *terre* and is certainly not the sum of the two.

Here it should be noted that orthographic criteria cannot, strictly speaking, be used to define or delimit grammatical or lexical units. Most European languages have their conventional rules of orthography: the use of the full stop, the space, capital letters and so forth. Some of these rules are generally considered as decisive for grammar. There exist, as is well known, hundreds of definitions of the word and the sentence; but for most people the sentence, if one thinks about it, or perhaps if one does not think about it, is 'what in orthography would have begun with a capital letter and ended with a full stop', while a word is 'what is found between two spaces or between a space and a hyphen'.

This custom has its practical usefulness, and rather than abandon it some would seek to reform the orthography. But it should not be forgotten that orthographic usage is often deceptive. French of course has not only been codified orthographically, but has also an academy to give rulings on spelling and other features; as a result it has a fairly coherent orthography, more obviously systematic than that of English. Yet French too is not without its contradictions. These contradictions are difficult to resolve precisely because they are due to the complexity of language; to return for a moment to our *pomme de terre*, given that *pomme, terre* and *pomme de terre* are three different lexical items, how can one achieve orthographic consistency? Perhaps one could standardize the use of the hyphen as in *pèse-lettres*. We should need it in English to distinguish between, for example, *run up* as two lexical items, in *he ran up the hill*, and *run+up* as a single lexical item, in *he ran-up a bill*.

The reason why it is important to be aware of the conventions of orthography is that different levels are involved, and these should not be confused. We have distinguished lexis from grammar: not that there is no relation between them—on the contrary they are very closely linked —but because they involve different items and relations and consequently require different methods and categories of description. The same applies to the two varieties of substance, phonic and graphic. In the nineteenth century the spoken language was rather neglected, and even considered unworthy of study, so that at the beginning of the twentieth century some linguists tended to reverse the situation, concentrating exclusively on the spoken language. Now, perhaps, attitudes have become more balanced: speech and writing are recognized to be equally important. From a historical and logical standpoint, speech is primary, writing being derived. But linguistic documents, the records of language in action, include both spoken and written texts; and as far as language teaching is concerned the student wants to learn how to read as well as to listen, to write as well as to speak. One should thus recognize the two kinds of substance and know wherein lies the difference, so that one can clarify the relation between substance and form.

I should now like to turn for a few moments to a consideration of this relation. I shall confine myself to phonic substance, since it is here that the special problems of phonology come into focus. The treatment of the problems raised by orthography, although they are by no means simple, has not demanded a parallel body of specialized theory.

4 Phonology

Other than in cases of lexical or structural ambiguity, a change of form involves a change of substance. If it is accepted for example that singular and plural are different terms in the grammatical system of a particular language, then it follows that there must somewhere be differentiated sounds to manifest or *expound* this system. (It may be noted in passing that *one* of the factors which suggest that the number system in modern French should be attributed to the nominal group, and not to the noun word, is that its exponence for the most part involves the article.) However, we do not relate the formal distinctions directly to the phonetic data. In describing for example the difference between the two forms *je chante* and *je chantais*, we do not say that it consists in the addition, after the voiceless unaspirated apico-dental plosive, of a half-open unrounded front oral vowel; we say rather than an /ɛ/ is added.

What is this element /ɛ/? Formally, in grammar, it is the fused exponent of the categories of number, person and tense (first, second and third person singular, and third person plural, of the imperfect). As for its nature as phonic substance, it is perfectly true that it is a half-open unrounded front oral vowel. In grammar, and lexis, we account for the meaningful contrasts in the language. In phonetics we account for the nature and production of the sounds. What is needed finally is a discipline that can state which are the sounds used in the particular language as exponents of all such contrasts; one, that is, that can link substance to form. This discipline is phonology. Languages exploit their phonic resources in ways that are too complex to allow us to match phonetic statements directly to grammatical and lexical statements; the bridge is provided by phonology. This is why phonology is where linguistics and phonetics meet.

The variations in the sounds of language, though not infinite, can be infinitely subdivided or graduated. Acoustically, there is variation in fundamental frequency, harmonic frequency, amplitude and duration; to these correspond (in total, but not one to one) what are perceived as pitch, quality, loudness and length. It is not surprising that no two languages use these various resources in the same way. It often happens that a difference in sound which counts in one language (which realizes, or expounds, a formal distinction) does not count in another (does not expound any formal distinction); and it regularly happens that a phonetic distinction is used in one way in one language and in a quite different way in a second language. For example, in French, *vowel* nasality is generally distinctive: *presse* is distinct from *prince*. In English it is found only as a by-product and is nowhere distinctive: *man* is pronounced [mæn] or [mæ̃n] without any formal change. But, on the other hand, *consonant* nasality is distinctive in English as in French and, moreover, also in certain structural positions where it is not found in French: *pat* is distinct from *pant*. The two languages use the contrast between nasal and non-nasal articulation in different ways. Phonology is concerned with the phonetic resources as they are used in the given language. Here we can recognize a second series of units: phonological units. These, like grammatical units, carry patterns; but this time the patterns lie in the distinctive sounds. The units naturally differ from language to language just as the phonetic features vary; but there are general tendencies, since human beings are all very much alike from a physiological point of view.

For each language we recognize one which is the smallest of the phonological units: the minimal contrastive segment of speech sound. This is the well-known *phoneme*. Normally contrastive at this rank are the articulatory features which shape the consonants and vowels. What the English or French speaker as a rule recognizes as a 'sound', a vowel or consonant, is a phoneme; we may note in passing that this is not true of the Chinese, who in general are conscious of the syllable but not of the phoneme: the latter plays a different part in their language. Above the phoneme, it is said that every language has the unit *syllable*; but even in the role of this there is considerable variation. In Japanese as in Chinese, the syllable is usually felt to be the basic phonological unit; yet the Japanese syllable is totally different from that of Chinese, being indeed much more like that of French. The syllable often carries stress contrasts and thus enters into rhythmic patterns; yet there are languages, such as Vietnamese and Cantonese, where the syllable carries pitch. In English, above the syllable we have the foot and above this the tone group; the former carries the rhythm and the latter the intonation system. The impression is that in most languages the phonetic resources are organized into three or four phonological units.

Once the phonological patterns have been stated they are brought into relation with the formal levels: we need to show what formal contrasts are realized by what phonological distinctions. In English, where pitch is distinctive at the rank of the tone group, the intonation system expounds, at the level of form, a grammatical system, or rather a number of grammatical systems.[4] In Cantonese, on the other hand, where the syllable is the unit which carries pitch contrasts, the intonation system is the exponent of distinctions at the lexical and not (with two exceptions) at the grammatical level. Cantonese syllables ending in a stop have three 'tones' (three tonic possibilities), those not ending in a stop have eight; in each case the value of the terms in the tone system is like that of the features of articulation: variation produces different lexical items (e.g. ⁻yat 'one', _yat 'day'; _yan 'to print', ⌄yan 'man', ⁄yan 'to lead'). The phonological system is closed, but the formal contrasts expounded by it belong to open sets.

In the same way, languages differ as regards the relation between their phonological and grammatical units, and in the extent to which there is regular correspondence between the two. In Cantonese the correspondence between the *syllable* (a phonological unit) and the *morpheme* (a grammatical unit) is almost absolute: one syllable, one morpheme. Such a regular correspondence is not met with in the Indo-European languages: the English tone group, for example, often coincides with a clause, but we also commonly find the tone group covering a whole compound sentence (two or three clauses) or on the other hand

---

[4] Cf. Paper 7 of this volume.

concentrated as it were on a (grammatical) group or even a single word.

Phonology, like grammar, deals with closed systems: no doubt the number of contrastive sounds that can be produced and identified at a particular moment in the chain of speech is very limited. A speaker may have at his disposal an infinite variety of consonantal sounds but he has only a small set of consonant phonemes. For example, in French a plosive is voiced or voiceless: we may have either *bas* or *pas*, and there is no third possibility for a bilabial plosive. If then an Englishman speaking French produces an English [b], which is different from either of the normal French plosives, a Frenchman has to identify it with one or other of the two possible phonemes. The number of possibilities may be further reduced by restrictions as to position. In Cantonese, for example, there are nineteen consonant phonemes that may occur in syllable-initial position, but in syllable-final only six. We treat the positional distribution of phonemes in the syllable, or that of syllables in the unit next above, whatever it happens to be, by methods parallel to those of grammar: that is, by recognizing structures. The elements of structure of the syllable may be simply the places where consonant and vowel phonemes occur, say C and V. Every language has a certain number of possible structures at syllable rank: in Japanese, for example, the only permitted structures are V and CV, giving *a i u e o ka ki ku ke ko* and so on. In Cantonese we find CV, CVC or CVVC. Some languages, such as the Slavonic group, allow complex consonant clusters in syllable-initial position; even in English we find such forms as CCVCCCC 'glimpsed'. In French, syllable structure is much more restricted.

For each of these structures there is a system of exponents for every element: an English syllable beginning with CCC can have only /s/ as its first element. As far as language teaching is concerned, one importance of phonological structure is that it conditions the phonetic realization of the elements entering into it. For example, in English syllables beginning with a single stop consonant, such as /p/ in *pan*, there is an opposition between voiced and voiceless: between *pan* and *ban*. On the other hand, where the syllable begins with CC, the first being the phoneme /s/ and the second a plosive, there is no longer any opposition between voiced and voiceless: one only is possible. We find a syllable written *span*, but with no contrasting form such as might be written *sban*. There is thus no need here for the /p/ to be distinguished from a /b/. Now in cases where /p/ and /b/ are distinguished, they differ from each other in respect of two phonetic features, voicing and aspiration: the /p/ is voiceless and (lightly) aspirated, the /b/ voiced and unaspirated. After /s/ there is only one possibility, and it is phonetically identical with neither /p/ nor /b/. It is in a sense a sort of mixture of the two: voiceless but unaspirated. In orthography it is always represented by the letters standing for the voiceless consonant phonemes: p t k/c, never b d g; but this is an accident as far as the language as such is concerned. It is idle to ask the question: 'is the /p/ of *span* a /p/ or a /b/ ?', since different elements in the structure of the syllable are involved.

These phonological categories derive, of course, from a process of abstraction from the linguistic material, just as do the categories of grammar. Speech does not consist of a succession of discrete units: we do not finish pronouncing one syllable and then retire to regroup for an assault on the next one. A phonetic feature may persist across several phonemes: some, such as pitch contour, always do, while others may or may not. In the French word *néanmoins*, for example, nasality is usually present throughout. This is an isolated example; but if such a thing happens as a regular pattern in the language the feature is abstracted as a *prosodic* feature and assigned to a segment larger than the phoneme. Some modern linguists have developed very fully the concept of prosodic features; their work in this field is sometimes referred to as 'prosodic phonology'. It is important always to recognize that speech, and in fact language itself, since a spoken language is a set of actual and potential speech events, is a form of activity. One breaks it down in order the better to understand it and to talk about it; but the reality remains in the whole, not in the segments such as the phoneme or the morpheme.

I have cast here only a rapid glance at the theories and methods of the formal description of a language. It is not of course possible in so short a space to explore all the corners of the linguistic landscape. I have not been able to touch on statistical linguistics, a subject likely to be of importance to the language teacher if it treats not only of statistics but also of linguistics. I have left aside the level of context; not only for the sake of brevity but also because it is less systematized and more controversial. Much of the theoretical work in the next ten years may well be devoted to the search for generalized semantic categories and to the systematic description of the relation between linguistic and situational features. Up till recently work in semantics has tended to remain somewhat unintegrated with descriptive linguistics as a whole; the integration of the two, and the development of 'contextual' semantics, is of importance not only for linguistic theory but especially, perhaps, for its pedagogical applications. Meanwhile it is useful to remember that as soon as one gives informative labels to a grammatical system and its terms, for example 'system of number; terms: singular and plural', one is already making observations, however approximate, about contextual meaning.

5 The comparison of languages

In touching on the formal levels of descriptive linguistics and also a little on the level of phonology, which links form and substance, I have tried to show that just as the sounds of a language may be described, with the help of phonetic methods, in such a way as to be of benefit to the student, so a description of the form of language, if based on general linguistic theory, can provide language teachers with a useful and efficient tool. Needless to say, it is not phonetics and linguistics as such that are relevant to the language student, but the results of phonetic and linguistic analysis. I have devoted the major part of this paper to this topic because the description of the language concerned is in my opinion the main task for which general linguistics can be applied to language teaching.

But there remains another aspect to be considered: the comparison of languages, and, in particular, the comparison of the foreign language with the mother tongue. There are different points of view on this question. Some teachers are convinced that one should pay no attention to the learner's mother tongue; that one should keep one's gaze firmly on the foreign language throughout. There are of course cases where no use can be made of the mother tongue, for example if one has a class of twenty students with twenty different native languages; such instances are clearly outside the discussion. This point of view is no doubt partly a reaction against some former methods which were not perhaps very useful: the translation of isolated uncontextualized sentences, the learning of word-lists with translation equivalents and so on. And if the native language itself is not well described, it is difficult to use it effectively. However, given the right conditions one can make positive use of the student's mother tongue; and in such cases to neglect it may be to throw away one of the tools best adapted to the task in hand.

The question is one of priorities. Sooner or later the time comes when one wants to explain to the English student the tenses of the French verbal group. By making a comparison with the English tense system, bringing out both the similarities and the differences, we can take advantage of the adult student's ability to make generalizations and abstractions, which is one of his greatest assets.

It is impossible to specify at what stage the native language comes in; the answer depends on the pedagogical principles adopted. On the one hand, one might attempt to make an overall comparison of the grammatical structure of the foreign and native languages; on the other hand, one might take account only of cases of equivalence, cases where there is a high probability that an item in the native language will always be translated by one and the same item in the foreign language. In any case, whatever the stage of teaching at which it is proposed to use the mother tongue, valid methods of comparison will be needed, and these methods too depend on general linguistic theory.

What is the nature of the equivalence between two languages? We take it for granted that there can be such an equivalence; that in some sense at least, and despite the Italian proverb 'traduttore—traditore', an utterance in language 1 may be *translated* into language 2. If we take two texts in different languages, one being a translation of the other, at what rank (among the grammatical units) would we be prepared to recognize 'equivalence'? In general, this would be at the rank of the sentence, this being the contextual unit of language; it is the sentence which operates in situations. In other words, as could be expected from what is said about the way language works, it is generally the case that (1) a single sentence in language 1 may be represented by a single sentence in language 2: if we have an English text consisting of forty-seven sentences, the French translation could also consist of forty-seven sentences, divided at the same points; and (2) a particular sentence in language 1 can always be represented by one and the same sentence in language 2.

But this equivalence of units and of items is lost as soon as we go below the sentence; and the further down the rank scale we go, the less is left of the equivalence. Once we reach the smallest unit, the morpheme, most vestige of equivalence disappears. The morpheme is untranslatable; the word a little less so, but it is nevertheless very rarely that we can say that a particular word in language 1 may always be translated by one and the same word in language 2—this being condition (2) above; even condition (1) is not always fulfilled for the word, since *one* word in language 1 is often the equivalent of part of a word, or of several words, in language 2. The nearer we come to the sentence, the greater becomes the probability of equivalence; yet it remains true to say that the basic unit of translation is the sentence.

As an illustration, here is an example of a sentence in French translated 'rank by rank' into English. First, each of the French morphemes is translated into English, by what as far as one can say would be the most probable equivalent (if one can be found) for that item irrespective of its environment. The translation is incomprehensible and meaningless. Next the same process is repeated at word rank: this shows more meaning but is still not English. Then in turn at group, clause and sentence rank. What is for some reason called 'literal translation' is translation at, roughly, the rank of the group.[5]

It may be useful here briefly to comment on the process of translation from a theoretical point of view: the theory of translation is an important, if somewhat neglected, aspect of general linguistics. Translation can, I think, be divided into three stages. This does not mean of course that the human translator carries out these three operations in a fixed order, or even that he separates them from each other. Note, however, that in machine translation they might have to be separated: the basic problem of machine translation could be said to be to devise categories drawn from certain aspects of general linguistic theory (description, comparison and translation) whose exponents are such that a machine can be programmed to recognize them.[6] The three stages of the translation process are distinct, rather, from a logical point of view.

In the first stage, for every item at each of the units (every morpheme, every word and so on) there is one equivalent in language 2 that is the most probable: the equivalent which, were one able to amass a large enough sample, would be the most frequent. For example, the French verbal group *ont été choisis* probably has as its most frequent English equivalent *were chosen*. But under certain given conditions other equivalents will be found, such as *have been chosen*; and similarly in the move from English to French there will be a number of equivalents, one being the most probable. The human translator has, as it were, a scale of probabilities recorded in his brain. In the second stage, the choice of equivalent is reconsidered in the light of the linguistic environment: we examine the units above, going as far up the scale as the complete sentence. For example, in the clause 'les délégués ont été choisis hier soir', we would keep in English the most probable equivalent *were chosen*, whereas in the clause 'les délégués ont été déjà choisis', it must be replaced by *have been chosen*. To take another example: the most

---

[5] The description of French grammar which forms the basis of this illustration, as well as of other examples cited in this paper, is the work of R. D. Huddleston.

[6] Cf. Paper 8 of this volume, p. 135; and Paper 9, *passim*.

	la	jeune	fille	avait	+	+	raison	je	vais	+	lui	demand	+er	pardon
M	X	young	daughter	have	X	X	reason	X	go	X	X	ask for	X	pardon
W	the	young	daughter	had			reason	I	am going	him	to ask for			pardon
G	the girl			had			reason	I am going to ask him for						pardon
C	the girl was right							I am going to apologize to him						
S	The girl was right; I am going to apologize to her.													

X = grammatical morpheme

+ = fused morpheme (e.g. *avait* consists of three fused morphemes)

M = morpheme equivalents

W = word equivalents

G = group equivalents

C = clause equivalents

S = sentence equivalent

frequent French equivalent of the English word *head* is *tête*, but if the nominal group in English were 'head of the department' we should have to translate by *chef de section*. Here again it is the unit immediately above that provides the necessary information. In the third stage we take account of the internal grammatical and lexical features of language 2: of grammatical concord (of gender, number, etc.), verbal tense sequence, fixed collocations, idioms and the like. It is interesting to note that in this stage language 1 no longer provides any information; it is only the features of the language into which we are translating that count.

A translation is, then, the final product of these three stages in the process. We may add in passing that the second stage, where we take account of the linguistic environment, extends in fact to a consideration of the situation. It is the stage where we examine the entire environment, formal and contextual. If we are translating a written text, the environment is purely formal: the linguistic entities surrounding the given item. A spoken text on the other hand is already contextualized: that is, it is operating in a situation, and this is part of the environment we consider with a view to determining the choice of equivalent. But as soon as the spoken text is recorded on tape, there is no longer a situation; it becomes decontextualized, just like a written text. Hence the usefulness of film-strips in language teaching; they enable us to recontextualize the spoken text.

This brief outline of the nature of translation is not unrelated to the problem of the comparison of languages. The type of comparison with which we are concerned is of course descriptive and in no way historical. This means that no historical relationship is implied between the languages under comparison. Any language at all may be compared with any other. If one is teaching French to a Vietnamese one can compare, from a purely descriptive standpoint, Vietnamese and French. The aim of such comparison is to bring out their similarities and their differences. We cannot give any reason for similarities and differences between languages. One of the great problems of linguistic typology is to know why it so often happens that languages belonging to the same region, and spoken by communities showing similar patterns of culture, have resemblances in their structures, without there being any lexical correspondences or other evidence of historical relationship.[7]

When we undertake a comparative description of two languages, we have as it were two kinds of evidence at our disposal. The first is transla-

[7] Cf. Paper 10 of this volume, p. 173.

tion equivalence; the second is formal comparison. The translation equivalents are linked to the category of grammatical unit, and they enable us to say that each particular item or category in language 2 is the normal (that is, most probable) equivalent of an item or category in language 1; this means, or at least suggests, that the two items or categories are comparable. The *possibility* of translation equivalence is of course a prerequisite of comparison: if two items can never translate each other, it is of no interest to compare them. Translation can thus be considered as a contextual comparison: if we say that an item $a(1)$ in language 1 can be translated by an item $a(2)$ in language 2, this means that the two items would have the same role in the situation. But we need to complete this observation by a formal comparison: we must know not only that the two items are the equivalent of each other in their contextual meaning, but also whether or not they operate in the same way in the formal structure of the two languages: whether or not they have the same formal meaning (which is also, as I have throughout tried to emphasize, part of the total linguistic meaning).

We must, then, compare the position of the items within the framework of the categories of the grammar: units, structures, classes and systems. One might ask here whether the two languages have a comparable set of units. If not, if for example language 1 does not distinguish between word and morpheme while language 2 does, the student's problem will be greatest at word rank, for the words of his own language will have two sorts of equivalents. Suppose, on the other hand, the two languages have the same set of units, as French and English have: then is *one* French clause translated by *one* English clause, and so on? 'Le médecin est venu', 'the doctor has come'; in both languages we have here one clause, which consists moreover of two groups || *le médecin* | *est venu* ||, || *the doctor* | *has come* ||; they are identical as far as the category of unit is concerned. Consider now 'le médecin de campagne', in English 'the country doctor'. They are both nominal groups. But in English the group is made up merely of words, whereas in French there is a rankshifted adverbial group *de campagne* functioning as qualifier in the structure of the nominal group. The important thing from the student's point of view is that English also has nominal groups with the structure: head (noun) plus qualifier (rankshifted adverbial group), for example 'the doctor at the hospital', but that this structure is not used in *the country doctor* and similar cases.

This non-equivalence in the structure of the nominal group in the two languages is quite normal; and therefore it should be handled systematically. Similarly the nominal and verbal groups in 'le médecin est venu' and 'the doctor has come' have the same structure, yet *ce matin* added to the French clause would produce a change of structure in the English verbal group: *has come* would have to be replaced by *came*. Now the two *clauses* have the same structure SPA: it is important to note that the clause structure remains the same in the two languages; but the two verbal *groups* are different: we have a simple group in English, a compound one in French. None of this is at all new; it merely serves to show that descriptive theory provides a way of establishing precisely what is identical and what is different in the utterances to be compared.

The same applies to lexis. The conventional method of comparing the lexis of two languages is the bilingual dictionary: equivalence is shown by translation, that is by contextual comparison. To say that the French word *venir* is translated in English by *come* means that in a context where a Frenchman uses *venir* an Englishman would have used *come*. In a bilingual dictionary the translation replaces the definition of the monolingual dictionary. But note that we have here translation *at word rank* which, as we have already seen, is very far from translation proper; this is why a comprehensive dictionary may offer us up to fifty equivalents for a single word. It goes without saying that the part played by the citation is here even more essential, if this is possible, than in a monolingual dictionary: not only is the range of contextual meaning of words radically different from one language to another, but so too is their collocational spread. Take for example the translation of a French word in a French–English dictionary, the word *relever*: one well-known dictionary offers us the following list: *raise again*; *set up again*; *restore*; *raise*; *take up*; *pick up*; *lift up*; *draw up*; *turn up*; *curl up*; *twirl up*; *heighten*; *enhance*; *relieve*; *set off*; *adorn*; *give a relish to*; *extol*; *exalt*; *revive*; *notice*; *point out*; *criticize*; *reply to*; *take up*; *free*; *release*; *absolve*; *collect (letters)*; *clear (letterboxes)*; *remove (a dish)*; *recover*; *depend, be dependent (on)*; (law) *be amenable (to)*; *step high*; and some others. If one then translated English clauses containing these words into French one would find oneself saying for example: 'je vais (me) relever (=*m'installer, me pelotonner: curl up*) dans un coin avec mon livre' 'ça a relevé (=*occupé: took up*) tout l'après-midi', 'on est en train de relever (=*reconstruire: restore*) le château', 'je relevais le service (=*me plaignais du service: was criticizing the service*) de ce restaurant'. All these examples represent normal usage of the English words; they are not idioms. It is clear that, for showing the meaning, formal or contextual, of the French word, translations without citations are of limited use.

Another problem in lexical comparision arises from the fact that the relations between words forming a lexical set are very varied. Let us return to what I called the vehicular set:

FRENCH	ENGLISH	CHINESE
train	train	huoche
auto	car	qiche
autobus	bus	gonggongqiche
taxi	taxi	sirenqiche
bicyclette	bicycle	zixingche
'tram'	tram	dianche

In Chinese, however, there is another term 'che', corresponding in some degree to the French word 'voiture' but without any equivalent in English. The word 'che' is the neutral term in the set, and is used in situations where the object in question is obvious or unimportant. If the bus stops in front of you, you would not say 'kuai shang gonggongqiche ba!' ('hurry up and get on the bus'), which would be too specific, but 'kuai shang che ba!'. In English there is no choice: in this set we have only specific words, no general or 'neutral' term. In French there is the word *voiture* which is partly general, but partly specific: one says 'voici l'autobus qui arrive' rather than 'voici la voiture qui arrive'. The important point to note in this respect is that this is a systematic feature of one section of the lexis of Chinese: many sets of items are related in this way, most of them being grammatically nouns. With verbs, in fact the comparative situation tends to be exactly the reverse. English has a word *cut*, French the corresponding *couper*; Chinese has as equivalents some fifteen terms—to cut with a knife, with scissors, with an axe, with a scythe and so on—but no non-specific word *cut*. To oversimplify, in English, generally speaking, sets of items which are verbs tend more often to have a non-specific member than do those made up of nouns, whereas in Chinese it is the other way round. French seems to have more non-specific nouns than English: thus lexically Chinese seems to resemble French more than it does English or the other Indo-European languages, although in its grammar it seems closer to English.

As a last example of comparison, I should like to consider the personal pronouns of French, English, Chinese and Italian:

CONTEXTUAL COMPARISON

I Principal system: reference to participant(s) in situation

	FRENCH	ENGLISH	CHINESE	ITALIAN
1	moi	I	wo	io
2	toi/vous	you	ni/nin	tu/Lei
22	vous	,,	nimen	voi/Loro
3	lui/elle	he/she	ta	lui/lei
12(2)	nous	we	zamen	noi
1(2(2))3(3)	,,	,,	women	,,
33	eux/elles	they	tamen	loro

1 = speaker
2 = addressee
3 = other participant
22 = two or more addressees
33 = two or more other participants
() = optional

II Sub-systems:

A *sex of participant(s)*

	FRENCH	ENGLISH		ITALIAN
	3 33	3		3
M	lui eux	he		lui
F	elle elles	she		lei

M = male, including mixed company if more
than one
F = female

B *social relationship of participant(s) to speaker*

	FRENCH		CHINESE	ITALIAN
	2		2	2 22
I	toi		ni	tu voi
E	vous		nin	Lei Loro

I = interior to social group
E = exterior to social group

FORMAL COMPARISON

Number of different systems:

	FRENCH	ENGLISH	CHINESE	ITALIAN
verbal	3			3
nominal	1	2	1	2
total	4	2	1	5

A Verbal systems: personal pronoun as (bound) word in structure of verbal group (exemplified by forms for 1 and 3M)

	FRENCH			ITALIAN
	1 3M			1 3M
(a)	je il			
(b)	me le			mi lo
(c) (cd)	} me lui {			mi gli
(d)				me glie-

(a) = verbal subject
(b) = verbal direct complement
(c) = verbal indirect complement (independent)
(d) = verbal indirect complement (dependent)

In French there is only one system (cd), but this incorporates a sub-system (cd*) operating in the structure in which the personal pronoun follows the verb. Examples:

il le lui présentera   je te le donne   donne-le-moi
a b cd   a cd b   b cd*
lo conosco   gli parlo   glielo presento   dammelo
b   c   d b   d b

B Nominal systems: personal pronoun as nominal group, operating as subject or complement in clause or as complement in adverbial group (exemplified by forms for 1 and 3M)

	FRENCH		ENGLISH		CHINESE		ITALIAN	
	1	3M	1	3M	1	3M	1	3M
(x) ⎱ (xy) (y) ⎰	⎱ moi	lui ⎰	I me	he him	⎱ wo	ta ⎰	io me	lui lui

(x) = clause subject
(y) = clause complement or adverbial group
        complement

French and Chinese have only one system (xy); in French, pronouns of this system operating as clause subject or clause complement under most conditions require a verbal pronoun in concord. Examples:

moi je sais bien   je le connais, lui   c'est moi   c'est à lui
xy a   b   xy   xy   xy

In Italian, pronouns of system (y) operating as clause complement may be accompanied by a verbal pronoun in concord. Examples:

io non so   non so, io   l'ho visto, lui   e lui   e per me
x   x   b   y   x   y

For the sake of simplicity the reflexive pronouns of Italian and French have been omitted, as also the Italian forms *egli*, *ella* etc. (which are rare in the spoken language). The non-personal pronouns of French, English and Italian have likewise been left out of consideration, as these require partially separate treatment.

The distinction in Italian between *lei* and *Lei*, *loro* and *Loro* is purely orthographic. The now somewhat rare use of *Voi* as 2E ('polite second person singular') has been ignored.

In the comparison of languages we may take advantage of the fact that, as mentioned above, there are always several different ways of describing the same linguistic phenomenon; it is thus possible to adapt the description of one language to that of another. The aim of this 'transfer comparison' is to draw attention to the resemblances between the two languages. For example, Chinese has no word class corresponding to the preposition in French and English; to translate into Chinese adverbial groups of structure 'preposition—complement', such as *into the garden, on the table* (*dao huayuan li, zai zhuoz shang*) we must use one or both of two sub-classes, of the verb and the noun respectively. But the contextual equivalence to English prepositions is so exact that in teaching Chinese to English students one can combine them both into a single distinct class, subdivided of course, and call it the class of prepositions, thus emphasizing the regularity of the equivalence we find in translating from English into Chinese. Transfer comparison is an example of the description of a language made with a specific aim in view, namely foreign language teaching.

6 Conclusion

Most of the first part of this paper was devoted to discussing the description of language at the formal levels. In the last section, speaking of the comparison of languages, I have devoted more time to contextual considerations, since comparison presupposes contextual equivalence, which can be established by translation. At the same time effective comparison depends on description, so that linguistic form cannot be neglected here either. Whether we are concerned with linguistic theory or with its application to language teaching, the foundations of the linguistic study of language will involve grammatical and lexical theory.

It is important here to avoid the impression that the 'formal' study of language is something mechanical or lifeless. It is perhaps unfortunate that the word 'formal' should have been chosen, for it may carry a connotation of devitalization, as though one were dealing only with the skeleton of language. Nothing could be more untrue. The grammatical and lexical study of English poetry, for example, in the light of general linguistic theory, can, it seems to me, be successful in throwing some light on the problem of how poetry, or rather a particular poem, achieves its effects so that it is recognized as a work of art.[8] The analysis of lin-

[8] Cf. Paper 2 of this volume, p. 48.

guistic form is an integral part of stylistics which, far from impairing the aesthetic appreciation of literature, can contribute positively towards it. This is not to imply that we can replace literary criticism by linguistic description. On the contrary, the critic himself, starting from the linguistic analysis of a work, finds his own field of action enlarged, since he has more material on which to base his judgements and the comparisons he makes between literary works.

We must admit, however, that general linguistics has sometimes given the impression of dehydrating language; the fault perhaps lies with our own interpretation of those who sought, understandably, to free themselves from the tyranny of mentalism and of ideas, from the demand that 'the ideas behind' language, rather than language itself, should be described, and thus attempted to exclude considerations of meaning. They said in effect: 'Our predecessors failed to solve the problems involved in describing a language because they based their categories on conceptual criteria; if we are to avoid making the same mistakes, we must exclude concepts, exclude all consideration of the "meaning" of language, all reference to non-linguistic facts; our analysis will be rigorously formal.' But, as I have tried to show, the formal analysis of language is itself a study of meaning. It is impossible to describe language without taking into account the meaning. We entirely agree with those linguists in demanding formal—that is, linguistic—criteria for linguistic categories; but what we cannot accept is this dichotomy between form and meaning, for it is a false opposition. It can I think fairly be claimed that linguists such as J. R. Firth and others have avoided both these extremes; they have rejected the principle that as soon as one begins to speak of linguistic form, one is no longer concerned with meaning. This is why, although making a structural (or rather structural-systemic) analysis of language, Firth never admitted the designation 'structuralist'.

But if we speak of the views of particular linguists, we should add a word of explanation in case of misunderstanding. I would certainly not want to give the impression that linguistic theory has a fragmented character. There are, of course, as in all sciences, especially when they are expanding, different approaches. In the recent history of linguistics, the Prague linguists, the Saussurian group at Geneva, Hjelmslev and the Copenhagen circle, those who followed Bloomfield and Sapir, in America, Daniel Jones, Firth and their colleagues in London, and many others have all contributed to the development of ideas. There are still, certainly, differences of approach; but the point has already been reached where what is held in common by linguists everywhere is much more fundamental than what they disagree about. In those parts of the theory where there are important divergences of opinion I have represented here my own views keeping in mind the question of relevance to language teaching. I have attempted to avoid both the so-called 'mechanism' of some structural linguistics, with its emphasis on 'procedures of description' rather than on a comprehensive theory of language, and on the other hand the more rarefied atmosphere of the Copenhagen circle, whose methods are somewhat difficult to apply to the practical description of a given language. At the same time it is their work no less than that of other linguists that has contributed to an overall theory of language which is both valid from the point of view of contemporary scientific thought and at the same time capable of being applied, not only in the description of any particular language but also in the use of a description for important practical or educational needs such as modern language teaching. A description of a language, if it is to be of practical use, must be based on a general theory; a theory of language, if it is to remain in touch with reality, must be tested in the description of languages. There is no cleavage between the pure and the applied in linguistics; on the contrary, each flourishes only where the other is also flourishing.

Two

Linguistics
and English studies (1959)

1

I shall be concerned here not with the place of linguistic work in English studies as a whole but rather with its place in relation to literary studies. My purpose will be to suggest that we need to narrow the gap between language studies and those falling under the general heading of literary criticism and appreciation. As I proceed, I shall touch on some problems which seem to call for closer collaboration. Speaking on a somewhat similar subject not long ago in Oxford, I mentioned my rejection of a possible title for a talk of this kind: 'Two cheers for philology'. Two cheers, I would rather say, for the somewhat half-hearted attempts of the two factions to achieve a fruitful integration. I am not thinking here of the world of mediaeval English, where integration of a sort is more forced upon one; I shall be concerned rather with studies relating to the last four centuries or so.

I am not altogether happy about acknowledging the dichotomy implied by the terms 'linguistic' and 'literary' at all, but one cannot easily avoid using them. One can however at least try to avoid allegorical imagery like 'The Muse unchained', noting in passing that it was at no time the *Muse* who was in chains but (if anybody) her humble gossips and hand-maidens. For 'Muse', therefore, even to keep the allegory right, we should in any case have to substitute some phrase with the appropriateness in that context which the phrase 'gentleman's gentleman' has in another. I wish then to examine the case for a thorough interpenetration of our disciplines and to consider (at least by implication) whether future progress in the field in general does not to a large extent depend on such interpenetration.

This being my aim, I hope I shall be forgiven if, among other things, I provide one or two instances of the way in which primarily literary scholars sometimes attack problems which directly involve language without having a wholly adequate understanding either of theory or method. But I should add a strong word on the other side: scholars specializing in the study of the language are too often reluctant to embark on such investigations at all. This is to be regretted, not merely as a loss to the subject as a whole, but because the rigorous exploration of new problems, which are quite often what we might call problems in applied linguistics, is always likely to produce advances in linguistic theory. I recall Sir George Thompson once saying on the Brains Trust that though pure science can readily be justified on its own terms, we must never forget that the consideration of new problems in applied science often leads to striking advances in pure mathematics and the like. I would indeed suggest that the main impetus to advances in linguistic theory must come from the tackling of new problems. And such advances are at least as likely to be made within those areas of language study which are of direct interest to students of literature as they are anywhere else. It is not therefore just a question of performing a possibly useful service, and it is beside the point to ask whether the resulting theoretical advances in a given case are likely to be earth-shaking or of a very minor significance.

My own observations within the field of English would lead me to suggest that professional linguists have in the main confined themselves to studies which certainly do not in any sense fully solve those many problems with linguistic aspects which so frequently confront students of literature. There are of course numerous works—dictionaries, concordances, historical and descriptive grammars and the like which everybody takes for granted; these are indeed hardly felt to belong to linguistics at all, they are somehow not difficult or mysterious enough for that. But though they certainly do so belong, and are of great importance, they should not blind us to the existence of many problems which they themselves do not begin to solve.

A real drawback about the very existence of such works, and this in rough proportion to their magnitude, is that they often give a spurious impression of finality and once-and-for-allness. This often seriously inhibits further work of a similar kind, even when it is quite obvious that further work is necessary. But we must squarely face the simple fact that new dictionaries, concordances, thesauri, grammars and the like must continually be created; such as Johnson is shall Onions be. This is not just because of a frequently clear need to incorporate new 'facts'; it is even more a matter of making the available 'facts' accessible in new and illuminating arrangements in the light of advances in linguistic theory and its application. In another realm of scholarship Buck's *Dictionary of Selected Synonyms in the Principal Indo-European Languages* is a notable example.

Besides such works as I have mentioned, there are of course numerous instances of much more restricted linguistic investigations, studies with highly limited and specialized objectives; one may cite, for example, the attempts which have been made to attain a thorough understanding of what certain earlier English writers meant when they used words like 'enthusiasm' or 'sensibility'. I would stress the need for more and more such studies, both of a historical and of a descriptive kind, and not of course confined to lexical matters.

To mention a single problem, I have been struck recently, purely as a bed-time reader, by the extraordinary interest of Jane Austen's dialogue. I continually find myself asking: what is the nature of the *selections*, grammatical as well as lexical, whereby she contrives to impart so individual a flavour to the conversation of this or that character? Much of value could be done on this subject. In advocating (as I should wish to) the pursuit of such limited objectives, I am taking into consideration the fact that so many more ambitious schemes simply never get completed. And though it is true that the arbitrary abstraction or delimitation of any such objective has its dangers, linguistic theory is not ill-equipped to meet situations of precisely this kind. Besides, unless linguistic theory proves adequate to handle such matters, it is scarcely likely to be of greater avail in some more comprehensive and ambitious study. It is remarkable indeed how *wide* the theoretical implications of even a small practical or 'applied' study are; such investigations are therefore, or can be, admirable proving grounds.

But there is a kind of inhibition here, comparable to that exerted by large dictionaries and grammars. For the very considerable amount of linguistic work which has been done with innumerable limited objectives in mind seems to give many people the impression that most of the 'real stuff' has been covered and that further excursions can hardly be counted as linguistic in the same fundamental sense at all, and are not therefore amenable to the same kind of discipline. It is both the sheer quantity of work done and the limited number of 'respectable' modes of approach that are inhibiting. As a result, in the unhappy hunting-ground in the no-man's land between traditional philology and traditional literary studies we tend to have a sort of free-for-all in which the weapons of analytical procedure are brushed aside as inapplicable or unnecessary. I have said enough already to suggest that professional linguists must take a considerable share of the blame for this since they themselves too often shy off from, and even despise, many exciting fields of study; such criticism as I now propose to offer is not therefore focused entirely on those whose work I shall be considering.

I shall begin with a problem which is explored by Francis Berry in *Poet's Grammar*,[1] a work that illustrates the importance which at least some literary critics are beginning to attach to certain kinds of linguistic scrutiny. Among other matters, Mr Berry considers Shakespeare's use of the pronoun of the second person; in particular, he investigates his shifting use of *you* and *thou* in those sonnets where Shakespeare is addressing the young man.[2]

Now it is a linguist's normal experience that the tackling of any such problem calls for a solid theoretical basis and then often demands of the investigator a great deal more sheer analysis than is ever fit to appear in a final statement. Furthermore it is important that such a statement be accompanied by enough information about both theory and material to enable the reader to assess the validity of the conclusions that are reached. In the case of Mr Berry's work, and it is typical of many such studies, I do not feel able to do this. One is asked, in fact, to accept a rather remarkable conclusion: that the pronoun *thou*, with which the sonnet sequence begins, is more formal than the *you* which (intermittently) appears thereafter, and also that (as Mr Berry puts it)[3]

> the one previously saluted as "thou" and a unity, has become a compound of body and soul, where the body can betray the soul's will or wish. Through the plural form a sense of duality is broached in the poetry.

This, incidentally, might suggest why a doctor says to his patient: 'And how are we this morning?' For could we not similarly maintain that what we have here is a special kind of 'exclusive *we*' which by excluding the doctor himself reserves its duality of reference for two sides of the patient himself, thereby indicating a sound appreciation of psychosomatic realities? What the doctor really means then is something like: 'And how are the wretched body and mind this morning?' My

---

[1] *Poet's Grammar; person, time and mood in poetry*, London, 1958.
[2] For an approach to a related topic see Paper 4 of this volume, and the bibliographical references in notes 1 and 2 to that paper.
[3] Op. cit., p. 36.

main point here is simply this: that on the evidence presented to us, I feel we are in no position either to accept or reject Mr Berry's conclusion. If he is right, therefore, he has done himself less than justice.

I take—almost at random—another example relating to a different kind of linguistic analysis, this time involving types of sentence-pattern in English. In her book *Eras and Modes in English Poetry*, Josephine Miles has constructed a sort of linguistic framework which we are asked to accept as quite fundamental to our understanding of the history of English poetry and our appreciation of that poetry. This framework is based on a rather ill-defined and puzzling analysis of two broadly contrasting kinds of sentence-patterns which are said to be favoured by various poets over the last four hundred years:

> The distinction (she writes)[4] which I have found pertinent in kinds of sentence structure is between the sort which emphasizes substantival elements—the phrasal and co-ordinative modifications of subject and object—and the sort which emphasizes causal co-ordination and complication of the predicate. The first or phrasal type employs an abundance of adjectives and nouns, in heavy modifications and compounding of subjects, in a variety of phrasal constructions, including verbs turned to participles; it is a cumulative way of speaking. The second or clausal type emphasizes compound or serial predicates, subordinate verbs in relative and adverbial clauses, action, and rational subordination; it is a discursive way of speaking. The first might say, "Rising and soaring, the golden bird flies into the stormy night of the east"; the second, if given the same terms, would say "The golden bird rises and soars; it flies into the night which storms in the east".

I should add that this is the only explanatory example that I can find anywhere in the book. Once again I feel that the writer has not done herself justice or sufficiently considered the difficulties which confront the reader in a situation of this kind. He is entitled to explanations, and no enthusiasm on the part of the writer can replace them or make them unnecessary.[5]

---

[4] Josephine Miles, *Eras and Modes in English Poetry*, University of California Press, 1957, p. 2.

[5] For a much more illuminating discussion of what I take to be basically the same distinction, see Rulon Wells, 'Nominal and Verbal Style', *Style in Language*, ed. Thomas A. Sebeok, New York and London, 1960, p. 213. See also H. and Mrs A. Thornton, *Time and Style; a psycho-linguistic essay in classical literature*, London, 1962.

A serious difficulty in such work lies in the handling of the terminology. I find it difficult, for instance, to understand what Miss Miles means when, in her introductory discussion, she talks of 'figure, symbolic connotation and association, or of normative intensification'. All such terms require the most careful definition and exemplification; only then can one appreciate and evaluate the conclusions which in a very real sense derive from their use.

The problems I have touched upon are in different ways related to style. Each such problem requires a linguistic approach which is carefully adapted to it. For example, the assessment of what is individual in a man's style requires that we should be in possession of some sort of yardstick by which we can assess or measure his use of language. If we say that the later prose of Carlyle is remarkable, this must be *in comparison with* something, and there is scarcely much point in trying to correlate it with the man and his personality until we have managed in some way to put our fingers on those characteristics which *are* remarkable. Of course everybody realizes this, but it is extraordinary how rarely anyone takes the trouble to apply the techniques of linguistic description and comparison to such a problem. I remember once submitting some remarks to Professor Bazell in which I had written that something or other was palpably different from something else. His chastening reply, that I seemed to have established no criteria of palpability, leads me to suggest that—in studying the style of a writer—we must have some kind of criteria of remarkableness.[6]

I would not deny that contributions on these lines have been made. But they have not usually been very systematic, and such studies in reference to English are still in their infancy. If we choose to be specially preoccupied with the question of personal flavour, then we are looking at something which, being personal, must in some measure be unique; and if it is so, we ought to be able to make at least *some* valid linguistic statements about the nature of its uniqueness. But if we begin (as I insist we must in such cases) with description, this, if it is to be stylistically enlightening, must be accompanied or followed up by comparisons of some kind. This kind of approach might be likened to the way one

---

[6] For some penetrating work on certain lexical aspects of this kind of problem, see two works by Alvar Ellegård: *Who was Junius?*, Stockholm, 1962, and *A statistical method for determining authorship: The Junius letters, 1769–1772*, Gothenburg Studies in English No. 13, Gothenburg, 1962. For references to other recent work of the same kind, see the review by C. D. Chrétien, *Language*, Vol. 40, 1964, p. 85.

reads 'character' from handwriting; I can only *evaluate* the distinctive and revealing features of one man's hand after I know from my experience of other hands what is in fact distinctive about it.

I do not suggest that it is the obligation of the linguist who has succeeded in applying his criteria of remarkableness to take the further step of relating the linguistic ingredients of the 'flavour' of a writer to his personality or his genius. At the very least, however, he can provide a frame of reference within which it becomes possible to pinpoint certain stylistic characteristics as a *prelude* to the assessment of their significance and effect, whether this assessment be made by himself or by someone else. But I believe further that the linguist can on occasion say something useful about the significance of certain stylistic features—something which might well escape those who had not themselves thought so seriously or critically about linguistic analysis and description.[7] We do not deny him the professional right to say quite specific things (e.g. in dictionaries) about the different implications of the words *tiger* and *elephant*. Why then should we debar him from the right to a concern with the differing implications of more subtle but equally 'linguistic' nuances of a stylistic kind? This second part of my paper will consist of some very diffident and tentative remarks which may help to bring out what I mean; they relate to some aspects of the language of Hopkins.

2

Father Peters, in a book he wrote on Hopkins in 1948,[8] furnishes us with a starting point when he says in effect (though not in these words) that Hopkins was struggling continually against some of the basic conventions of the system of normal English because they ran distinctly counter to his own conceptualizing of reality.

> I start (he says)[9] from Hopkins' peculiar perception of external objects and study how its precise expression necessitated the employment of (his) peculiar form of language.

He goes on to show how Hopkins' use of the word *inscape* helps us here. His analysis—earlier in the book—of this word (which is not in the *Oxford English Dictionary* or in the *Supplement*) is most revealing. He

---

[7] Cf. Paper 3 of this volume, p. 56 ff.

[8] W. A. M. Peters, *Gerard Manley Hopkins. A critical essay towards the understanding of his poetry*, London, 1948.

[9] Op. cit., p. 107.

examines *all* the collocations of the word and discusses in detail over a score of the many dozens of instances of it which occur in his writings.

> Hopkins (he says)[10] habitually looked at objects with the fixed determination to catch what was individually distinctive in them in order thus to arrive at some insight into their essence as individuals. To express this set of individuating characteristics in a suitable term he coined the word 'inscape'.

There are no trade-union rules which forbid me according the full three cheers to Father Peters for the unusually perceptive and detailed analysis set forth in this chapter, though I shall suggest later that a failure to see the full implications of certain linguistic data has led him slightly astray in one particular.

Hopkins' constant use of *inscape* suggests a preoccupation, as he looks at aspects of the world around him, with that set of individuating characteristics of an object which mark it off from all others.

> Inscape (Peters says)[11] is individually distinctive and unique, and as such it cannot be expressed in words which, with the exception of proper names, by their very essence as lexical elements of the given language, are universal terms . . . Words as symbols of universals were of no use to Hopkins. He could not describe an object by indicating the genus to which it belongs and then limiting this genus to a species by the addition of a specific difference: (e.g.) 'an oaken chest'. For such description indicates the universal nature of the object, and its specific essence, but gives no direct information whatever about its individual essence,[12] and this is precisely what Hopkins is so anxious to express in words . . . Hopkins did not attend to what this object had in common with others. Inscape is the denial of universality and consequently description by way of limiting the universal was useless.

I must necessarily speak in rather primitive terms here but what I think Peters does not develop quite enough (though as I shall show later he comes very near to the heart of the matter at one point) is that *inscape* relates quite often to the uniqueness and individuality not of objects, but

---

[10] Ibid., p. 2.

[11] Ibid., pp. 107 ff.

[12] Hopkins is interestingly similar to Tolstoy in this matter, despite Tolstoy's theoretical views to the contrary. Cf. Isaiah Berlin, *The Hedgehog and the Fox*, New York, Mentor Books: 1957, pp. 63 ff.: 'The celebrated life-likeness of every object and person in his world derives from this astonishing capacity of presenting every ingredient of it in its *fullest individual essence* (italics mine) . . . always . . . set in an absolutely specific context in time and space.'

of what might loosely be called processes or events. I would stress here that it is an examination of his own way of using language, both in prose and verse (and not merely in passages where the word *inscape* occurs) which leads me to say this. Just as Hopkins could not in his verse (except for certain special purposes which Peters deals with) use a phrase like 'oaken chest', so also was he worried by the way ordinary language seemed perpetually to force him arbitrarily to split up the concept 'process' or 'event' by compelling him to use what in this context we may describe as object-words on the one hand and action-words on the other, that is to say (very roughly) substantives and finite verbs.

It is true that in his prose Hopkins never discusses this openly, though I suspect he gets rather near to it in his early paper on Parmenides (?1868).[13] But (so far as I can discover) he never, intellectually, sees even the 'oaken chest' problem either; this only comes out clearly in the language of Hopkins the poet—clearly, at least, once Father Peters has pointed it out to us. We need not be surprised therefore if in his notebooks and elsewhere Hopkins often uses *inscape* in reference to objects rather than events, for instance Spanish chestnuts, Edinburgh Castle Rock, a bluebell, seaweed, a glacier, a horned violet, various details of architecture, and so forth. But it is revealing how extraordinarily numerous are the additional cases in which it is applied to what one can only call events, with movements and action and flux and change deeply involved. For example:

> Note that a slender race of fine flue cloud inscaped in continuous eyebrow curves hitched on the Weisshorn peak as it passed.[14]

Or of the development of a flower:

> A beautiful instance of inscape sided on the slide, that is a *successive sidings of one inscape* (the italics are mine: the phrase 'sided on the slide' seems to mean 'with different aspects successively revealed') is seen in the behaviour of the flag flower from the shut bud to the full blowing: each term you can distinguish is beautiful in itself and of course if the whole 'behaviour' were gathered up and so stalled[15] it would have a beauty of all the higher degree.[16]

[13] *The Journals and Papers of Gerard Manley Hopkins*, ed. Humphrey House and Graham Storey, London, 1959, p. 127.

[14] Ibid., p. 181.

[15] The word *stall* is also used elsewhere in the *Journals*, see pp. 194, 196. The basic meaning would seem to be 'fix' or 'hold'. Hence 'gathered up and stalled' means 'apprehended as a single experience rather than as a succession of separate experiences'.

[16] *Journals*, p. 211. 'Sided' and 'siding' appear elsewhere in his writings, see

The word 'behaviour' here is significant and we shall see in a minute that it comes into his verse too. And to me his final remark is of striking interest:

> if the whole behaviour were gathered up and so stalled it would have a beauty of all the higher degree.

Is it fanciful to suggest that this is startlingly like the concept in modern physics whereby we can regard an event as a static picture in a time-space continuum instead of the older classical concept of a dynamic picture in a merely space continuum?[17]

One thing that strikes me above all others in the poetry of Hopkins (and it is present to a marked degree in his descriptive prose) is the linguistic evidence for a preoccupation with the flow and agitation of process and change. Cloud movements obsessed him; he refers to them scores of times in his prose. Hear him in verse about them, and how he brings in the word 'behaviour' again:

> . . . up above, what wind-walks! What lovely behaviour
> Of silk-sack clouds! has wilder, wilful-wavier
> Meal-drift moulded ever and melted across skies?[18]

Who can doubt that it is the whole of what we perceive (in the framework of ordinary concepts of time) as an active changing process which he is striving here and elsewhere to capture and present as a sort of indivisible unit, a glimpse of the 'eternal image' which Plato describes so movingly in the *Timaeus*?[19]

Now it is a normal consequence of the structure of English grammar (and indeed of Indo-European grammar in general and that of many other languages) that events are usually 'conveyed' by a procedure involving the use of substantives and finite verbs. And this procedure

[17] See A. Einstein and L. Infeld, *The Evolution of Physics*, Cambridge, 1938, Chap. iii, and especially the sub-section headed 'The Time-Space Continuum'.
[18] *Poems*, 3rd ed. p. 74.
[19] See Benjamin Jowett's translation in *The Dialogues of Plato*, Oxford, 1892, Vol. iii, p. 456. Cf. Miguel de Unamuno, *Del Sentimiento Trágico de la Vida*, Chap. ix: 'Ante nosotros pasan las escenas como en un cinematógrafo, pero la cinta permanece una y entera más allá del tiempo.' See also C. G. Jung, *Memories, Dreams, Reflections*, London, 1963, Chap. x.

Journals, pp. 130, 155, 267. 'Siding' would appear to mean something like 'aspect'. The most illuminating examples appear in the essay on Parmenides, *Journals*, p. 130.

does not reflect or do justice to what (borrowing Peters' phrase about objects) we may call the 'individual essence' of a particular event. In his own intellectual discussions of these matters in his prose writings, Hopkins (as I have already suggested) is sufficiently hidebound to accept the use of substantive and finite verb as corresponding in some quite direct way to reality. Like most of his later critics, though for better reasons, he had not read Whorf's book on *Language, Thought and Reality*[20] or the numerous papers in the *International Journal of American Linguistics* and elsewhere which might have helped him to bridge the gap between his intellectual and his more intuitive and poetic self.

'All words mean either things or relations of things' he says,[21] as if the terms 'things' and 'relations of things' had a firm extra-linguistic validity. This is in an early paper written when he was still only twenty-three years old, but there is nothing elsewhere to show that he ever abandoned this position intellectually. But the very frequency with which he writes, in prose, about comets, clouds, sunsets, eclipses, the Aurora Borealis, rain, wind, waves, running water, burning candles, fireworks, rainbows, thunderstorms, lightning and the like shows that, even intellectually, this does not quite satisfy him; as a poet he can be seen much more clearly struggling to break away from this position. We may now consider a little further in just what ways the language of his poetry reflects and demonstrates this struggle.

I have already touched upon the vocabulary, and I shall confine my remarks on grammar to three points. Father Peters has himself called attention, first of all, to the unusual rarity of adverbs in his poetry: It seems that there are only twelve ending in *-ly* in all his poems.[22] Hopkins much prefers what, formally speaking, would normally be regarded as an adjective:

> . . . the bright wind boisterous ropes, wrestles beats earth bare[23]
> . . . then off, off forth on swing,
> As a skate's heel sweeps smooth on a bow-bend:[24]

[20] Benjamin Lee Whorf, *Language, Thought and Reality*, New York and London: MIT Technology Press and Wiley, 1956.

[21] *Journals*, p. 125 (1868). John Locke had long before, but with more sophistication, said something on similar lines: 'Besides Words, which are Names of *Ideas* in the Mind, there are a great many others that are made use of to signify the *Connection* that the Mind gives to *Ideas, or Propositions*, one with another.' *An Essay concerning Human Understanding*, Book III, Chap. vii, para. 1.

[22] In a full study one would naturally wish to verify that this *is* in fact a remarkably low frequency.

[23] *Poems*, p. 111.

[24] *Poems*, p. 73.

In his discussion of this problem,[25] Peters writes:

> The best approach to this question why Hopkins was so keen on the use of the predicative adjective is first to show why it was that he had no use for the adverb proper, that is, the adverb belonging to the verb. The modal adverb proper determines the nature of the verb ... In a complete sentence of the type 'the candle burns clearly', the group 'burns clearly' is predicative of the subject, and the adverb 'clearly' has no direct connexion with the subject. But in Hopkins' perception of inscape the quality did not only affect the activity as expressed by the verb, but it directly inhered in the subject as well. When Hopkins inscaped a burning candle, the quality of clearness did not exclusively belong to the burning; as the burning was of the individual essence of this candle as here and now perceived, as consequently, in his perception there was no separation of activity and essence. 'Some candle *clear* burns'[26]: because it defines the nature of the burning, it defines the nature and the essence of the inscaped candle as well: the burning is clear, but the candle is clear too. The quality cannot be sundered from the activity; and because activity and essence are one here, the quality consequently points to both the activity and the thing; it looks both ways. Unless we take it in this twofold function—of course the functions converge and fall together—we cannot understand the exact expression of the inscapes of this world.

Here Peters gets very near to what I have been trying to bring out. But he speaks throughout as if 'individual essence' on the one hand and 'activity' on the other, though not to be sundered, were somehow two separate realities, and as if Hopkins' attempt to link them more closely were therefore a linking of two separate realities. Peters is wedded to the doctrine of substances and relations between substances and unquestioningly sees these directly mirrored in what Bertrand Russell calls term-words and relation-words.[27] As a result his account of all this falls, as it seems to me, a little short of the mark; it does so precisely because of his having much the same intellectual preconceptions as are characteristic of Hopkins himself when *he* tries to be analytical.

A second way in which the language of Hopkins the poet reveals his

[25] Op. cit., p. 137 ff.
[26] *Poems*, p. 89.
[27] Bertrand Russell, *Human Knowledge*, London, 1948, p. 88.

preoccupation with the *inscape* (i.e. with the individuating characteristics) of processes and events, is the role played in it by the verbal
noun.[28] For the verbal noun in English has frequently to be called into
use when we try to translate closely into English sentences from languages where there is a less sharp distinction between object-words and
action-words, and readily suggests itself as a bridger of the gap in
question:

> There is one, yes I have one (Hush there!);
> Only not within seeing of the sun,
> Not within the singeing of the strong sun,
> Tall sun's tingeing, or treacherous the tainting of the earth's air,
> Somewhere elsewhere there is ah well where! one,
> One.[29]

Finally, though I shall not pursue this, one may suspect that the total
omission of finite verbs in certain passages has a similar motivation:

> Happy the father, mother of these! Too fast:
> Not that, but thus far, all with frailty, blest
> In one fair fall; but for times aftercast,
> Creatures all heft, hope, hazard, interest.[30]

There were times, it is clear, when the tidy conventional relationships of
subject and predicate ran counter to his modes of thought. His was a
continuous struggle to come to terms with a medium which he felt was
fundamentally unsuited in certain ways to the expression of some of his
deepest perceptions.

I have ventured to present these very sketchy and tentative remarks
about Hopkins because they would seem to indicate the interesting
possibility that a knowledge of the system of certain non-Indo-European
languages might throw a little new light on one of our own poets. I
suggest that a carefully chosen American Indian with a first-class English
degree from Cambridge could do distinguished work on Hopkins. If he
had also a degree in theoretical physics from M.I.T. so much the better.
Can it even be, it suddenly strikes me, that we have hit here on a further
exciting possibility? In view of the Middle English shortening of a long
stressed vowel before two or more consonants in dissyllabic words,
(compare *wisdom*, *chapman*, *bonfire*) can we afford to dismiss the *Hŏp-* of

[28] Cf. Peters, op. cit., pp. 135 ff.
[29] *Poems*, p. 97. This should be examined in connection with the essay on
Parmenides, see footnote 13, p. 50.
[30] *Poems*, p. 164.

Hopkins and the *Hōp-* of *Hopi* as mere coincidence? Surely, rather, Hopkins, 'the little Hopi', was himself an American Indian on his father's side.

I am conscious of having in this paper merely scratched here and there at one or two types of problem. I conclude with a brief plea for the attainment of a number of well-defined objectives. We need more work on dictionaries and concordances and more still on thesauri; we need more 'period' grammars and grammars covering the work of single writers; we need a closer integration of linguistic work and textual criticism; we need more work on versification and still more on the underlying problems relating to the rhythms of prose; we need more understanding of the correlation between remarkable language and remarkable processes of thought; we need to overhaul and bring up to date our cumbersome and confused technical vocabulary. In all this we need constant interdisciplinary collaboration, and it is my hope and belief that the Cambridge Linguistic Society will among many other things act as a constant stimulus in these directions.

Three

Descriptive linguistics
in literary studies (1962)

In any discussion of the application of linguistic theory and method to the study of literary texts, one of the difficulties that arise is that there is so much background to be filled in before one actually reaches the text. I am not referring to the linguistic theory itself, the exposition of which is clearly outside the necessary scope of such a discussion, although it may be useful to specify what areas of linguistic science are relevant. But while it can be taken for granted that there are within linguistics theories and methods for describing the language of any text, many other things cannot be taken for granted: the place of linguistic statements in literary analysis, the relation between literary and non-literary texts and the question whether literary texts require special linguistic methods, to name only a few.[1]

So much that is of underlying importance still needs to be said on all these subjects that one runs the risk of devoting all one's time to the discussion of principles. I propose to avoid that danger by reversing the more usual order of procedure and starting with some texts, leaving theoretical points to the second part of my paper. Although this may make it less clear what is being illustrated, it will at least ensure that the illustrations are not left out.

Immediately another problem arises: all illustrations in linguistics are misleading. Language does not operate except in the context of other events; even where these are, as with written texts, other language events, any one point made about a piece of text which is under focus raises many further points extending way beyond it into the context. This does not mean that no linguistic statements can be self-sufficient, but that the only ultimately valid unit for textual analysis is the whole text. It takes

[1] See in particular the discussion in Paper 2 of this volume.

many hours of talking to describe exhaustively even the language of one sonnet.

However, if students can be asked to comment on the language of literary texts within the time limits of an examination, it should be possible to give selective illustrations of what would be regarded as a good answer to a question on the language of particular short texts. I propose here to refer to W. B. Yeats's poem *Leda and the Swan*, and to three short passages of modern English prose, by John Braine, Dylan Thomas, and Angus Wilson.

LEDA AND THE SWAN

A sudden blow: the great wings beating still
Above the staggering girl, the thighs caressed
By the dark webs, her nape caught in his bill,
He holds her helpless breast upon his breast.

How can those terrified, vague fingers push
The feathered glory from her loosening thighs?
And how can body, laid in that white rush,
But feel the strange heart beating where it lies?

A shudder in the loins engenders there
The broken wall, the burning roof and tower
And Agamemnon dead.

Being so caught up,
So mastered by the brute blood of the air,
Did she put on his knowledge with his power
Before the indifferent beak could let her drop?

(W. B. YEATS)

The first example will be the use of 'the' in *Leda and the Swan*. The relevant grammatical background can be summarized as follows. The primary (least delicate) structure of the English nominal group is (M)H(Q): a head, which may or may not be preceded by a modifier and followed by a qualifier. Nearly everything occurring in the qualifier is rankshifted: that is, is of a rank (in fact always clause or group) above or equal to the unit in whose structure it is operating (here the group). In the modifier, on the other hand, only compound 'Saxon genitives' and some modifiers of measurement are rankshifted; in general the modifier is an ordered sequence of words (the word being the unit immediately below the group in rank), proceeding from the most grammatical to the most lexical. The first place in the structure of the modifier is occupied by the word class known as 'deictics', consisting more delicately of three sub-classes of which one contains the items 'the', 'a', 'this', 'that', the personal deictics 'his', 'her', etc., and certain other words. The contextual function of the deictics is to identify, and among them 'the' is unmarked and specific: that is, its function is to identify a *specific* subset but to do so by reference to something other than itself; unlike 'his' or 'that', 'the' carries no power of identification but indicates that something else present does. This 'something else' may be either (1) in the M/Q elements of the nominal group, (2) in the context, linguistic or situational, or (3) in the head of the nominal group itself. There are thus three distinct relations into which 'the' as deictic enters, respectively 'cataphoric', 'anaphoric', and 'homophoric'. These can be illustrated from the following passage:

> Accordingly, after a peace-offering of tobacco, in return for a draught of foaming milk, I took leave, and turned to the ascent of the peak.
>
> The climb is perfectly easy, though I contrived to complicate matters by going the wrong way. The absence of guides generally enables one to enjoy a little excitement, the more agreeable because not contemplated beforehand. Indeed, to confess the truth, a former attempt upon the mountain had failed altogether by reason of my ingeniously attacking it by the only impracticable route. It was with all the more satisfaction that I found myself on the present occasion rapidly approaching the summit, and circumventing the petty obstacles which tried to oppose my progress.
>
> (LESLIE STEPHEN: *The Playground of Europe*)

For example:

Cataphoric:
  The absence *of guides*
  the only impracticable route

Anaphoric:
  turned to the *ascent* of the peak. *The* climb

Homophoric:
  the truth

In two instances, 'the more agreeable' and 'all the more satisfaction', 'the' is not a deictic at all but a distinct formal item which operates as submodifier in the nominal group.

The complete statement of the formal properties of these relations, such that they can be recognized as distinct structures, is complex and involves lexis as well as grammar—though in spoken English, since tonicity (the placing of the tonic in the tone group) can be observed, it is possible to make a purely grammatical statement that accounts for most occurrences. In written English the general picture is as follows: there is a high probability that

(a) if, following 'the', there is a modifier or qualifier in the nominal group, 'the' is cataphoric,
(b) if there is no modifier or qualifier, then

    (i) if in the preceding context there has occurred a lexical item which is either the same item as, or from the same lexical set as, the head of the nominal group, 'the' is anaphoric,

    (ii) if not, 'the' is homophoric.

Table I[1] shows all the nominal groups, other than those consisting only of pronoun or personal name, in *Leda and the Swan*. Out of a total of 25, no less than 15 have *both* a specific deictic (10 'the', 5 others) *and* a modifier (other than the deictic) or qualifier or both. This contrasts, for example, with Yeats's poem *His Phoenix*, which contains 81 nominal groups of which only 17 are of this type. In nominal groups with modifier or qualifier, if 'the', or other specific deictic, is present it is usually cataphoric; moreover, samples of modern English prose writing show that the most frequent use of 'the' is in fact cataphoric reference to modifier or qualifier, not anaphoric reference ('second mention') as often supposed. In *Leda*, however, out of ten nominal groups having 'the' and a modifier or qualifier, only one, 'the brute blood of the air', had 'the' in cataphoric use. The remainder, although they have both (*a*) items whose place in structure (at M or Q) makes them potentially defining, and (*b*) the item 'the' whose function is usually to show that such potentially defining items are in fact defining, yet have non-cataphoric 'the'. That is to say, in spite of the 'the', 'the dark webs' are not identified by their being dark—like 'the loins', they are to be identified anaphorically, in fact by anaphoric reference to the title of the poem. The only other type of writing I can call to mind in which this feature is found at such a high density is in tourist guides and, sometimes, exhibition catalogues. (I hope I need not add that this is in no sense intended as an adverse criticism of the poem.)

[1] The Tables are printed at the end of the article, pp. 68 and 69.

The second example is the distribution of verbal items in *Leda and the Swan*. Most of this poem, especially the first ten and a half lines, is organized in nominal groups; they account for 69 of the 83 words in this first part. There are 15 verbal groups in the poem, and in addition four words of the class 'verb' operating directly in the structure of (as opposed to being rankshifted into) nominal groups ('staggering', 'loosening', 'burning', 'broken'). The distribution of verbal groups, finite and non-finite, into the primary clause classes of 'independent', 'dependent' and 'qualifying', is shown in Table II.

The table represents a sort of scale of 'verbness' in the use of verbal items—the 'cline of verbality', to give it a jargonistic label. On the extreme left, most 'verbish' of all, is the finite verbal group in free clause; the further over to the right, the more the status of 'verb' is attenuated, until finally it is subordinated altogether to the nominal element without even the formality of a rankshift. In *Leda*, with its preponderance of nominal groups, the verbal items are considerably deverbalized: contrast again *His Phoenix*, and also the sixteen lines from Tennyson's *Morte d'Arthur* beginning 'Then quickly rose Sir Bedivere, and ran' (columns as in Table II):

	1	2	3	4	5	6
Leda	5	2	3		5	4
His Phoenix	30	12	2	6	2	2
Morte d'Arthur (extract from)	17		3		2	

Of various short passages examined for comparative purposes, the only one showing a distribution at all comparable to that of *Leda* was a passage of prose from the *New Scientist* concerning the peaceful uses of plutonium.

I am not of course saying that the language of *Leda* is like that of the *New Scientist*. The two passages are alike *in this respect*: that is all. Again, no evaluation is implied: even if one criticized the highly nominal style of much scientific writing this is quite irrelevant to *Leda*, since (i) the two are quite different registers, and what is effective in one register may not be effective in another, and (ii) this feature cannot be isolated from other features in which the two are quite different—for example the lexical items concerned.

It is worth examining the lexical items in more detail. In the *New Scientist* passage, and also in *His Phoenix* (where however the *grammati-*

cal use of verbs is, as we have seen, highly 'verbal'), the *lexical items*
operating as verbs are in general weak: that is, they are items like 'be'
and 'have' which are collocationally neutral. In *His Phoenix*, for example,
out of 48 finite verbal groups, 40 are accounted for by the following
items: 'be' (13), 'have' (12), 'know' (4), 'do', 'go', 'say', 'find', 'hear',
'live', 'walk and talk', 'pick and choose' and 'please'. By contrast many
of those in the Tennyson passage are powerful items: that is, items with
restricted ranges of collocation, like 'plunge', 'brandish', 'wheel' and
'flash'. In *Leda*, the few verbal items are varied in power, though
medium rather than extreme. But they get lexically more powerful as
they get grammatically less 'verbal': in finite verbal group in free clause
we have 'hold', 'push', 'put on', 'feel'; while at the other end of the
scale, including some not operating in verbal group at all, are 'stagger',
'loosen' and 'caress'.

Lexical power is the measure of the restriction on high probability
collocations: the fewer the items with which a given item is likely to
collocate (put another way, the more strongly the given item tends to be
associated with certain other items), the more 'powerful' it is said to be.
This, of course, has no evaluative connotations, nor has it anything to do
with a denotation of violence or movement. But in fact in *Leda* the more
powerful of the verbal lexical items are items of violence; and it is
precisely these that perform nominal rather than verbal roles. Thus
while the Tennyson passage, a straightforward narrative, is characterized by a succession of fairly powerful lexical items denoting movement,
each constituting by itself a (generally monosyllabic) finite verbal group
in independent clause, in *Leda*, where there are lexical items of movement which are likewise fairly powerful, these either are not verbs at all
or are themselves verbs but subordinated to the nominal elements in
clause structure.

The third example is a comparison of one or two features in three
short passages of prose, which have in common the fact that each is the
description of a room. The passages, which are reproduced below, are
taken from *Room at the Top* by John Braine, *Adventures in the Skin Trade*
by Dylan Thomas and *The Middle Age of Mrs Eliot* by Angus Wilson;
they are referred to by the abbreviations JB, DT and AW.

> I looked at it with incredulous delight: wallpaper vertically striped
> in beige and silver, a bay window extending for almost the whole
> length of the room with fitted cushions along it, a divan bed that
> looked like a divan and not like a bed with its depressing daylight

intimations of sleep and sickness, two armchairs, and a dressing-table, wardrobe and writing-table all in the same pale satiny wood. On the cream-painted bookcase was a bowl of anemones and there was a fire burning in the grate, leaving an aromatic smell, faintly acid and faintly flower-like, which I knew but couldn't quite place. . . . There were three small pictures hanging on the far wall: *The Harbour at Arles*, a Breughel skating scene, and Manet's *Olympe*.

(JOHN BRAINE: *Room at the Top*)

Every inch of the room was covered with furniture. Chairs stood on couches that lay on tables; mirrors nearly the height of the door were propped, back to back, against the walls, reflecting and making endless the hills of desks and chairs with their legs in the air, sideboards, dressing-tables, chests-of-drawers, more mirrors, empty bookcases, wash-basins, clothes cupboards. There was a double bed, carefully made with the ends of the sheets turned back; lying on top of a dining table on top of another table there were electric lamps and lampshades, trays and vases, lavatory bowls and basins, heaped in the armchairs that stood on cupboards and tables and beds, touching the ceiling. The one window, looking out on the road, could just be seen through the curved legs of sideboards on their backs. The walls behind the standing mirrors were thick with pictures and picture frames.

(DYLAN THOMAS: *Adventures in the Skin Trade*)

Her little bedroom at the hotel was ugly—the more hideous for having been recently redecorated with a standard 'contemporary' wallpaper. All over the walls floated gay little blue and pink café tables, around them a few Vermouth and Pernod bottles and the word 'Montmartre' in pretty childish script. The design was no doubt carefully chosen to enchant cross-Channel travellers; it had no message for Meg. In the first weeks she had sought every excuse to be away from the room; but now suddenly the wallpaper, the pink, bevel-edged, modernistic mirror, and the furniture of shaded pink and silver began to give her a sense of anonymity. They were so remote from anything she knew or cared for that she felt free, safe, and hidden.

(ANGUS WILSON: *The Middle Age of Mrs Eliot*)

(*a*) Nominal groups. In DT, all 49 nominal groups have lexical item as head: there are no pronouns or other grammatical heads. Of these only 11 have any lexical modification or qualification, and of a total of 5 lexical modifiers only 'empty' has the value 'epithet' in the group structure. By contrast in JB, which has 36 nominal groups of which 4 have grammatical heads, of the remaining 32 with lexical heads 16 have modifier or qualifier (or both) and 22 have deictics. Likewise in AW, with 37 nominal groups of which 9 have grammatical heads, 12 of the 28 with lexical heads are lexically modified or qualified and 15 have deictics. The DT passage is a heap of mainly simple nominal groups (that is, ones consisting of a noun only), with also some heaping of clauses; in AW and JB we have the compound nominal group as the centre of attention. All this is 'obvious'; but the fact that it is obvious does not mean it should not be made explicit. Nor is it useful to count items or patterns without a linguistic analysis to identify what is to be counted.

The following table shows the number of nominal groups with lexical heads, and with lexical and grammatical modifiers and qualifiers, in the three prose passages. The last part of the table shows the distribution of 'head' items in the principal lexical sets (see next paragraph).

	JB	DT	AW
Nominal groups	36	49	37
Nominal groups with lexical head	32	49	28
with M/Q (lexical)	16	11	12
with D	22	19	15
Head from 'room' set	19	40	9
'furniture and décor'	14	34	5
'constructional'	5	6	4

(*b*) Lexical sets. Of the 49 lexical items as head of the nominal groups in DT, 40 are assignable to a lexical set under the heading 'room': 34 of these to a set (subset of 'room') 'furniture and décor'. Of the 32 lexical heads in JB, only 14 are furniture; and of AW's 28, only 5. Constructional items, however, such as 'wall', are distributed fairly evenly among the three passages. In AW especially the furniture is of little interest: even of the 5 non-constructional items, two are occurrences of 'wallpaper' and one, 'tables', refers to the design of the wallpaper—the tables 'float'; the other two items are 'furniture' and 'mirror'. It is interesting to note the different parts played by lexical items from the sets associated with the 'room' theme in the three passages.

(*c*) Cohesion. The principal types of cohesion are shown in Table III. The passages are too short to allow much to be said about their relative degrees, and use of different types, of cohesion; but some differences do emerge. In DT there is no grammatical cohesion at all across sentences or across orthographic sub-sentences (and only one instance even within a sentence: presupposition by dependence beginning at 'reflecting'). Cohesion is entirely lexical, by constant repetition of items or occurrence of items from within one set. JB is likewise not cohesive grammatically, except for some co-ordination between clauses and the anaphoric 'it' in the first sentence (and cohesion by structural parallelism, an important type of grammatical cohesion about which too little is yet known to permit accurate assessment); nor however is there much lexical cohesion in the passage. AW on the other hand is more grammatically cohesive; apart from clause co-ordination, there are the anaphoric pronouns 'it', 'she', 'they', and the anaphoric 'the' in 'the walls' and 'the design'; at the same time there is, as often in Angus Wilson, lexical cohesion by occurrence of items within a set, for example 'ugly . . . hideous'.

Other points of interest include: the distribution of lexical items in nominal groups as subject in clause structure; the use of original and of familiar collocations—compare JB: 'picture/hang' with DT 'picture/ thick'; the use of items from the lexical sets of colour and smell; the distribution of verbal groups and words in the 'cline of verbality' and the choice of lexical items, weak and powerful, operating in the verbal groups. But enough has been said to illustrate textual analysis, and by now perhaps the pass mark has been awarded. That the linguist can suggest how to describe a text is perhaps, from the point of view of the literary analyst, the main justification for his existence.

At the very beginning of this paper I used the term 'application' to refer to the study of literary texts by the theories and methods of linguistics, and I would stress that it is in fact an application of linguistics that is under discussion. We can be more specific than this. One branch of linguistics is descriptive linguistics, the study of how language works; this contrasts both with historical linguistics, the study of how language persists in time, and with institutional linguistics, the study of the varieties and uses of, and the attitudes to, language. Within descriptive linguistics, one kind of description is textual: the linguist describes a text, written or spoken; this contrasts with exemplificatory description, which presents the categories of the language and illustrates them, or, if formalized, generates a set of described sentences and derives others from them. The linguistic study of literature is textual description, and it is no different from any other textual description; it is not a new branch or a new level or a new kind of linguistics but the application of existing theories and methods. What the linguist does when faced with a literary text is the same as what he does when faced with any text that he is going to describe.

But all description involves institutional considerations, and literary description is no exception. When we describe language we have to find out and specify the range of validity of the description; this means taking into account the variety represented, both dialect (variety according to user) and register (variety according to use). Register and dialect differences are of course variable in delicacy: we may talk of the register of literature, subdivided into the registers of prose and verse, each subdivided further into the various genres. At any particular point on the scale of delicacy the total set of registers may form a continuum, and there will certainly be a great deal that is common, linguistically, to all; but there are also linguistic differences between them—otherwise they would not be recognized as different registers. And just as in dialect we eventually, by progressive refinement, reach the individual: every speaker his own idiolect, or bundle of available individual dialects: so also in register we come finally to the individual—every speaker, and writer, his own bundle of individual registers. Again, it does not need a new branch of linguistics to recognize and account for individual styles: all language is individual activity in a given variety, and thus there is an institutional basis, in the technical sense of institutional linguistics, in all description, literary or otherwise.

This does not mean, however, that for each text or individual writer we start again with a totally new description, with a new set of categories unrelated to what has gone before. Indeed, if some of the things written about the language of particular works of literature are much less useful than they might have been, this is more often than not because the writer, having neither made a description of the language himself nor used one made by someone else (other than the misty image of English that is still so often given in our schools), has invented a set of *ad hoc* categories for each text he has examined. What is said has therefore no relation to what was said about any other text, still less to any description of the language as a whole. If the linguistic analysis of literature is to be of any value or significance it must surely operate against the background of a general description of the language, using the same theories, methods and categories. A literary text has meaning against the background of the language as a whole, in all its uses; how can its language be understood except as the selection by the individual writer from the total resources at his disposal ? Yet all too often the observations about the language of a work of literature bear no relation to any descriptive account of those resources.

The same point applies to the comparison of texts: it is impossible to compare one text with another unless both have been described in the same way. All literary analysis, if one is at all interested in the special properties of the language of literary texts or of a particular genre, is essentially comparative. This makes it all the more essential to be consistent, accurate and explicit: to base the analysis firmly on a sound, existing description of the language. While this means restraining oneself from inventing new categories, a temptation to which the literary analyst must be especially exposed, it does not of course preclude new alignments of established categories, such as Professor McIntosh's use of 'involvement' in studying Shakespearean dialogue.[2] These may be required in any linguistic study, but they are perhaps especially fruitful in comparative literary studies. Another example is the relation of cohesion referred to above, which is very valuable in comparing long texts. The concept of cohesion has been developed especially for literary textual analysis; but every category brought together under this heading is drawn from the total description of English and has exactly the same range of application whatever the text to which it is applied.

Of course no amount of faithful adherence to the same description will be of any use if the description is not a good one in the first place. We are still plagued with steam grammars, with their ragged categories, their jumbled criteria and their fictions; descriptions of English which give little insight into the way the language works or indeed the way any language works, except perhaps the Latin they were originally modelled on. This kind of pre-linguistic linguistics is of no use for literary studies. It is no paradox that it is modern scientific, including statistical, linguistics that proves really illuminating when applied to the study of literature—no paradox at least to anyone who studies language seriously, since the study of language perhaps more than anything else shows up the artificial nature of the dichotomy between arts and sciences. Not only do we need to be able to state accurately the role of a particular pattern or item in the language, what it contrasts with, what it may and may not combine with and so on; we may want to know its probability of occurrence under various definable conditions. It is of no interest to show that nine-tenths of all clauses in a certain poem are, say, of the class 'interrogative' unless we know how this relates to the probabilities of occurrence of this and the other terms in the mood system. The originality of a person's use of his language consists in his selecting a feature not where it is impossible (has not been previously selected) but

[2] Cf. Paper 4 of this volume, especially pp. 76–7 and footnote 9.

where another would be more probable—and even more in his balanced combination of the improbable with the probable, as in the lexis of *Leda and the Swan*, which is an interesting blend of old and new collocations.

I have stressed grammar, but this is of course only one of the levels involved, and the usefulness of linguistic theory in application to literary studies depends on its ability both to comprehend and to integrate all the levels of language. That is another reason for insisting on the need for integrated linguistics: not only must the literary analyst have access to theories for the description of all levels of linguistic patterning— grammar, lexis, phonology and phonetics, and their graphic parallels— but he must be able to see them in interaction as they must always inter- act in any language event. He may want to analyse, for example, 'her loosening thighs' as a grammatical item, with a certain structure—is it the same as 'the staggering girl', or not?; as a collocation in lexis—is 'loosen' the same lexical item as 'loose'?; as a piece of English phon- ology—how does it exploit the patterns of English rhythm and intona- tion?; and in terms of its phonetic properties. He may feel he needs to do all this so that he can see what it is doing in the poem. I have not, for reasons of space, given illustrations of phonological and phonetic analysis; but this is a good place to point out that when we speak of 'linguistics' in literary studies, this is really a shorthand for 'the linguistic sciences', and is to be taken to include them both—linguistics and phonetics.

If it is considered that the meaning of a piece of literature lies between rather than within the lines, it seems likely that linguistics has no mes- sage. This is not to say that the literary allusion is outside the scope of linguistic analysis; on the contrary, all use of language is allusion, and textual allusion is only one endpoint on a scale the other end of which is the context of our whole previous experience of the use of an item or pattern: hence the insistence that a work of literature, like any other piece of language activity, is meaningful only in the perspective of the whole range of uses of the language. Similarly it is not to say that literary 'figures of speech' cannot be analysed; it is true however that they do need rigorous linguistic definition. Again there is no sharp line to be drawn between metaphor and non-metaphor; but if linguistics cannot describe certain parts of language it is likely to be of little use for any application. Linguistics is not and will never be the whole of literary analysis, and only the literary analyst—not the linguist—can determine the place of linguistics in literary studies. But if a text is to be described at all, then it should be described properly; and this means by the theories and methods developed in linguistics, the subject whose task is precisely to show how language works. The literary analyst is not content with amateur psychology, armchair philosophy, or fictitious social history; yet the linguistics that is applied in some accounts of literature, and the statements about language that are used as evidence, are no less amateur, armchair and fictitious. It is encouraging that literary

TABLE I

Deixis in nominal groups in 'Leda and the Swan'

Modifiers and qualifiers	+M/Q			−M/Q
Deictics	M	Q	MQ	
+D specific	the staggering girl the dark webs the feathered glory the broken wall the burning roof and tower the indifferent beak those terrified vague fingers that white rush her helpless breast her loosening thighs	the thighs caressed by the dark webs her nape caught in his bill	the great wings beating above the staggering girl the strange heart beating the brute blood of the air	the loins the air his bill his breast her nape his knowledge his power
+D non-specific	a sudden blow	a shudder in the loins		
−D				body

scholars are coming more and more to reject such statements, and to demand a standard of objective linguistic scholarship that is no less rigorous than the standard of literary scholarship which they expect, and exact, from themselves.

TABLE II

Verbal items in 'Leda and the Swan'

		Items in verbal group (i.e. functioning as 'predicator' in clause structure)				Items in nominal group (i.e. not functioning as predicator)
	I	2	3	4	5	6
(a)	Inde-pendent	Dependent		Qualifying (rankshifted)		(inapplicable)
(b)	Finite	Finite	Non-finite	Finite	Non-finite	
	hold push feel engender put on	lie let	drop catch up master		beat (2) caress catch lay	stagger loosen burn break

(*a*) Clause class
(*b*) Group class

TABLE III

Cohesion

A. Grammatical: 1. Structural (clauses in sentence structure):
    (*a*) Dependence
    (*b*) Co-ordination
    2. Non-structural:
    (*a*) Anaphora:
        (i) deictics and submodifiers,
        (ii) pronouns.
    (*b*) Substitution:
        (i) verbal,
        (ii) nominal.

B. Lexical: 1. Repetition of item.
    2. Occurrence of item from same lexical set.

Four

'As You Like It':
a grammatical clue to character (1963)

The main qualities of the overtones carried by the pronouns *thou* and *you* in Shakespeare's time have long been understood.[1] But it is remarkable how few critics have taken them into account, and how little scrutiny there has been, even in these days of close reading, of their precise implications in particular scenes or in particular relationships between characters.[2] I propose here to confine myself to an examination of what is conveyed by the use which Shakespeare makes of the *thou-you* distinction in his portrayal of the relationship between Celia and Rosalind through the course of *As You Like It*.[3]

[1] See especially E. A. Abbott, *Shakespearian Grammar*, 2nd edition, London, 1870, para. 232 ff., and W. Franz, *Shakespeare-Grammatik*, Heidelberg, 1924, para. 289 ff. References to a number of works on various aspects of this opposition in different European languages will be found in R. Brown and A. Gilman, 'The pronouns of Power and Solidarity', *Style in Language*, p. 253, ed. Thomas A. Sebeok, New York and London, 1960. Among these, particular mention may be made of Sister St G. Byrne, *Shakespeare's use of the pronoun of address*, (unpublished dissertation), Catholic University of America, Washington, 1936. For Middle English see also W. W. Skeat, *William of Palerne*, E.E.T.S., E.S. No. 1, 1867, pp. xli–xliii.

Additional note: A valuable analysis of Shakespeare's use of *thou* and *you* has recently been made in an unpublished dissertation '*Thou*' and '*You*': some *Pronominal Shifts in Shakespeare* by Mr Raymond Adlam, written for the Diploma in Applied Linguistics, University of Edinburgh, 1964. For a general survey see also T. Finkenstaedt, "*You*" and "*Thou*". *Studien zur Anrede im Englischen*, Berlin, 1963. For a discussion of the use of the two pronouns in *Sir Gawain and the Green Knight*, see the edition of Israel Gollancz, E.E.T.S., O.S. 210, note to line 1071. Further references are given by Norman Davis, 'The *Litera Troili* and English Letters', *R.E.S.*, New Series, Vol. xvi, No. 63, 1965, p. 243, footnote 5.

[2] Cf. Angus McIntosh and C. F. Williamson, '*King Lear*, Act I Scene 1: two stylistic notes', *R.E.S.*, New Series, Vol. xiv, No. 53, 1963, p. 54.

[3] I am of course considering *you* in its *singular* use. In speaking of *thou* and *you*

It should perhaps be noted that the conventions governing the choice of pronoun in English at that period—as indeed for a long time before—differed in an important respect from those which pertain in most European languages of the present day. For in earlier English, to a degree which does not seem to be paralleled elsewhere, the pronoun selected by a given speaker could in many circumstances vary from one moment to the next, even where that speaker is all the time addressing one and the same person. The selection is then often an 'expression of transient attitudes'[4]; this is well illustrated by the shifts in which both Celia and Rosalind indulge.

Before embarking on details, I wish, at the risk of seeming trivial, to consider what is involved in a study of this kind. Our task is to restore as nearly as possible the old awareness of the effects conveyed by the selection of one as against the other form. I say 'effects' rather than 'effect' because an instance of, say, *thou* in one context will not necessarily have the same implication as an instance of it in another.[5] This task involves the close scrutiny, case by case, of the relevant pronouns, always within the framework of a fairly adequate (if sometimes over-rated) knowledge of Shakespeare's language as a whole. And for each instance we must postulate as the intended effect something which most convincingly fits in with all the other impressions conveyed to us by those numerous other touches which (unlike the *thou-you* distinction) are still capable today of making directly something of their original impact.

In the last resort, we may regard the whole text as a complex of such touches, though these will be of very different orders of significance and of subtlety and will also vary greatly in degree of amenability to analysis. Furthermore some will be more or less self-evident even to a modern

[4] See R. Brown and A. Gilman, op. cit., pp. 253–4, 273–6.
Additional note: It has been brought to my attention by Professor E. Lapesa of the University of Madrid (in private conversation) that similar shifts take place in Classical Spanish; there are for instance striking examples in *Don Quixote*.
[5] Cf. footnote 8, p. 75. In the technical sense I attach to the word *use*, I should speak of two such instances exemplifying two different uses. Cf. p. 105 footnote 12.

I imply all related forms, *thy, thine, your*, etc. For convenience I shall sometimes refer to uses involving the *th-* forms as uses of the singular mode, those involving *y-* forms as of the plural mode. Line references are to the edition of the play in *The Comedies of Shakespeare*, Oxford, 1922. The passages which concern us are in I.2, I.3, III.2, III.4, III.5, IV.1, and IV.3. I have noted one hundred and five relevant second person pronouns in them; eight of these are used by Aliena and Ganymede when speaking in public, cf. footnote 13, p. 82.

reader, while others will not unless he can make some informed adjustment to earlier usage. But they may all have a bearing on the interpretation we seek to ascribe to instances of *thou* or *you*. In what follows I have not attempted except quite incidentally (cf. footnotes 9 and 11, pp. 76 and 80) to specify what it is about the text, linguistically or stylistically speaking, which has led me to the assumption of certain basic impressions as a background to such interpretation; this has been necessary in order to proceed at all within the scope of an article. But failure to specify implies no denial of the relevance of whatever I can learn from everything else in the text.

We naturally require, for any interpretation we may be tempted to make, some further support for it than that it seems to accord plausibly with the impressions we have from other touches. First, looking at our interpretations as a whole, we must assure ourselves that they form a workable and self-consistent system. We should certainly not reject the possibility of some system of considerable complexity, since both textual and extra-textual context[6] are always likely to produce significant variations of effect numerically far in excess of the basic two which one might, naïvely, expect from the operation of a two-term system like *thou/you*. At the same time we must not postulate an unbelievably complex set of effects, such that no contemporary of Shakespeare's could reasonably have been expected to find his way about in it, however admirably each of those we are tempted to postulate seems to us to fit a particular instance. And our means of control here must be to seek parallels elsewhere than in the text under immediate scrutiny for those effects we seek to justify. For it is not enough that the effect postulated in a given instance shall (at the least) do no violence to the impression made by all the other touches; it must also be an effect which squares with that suggested by any evidence which happens to be available about other instances of *thou* or *you* elsewhere which we judged to be relevantly similar in import. Again here, within the limits of this paper, I do not attempt to cite parallels. But I have not wittingly suggested any interpretation which I feel to be unjustifiable from this point of view.

We should not lose sight of one thing: that whatever we legitimately 'know' about Celia and Rosalind depends in the last resort on the text of *As You Like It* and our ability to interpret it. It is necessary to labour this point, because it is easy to fall into the delusion that we have some

---

[6] By these terms I mean 'what occurs in the passage under examination' and 'what occurs outside that particular passage'.

sort of non-textually derived acquaintance with such old friends. From here it is an easy step to a frame of mind where we refuse to allow any further evidence from the text (such as the demonstration of some hitherto unnoticed implication of a use of *thou*) to alter even in the slightest our ideas about the characters. And this is unfortunate, for we should always be prepared to go back to the text and re-examine it again and again without the drag of any such fixed ideas. Till we have caught in our text the whispered implication of every slightest linguistic nuance capable of yielding its import to us, our interpretation, however 'right' in a broad sort of way, must remain tentative.

A use of *thou* or *you* in Shakespeare is then a nuance to which we are trying to assign an import. And our procedure is to attempt to fit what is so far without any clear message to us into the pattern of those implications which the text *does* in various other ways succeed in putting across; it is a task of reconciliation, the conclusions from which must ultimately be verified in the ways I have already considered. But by 'reconciliation' it is not implied that such and such a use of the pronoun will necessarily achieve no more than the mere corroboration of an impression we have already picked up in full clarity from other things in the text. For every nuance is likely to make its own irreplaceable contribution. So we must be prepared to ask ourselves what, if anything, such a use *additionally* contributes. And if it does contribute something extra, we may find that this requires us to modify somewhat the interpretation of all the rest of the linguistic evidence from which we started. This kind of approach is familiar enough in lexicographical problems relating to past stages of the language.[7]

Our own problem is made the more difficult by the diversity of factors which may, in varying situations or relationships, as it were 'pull' a given speaker towards one or the other of the two modes. It is therefore easier to break into it in a preliminary way by choosing a set of cases where not all these complicating factors are present. It is partly for this reason that I have taken one where, though the situation of course changes, the same two persons are involved throughout. As I have already indicated, a full-scale attack on even this restricted problem

---

[7] It may be noted that many more straightforward and typical lexical problems than that of *thou* and *you* await a similar sort of delicate analysis in Shakespeare. Who at present for instance could with any assurance give a full account of the various implications of Shakespeare's uses of *accommodate* and *accommodation*? For a recent discussion of *one* instance of *accommodate* (Lear IV.6.82) see Hilda M. Hulme, *Explorations in Shakespeare's Language*, London, 1962, pp. 275–7.

would require that we hunt out many instances from elsewhere to support or corroborate the interpretation suggested for those under scrutiny. The present study attempts no more than to show the nature of the problem of interpretation and therefore, by implication, the kind of parallels which should be sought in a more comprehensive approach to the problem.

One may begin by observing that a certain atmosphere of relationship between Celia and Rosalind is quite clearly being built up by Shakespeare in the first scene where the two cousins are together (I.2). If we examine the pronouns which they use in addressing one another here, we find something which (whatever else it may be) is statistically somewhat striking. For with two exceptions (lines 17, 254) Celia regularly uses the *thou* form, of which there are fifteen instances. Rosalind, on the other hand, uses the plural mode with only one exception (line 40). She yields only five examples of *you*, but this is because of another touch: that she is much more quiet than Celia in this scene. Just what are we intended to catch from these pronominal uses?

I shall first consider Rosalind's addiction to *you*, since a general acquaintance with the conventions which governed Shakespeare's choice of pronoun at once suggests that this, in addressing a youthful girl cousin who is at the same time a close friend, is what is the more strongly in need of explanation. Rosalind is the daughter of the banished Duke; her position, as we are soon to find out, is insecure, and her status is to some degree inferior to that of Celia in the eyes of everyone except perhaps Celia herself. Rosalind is clearly aware of all this, and in normal circumstances (as here) she expresses her feelings by—among other things—a somewhat guarded protocol-observing and perhaps even slightly resentful *you*. We may at least say, I think, that her use of this pronoun strengthens and sharpens the impressions we pick up from all the other nuances in this scene.

Celia is in quite a different position. She is by nature impulsive and outgoing, she is at this time on top of the world, and she is in no way inhibited in her uncomplicated affection for Rosalind. We may say that her use of *thou* to Rosalind is in full accordance with these traits, and helps to adumbrate them. We may also suspect that the contrast of her *thou* with Rosalind's *you* should help to make us aware from the start of a certain uneasiness in their relationship.

In the English of the time a clear-cut convention such as we can observe in this scene may be expected to operate smoothly in what we may call 'normal rapport', but be broken if something happens to disturb

the normality.[8] We may not always be able to explain a shift of pronominal mode, but we shall certainly be in a better position to do so once
we have established what we can regard with some assurance as the
conventions of normal rapport. Thereafter, in individual instances, we
must always of course reckon, not only with textual error, but with the
possibility that there may be situations where opposing tendencies result
in there being at a given place no obviously 'right' and conversely
'wrong' form. Let us examine the deviations from the postulated norm
in this introductory scene, and see what impression we can gain of their
implications.

At line 17 Celia says:

> You know my father hath no child but I, nor none is like to have; and
> truly, when he dies, thou shalt be his heir.

If anything is to be concluded from the pronominal modes here, it is
that Celia opens with a momentary burst of impatience with Rosalind
(foreshadowed in her previous speech) which she cannot sustain beyond
the first fifteen words; thereafter she returns to, and for the present
maintains, the sweeter kind of attitude 'conveyed' to us by the very first
words she addresses to her cousin as the scene opens. The delivery of
the following words (lines 18 ff.), beginning with the almost wheedling
'and, truly', is therefore intended to contrast sharply with what she has
just said. The very quickness of the reversion to *thou* is itself a touch of
some significance.

In line 254 Celia says:

> Will you go, coz?

This is spoken to Rosalind while she is loitering behind with Orlando
in a somewhat unladylike manner. Celia has already (seven lines before)
bidden formal farewell to Orlando, and now she is hanging about
temporarily deserted by her beloved cousin in an unprecedented fashion.
As in line 17, a certain annoyance, mingled this time perhaps with an
ingredient of disquiet, would seem to be indicated by her shift to the
plural mode; we shall hear more later of such bursts of annoyance and

---

[8] It would doubtless not always be easy to define 'normal rapport', but there
are numerous cases throughout Shakespeare where we can establish it without
difficulty. Thus it is normal in *Twelfth Night* for Sir Toby to address Sir Andrew
as *thou*, and for Sir Andrew to address Sir Toby as *you*: it is instructive to note
(however obvious this may be) that the motivation of these uses by Sir Toby and
Sir Andrew is very different from that of Celia and Rosalind, though not totally
so.

exasperation on Celia's part. We must also reckon (though I think this is less likely) with the possibility that the access of formality is prompted by nothing more than her having to address Rosalind in the presence of a stranger.

In lines 40 and following we have the only speech in this scene wherein Rosalind addresses Celia as *thou*:

> Nay, how thou goest from Fortune's office to Nature's: Fortune reigns in gifts of the world, not in the lineaments of Nature.

Here it may be that the preceding fantasy of Celia's, which she has pursued to try to cheer Rosalind, has at last had the effect of jogging her, for the moment at least, out of her more reserved and guarded attitude. But I would stress that such suggested explanations as I here offer are mere first approximations. Such hypotheses must stand or fall according to the findings of a much wider scrutiny of related instances; I am merely sketching part of a frame of reference for a much more exhaustive study which is long overdue.

There is further dialogue between Celia and Rosalind in the next scene (I.3). Here Rosalind uses the plural mode regularly, though since (as usual at this stage of the play) she is for most of the scene both more silent and also more impersonal[9] than Celia, we have only four instances.

[9] By 'impersonal' I mean that, up to a certain point in the play, whenever Rosalind speaks she tends much less to involve Celia directly than Celia does when speaking to her. Apart from the use of second person pronouns, the main markers which indicate such involvement of the hearer are: (1) the use of *we, us, our*, etc.; (2) vocatives; (3) questions; (4) imperatives. Note that Rosalind's use of a mere five instances of these markers in lines 1–104 is by no means fully explained by her taciturnity. For Celia uses well over four times as many as Rosalind does for each hundred words spoken. It should be observed that the

	lines 1–104		lines 105–137	
	Rosalind	Celia	Rosalind	Celia
thou, you etc.	1	24	3	3
we, us etc.	0	6	6	6
vocatives	0	7	1	0
questions	0	12	5	1
imperatives	4	7	1	4
Totals	5	56	16	14
Total number of words spoken	124	303	142	117

Celia uses the second person pronoun no less than 27 times. She uses *thou* 17 times, *you* 10 times, and she makes eight shifts. This can be made clear in a table:

C sg.	4		13	21					89	90(2)	91(2)	92
pl.		10			24(2)	27	31					
C sg.	93(2)	96(2)					104(2)			122(2)		
pl.			101(2)	102(2)				112				

This contrasts remarkably both with the regularity of her use of *thou* in the previous scene and with Rosalind's still stable pronominal habits. And since we are regarding Celia's *thou* as her pronoun of normal rapport with Rosalind, it is her employment of *you* in this scene which requires special examination.

We should perhaps consider the first five instances separately, for these all come before the disrupting moment when Frederick orders Rosalind to leave the court. Up to this point Celia and Rosalind would at first sight seem to be in much the same sort of situation as in the previous scene; yet something must have happened. My own impression is that all these first cases of *you* carry once more an overtone of disquiet and annoyance, this time an annoyance related directly to Rosalind's preoccupation with Orlando. This is foreshadowed at the end of the previous scene, but the situation *has* in fact changed in that it is increasingly more clear to Celia that she has a rival to her own affections. One need not pursue the point here, but it may be suggested that this reaction of Celia's is the stronger because she seems from the beginning

---

whole pattern changes about line 105, where Rosalind's interest in a joint flight begins to quicken. Hereafter in the scene she not only speaks more than Celia, but in what she says there is now a far heavier incidence than before of these markers of involvement; for instance three of the four second person pronouns that she uses in this scene come in this short passage. Even here, however, Rosalind's 'score' still falls well below Celia's remarkable average (over the whole scene) of one marker or another to every six words she utters. The pattern at its two stages is demonstrated in tabular fashion on the previous page. For a marked change in the ways in which (in a subsequent scene) Rosalind involves Celia, see footnote 11, p. 80.

Additional note. I have touched on this question of involvement in 'Language and Style', *Durham University Journal*, June 1963, pp. 120–1. An even more striking case of imbalance in the involvement-relation between two characters is to be found in *Macbeth*, II.2.22–58; 65–73.

to be in greater need of Rosalind's affection than Rosalind of hers. And so it is only intermittently now that Celia can overcome her feelings about this and treat her cousin in quite the old carefree way. There will be more to say about this when we come to III.2.

The remaining cases occur in lines 101–102 and 112:

> Therefore devise with me how we may fly,
> Whither to go, and what to bear with us:
> And do not seek to take your change upon you
> To bear your griefs yourself and leave me out:
> For, by this heaven, now at our sorrows pale,
> Say what thou canst, I'll go along with thee.
>
> 99–104
>
> I'll put myself in poor and mean attire,
> And with a kind of umber smirch my face;
> The like do you: so shall we pass along
> And never stir assailants.
>
> 110–113

It may be suggested that lines 112–113 represent a short burst of anxious petulance, an impulsive taking of offence at the mere thought of Rosalind perhaps having it in mind to go off without her. But (rather as in the shift between I.2.17 and 18) Celia cannot sustain this mood and she modulates into an expression of devoted and dependent loyalty in the following two lines. As in the earlier instance, the selection of *you* and then of *thou* is, on this interpretation, a sort of key to the contrasting tone in which the first and second pairs of these last four lines should be delivered. As for line 112, I can suggest no very convincing interpretation; it is one of the rare cases where the pronoun selected is not accounted for by the present suggestions.[10]

The next relevant scene is III.2 (lines 156 ff.). Here we have a quite remarkable change, for *both* girls now depart from the pronominal conventions which characterized their normal rapport, and over a large

---

[10] It should be added that there may be circumstances where the choice of form is affected by grammatical or lexical factors. Abbott, op. cit., para. 234, touches on something of this sort (not relevant to the above instance) namely that *you* may be used in conditional and other sentences where there is no direct appeal to the person addressed in situations where *thou* would be used in statements and requests. Franz however makes no allusion to any such conditioning, and I have observed no clear instances of it.

Additional note: Since the above was written, Mr Raymond Adlam has discovered that Abbott's conjecture is erroneous, being based either on passages which are corrupt or (in one case) on a conflation in an eighteenth-century text.

stretch of text (lines 180 ff.) their modes are completely reversed. As before, what happens can be shown in tabular form:

	NORMAL	REVERSED
R pl. C sg.	156(2) 176 163 172 173	
R sg. C pl.	180 182 183	184 190 195 198 199 200 201

	REVERSED (*continued*)	NORMAL	REVERSED
R pl. C sg.		251 245(2) 249	
R sg. C pl.	203(2) 204 212 221 224 225 205(2) 226		253

This patterning is clearly no accident, however tentative any detailed explanation of it may have to be. Were it not that the opening part of the scene (up to line 179) displays their conventions of normal rapport, one might suppose that this of itself had once and for all shifted with the now radically different circumstances and relationship in which the two girls find themselves. But as things are this can hardly be the case.

The change, which is initiated by Celia, does not come till line 180:

ROSALIND. I was seven of the nine days out of the wonder before you came; for look here what I found on a palm-tree; I was never so be-rimed since Pythagoras' time, that I was an Irish rat, which I can hardly remember.

CELIA. Trow you who hath done this?

175–80

Hereafter we have an uninterrupted run of twenty instances of a reversal of their normal modes. So far as Celia is concerned, it is difficult not to connect this with something we have already noticed. Once more she is faced with the intrusion of Orlando into the cosiness of their hitherto undisturbed relationship and, as this becomes more and more of a menace, it more and more clearly introduces a note of huffiness into Celia's attitude and an element of estrangement foreign to her side of the original relationship. I have suggested that this is probably foreshadowed in I.2.254, I.3.10 and I.3.24–31.

Rosalind's reversal here must be related to the excited state of mind induced by Orlando. Her normal reserve breaks down: she is unprecedentedly loquacious, and she will now go to all lengths of girlish directness and unreserve to clarify her uncertainties, cf. 203–4:

> I prithee, take the cork out of thy mouth, that I may drink thy tidings.

This shift to *thou* from line 184 onwards contributes in its small way to the throwing of the main emotional interest now quite sharply on to Rosalind herself; she is more and more clearly revealed as being transformed by love. And, caparison'd like a man as she now is, the dramatic effect of this is the more telling.[11]

If this interpretation is more or less on the right lines, we are left with the problem of the reversion to the old pattern between lines 245 and 251. Again it is Celia who initiates it, this time (it would seem) rather in the mood of an impetuous child. Up to line 239 ('give me audience, good madam') she has, whether satirically or otherwise, been observing a certain distance and formality. But at line 254 she breaks down:

> Cry 'holla!' to thy tongue, I prithee; it curvets unseasonably.

In similar vein she says at line 249:

> I would sing my song without a burthen: thou bringest me out of tune.

[11] It is worthwhile presenting here an 'involvement table' similar to that which relates to I.3. (cf. footnote 9, p. 76):

	lines 180–254	
	Rosalind	Celia
thou, you etc.	15	11
vocatives	3	1
we, us etc.	0	0
questions	22	4
imperatives	11	5
Totals	51	21
Total number of words spoken	310	228

We may note that the incidence of second person pronouns is now about equal, but there is no more talk of *we* and *us*. Questions and imperatives now fall heavily on Rosalind's side. This is clearly a new kind of involvement, very different from that in I.3.105–37.

And when Rosalind replies (line 251), it is in a mood of calm more like her old self, but tinged now with a new touch of superiority:

> Do you not know I am a woman? when I think, I must speak. Sweet, say on.

Celia's final reply here (line 253) is in the plural mode:

> You bring me out. Soft! comes he not here?

The first four words are an aposiopesis, echoing her previous 'thou bringest me out of tune', but this time reflecting a huffier and more distant frame of mind probably directly brought on by Rosalind's rather patronizing previous words.

The next scene in which the cousins converse, III.4, tells us little: there are only three relevant instances of pronouns, a singular by Celia (line 2) and two plurals by Rosalind (lines 22, 28).[12] Rosalind is no longer keyed up, and her reversion to the plural mode seems appropriate enough here. So also does Celia's single *prithee*; I suspect however that if Celia had had occasion to use any second person pronouns after line 8 or thereabouts, they would have been plurals, to reinforce the impression of her exasperation.

In IV.1. we have another upset of the mode of normal rapport; the instances are not numerous, but there are no exceptions and the passage is of considerable interest:

C pl.	196(2)	197	198	204	
R sg.				201	210

Here, more clearly than in the middle of III.2, one has corroboration from other touches that Celia is voicing a certain feeling of estrangement from this disquieting new cousin of hers. In lines 196 and following, this implication of the *you*'s is in strict keeping with the whole tenor of what she says:

> You have simply misused our sex in your love-prate: we must have your doublet and hose plucked over your head, and show the world what the bird hath done to her own nest.

And Celia's sense of deprivation is offset now by still clearer signs than

---

[12] The *your* of Celia at line 12 is not of course relevant.

hitherto of a new superiority on Rosalind's side of the relationship (line 200):

> O coz, coz, coz, my pretty little coz, that you didst know how many fathom deep I am in love.

This is the last scene in which the two girls have any intimate exchanges. When they appear in IV.3, they are for a brief moment alone (lines 1–5) and they both use *you* once (lines 1, 3); no comment of much value can be offered on so short a passage. Thereafter all we have is three more plural forms from Celia (lines 161, 176(2)). But this is Aliena speaking to Ganymede in the presence of others, and this is probably in keeping with the public conventions of their rapport in this artificial role.[13] It is interesting that thereafter, throughout the whole of Act V, they never exchange another word. So from III.4 onward there is a steady toning down of their friendship; as we move through the latter part of the play, the girlish intimacy, never indeed completely secure and balanced, yet so much to the fore in the beginning, recedes into the background. For we are being prepared for Hymen and the honouring of high wedlock and the old relationship has had its day.

[13] We know at any rate that Ganymede always uses *you* to Aliena in such cases, cf. III.5.75; IV.1.118, 119, 123; IV.3.66.

Five

Some thoughts on style (1962)

1

I propose to consider in what sense stylistic problems can be regarded as the concern of the linguist, and how we might try to demarcate certain aspects of style and devise ways of looking at them so that as much light as possible may be thrown on them from one direction or another.

Without attempting to be too precise here, one may at least say that problems of style involve us in the close observation of longer and shorter stretches of text[1] in relation to some live situation in which they as it were have their existence. Someone, in a situation of some sort, had something to communicate and he made an effort to 'put it across'. What then, and from what points of view, can we say about this effort? And how far can we distinguish the various points of view? And can some of them be said to be more essentially 'linguistic' than others? And if so, just what linguistic factors should be taken into account in considering those that are?

When I speak of a 'live situation' I imply of course not only what, in the ordinary sense, is 'going on', but also the mentality, disposition, attitude and so forth of the speaker or writer on the one hand, and—in a different but relevant way—of the listener or reader on the other. A matter of central importance here, however trivial it may seem, is this: that if someone is to say things which are to fit into a given situation, he is involved in the selection of one of a quite small number of utterances, or sequences of utterances, out of a very large number of possibilities— 'possibilities' in the sense that none of these others would be branded as failing to comply with the rules of the language as a whole; they would

---

[1] I use this word to refer to something either written or spoken; the length implied will depend on the amount of material which happens to be within the focus of our scrutiny on a given occasion.

all be acceptable *somewhere*, no matter to what degree they might be unsuitable in *this* situation.

In speaking of selection I have been careful not to suggest that there is usually a unique 'right' choice; as we well know, there are many simple situations in which five or six alternative utterances would serve equally well. So what we are usually dealing with is degrees of suitability, not with anything unique or absolute. In stressing the fact that there is a process of selection, all I wish to bring out is that many utterances would simply *not* have served in the situation in question, and that we must therefore assess whether an utterance is 'good' (if I may use this vague word for the moment) according to the particular circumstances in which it has its being. Nothing is good without respect:

> How many things by season season'd are
> To their right praise and true perfection.

However obvious this may be, we must nevertheless acknowledge that it is often felt to be reasonable to ask the question: 'Is such and such good English?' as it were in a vacuum: we answer 'Yes' if we can call to mind *some* situation or situations where in our opinion this would have been a suitable utterance or part thereof. It is rather as if we were to enquire: 'Are corduroy trousers good garments?' without asking explicitly any such questions as 'Who for?' (Very old ladies living in Park Lane?), 'When?' (In bed? At investitures?), and so forth. I am not saying that such enquiries are pointless; only that a much more common practical question is: 'Would such and such be good English in such and such a particular situation?'. This would be comparable to a situationally-focused problem involving the selection of some article of clothing.

It does no harm, in considering such matters, to crawl before we run, and to give some thought to very simple and obvious cases. The sentence 'Can I buy a spanner from you?' is not wholly 'good' in some situation wherein what I really *meant* (in the most ordinary sense of that word) was 'Can I borrow a tyre lever from you?' I do not mean that it is totally useless in this situation, for it is not, but only that it scores a rather low mark. This case, of course, is not of a type that we should normally think of as having much to do with *stylistic* suitability; we should tend to associate such a 'misuse' with some rather elementary stage of language learning and treat it as subliminal from any stylistic point of view. But there are other cases where we might feel otherwise. For instance there are certainly situations (as with my other sentence) in which 'Well, friends, I'd better get cracking!' would be perfectly suitable. But eyebrows would be raised if I made it the opening sentence of a formal lecture. The unsuitability of this second sentence would be of a different order from that of the one about the spanner, an unsuitability this time which we should probably feel to be much more definitely of a stylistic kind; there is no need to go into the nature of the difference here, though it should not be overlooked or simply taken for granted.

I believe that not enough attention has been paid to the nature of the two very different kinds of question which can be, and often are, asked about 'good' English: the question asked in a sort of vacuum, and that asked in relation to a specific situation.[2] When we are considering some stylistic matter, as distinct from the resources of the language as a whole, we are likely to be mainly and more directly concerned with the second kind. Consider this in relation to the difference between a preoccupation we may have at some particular time with *the* game of golf and *a* game of golf. Speaking of *the* game of golf, and therefore from the point of view of the first kind of question, I can feel free to allude to the suitability, as part of the game as a whole, of a (or if you like 'the') two-hundred yard brassie shot straight down the middle of the fairway. But if I am speaking of a given game of golf, and therefore from the point of view of the second kind of question, I must be much more reserved. Which hole are you playing? How far are you from the green? How good are your wood shots anyhow? How does your opponent lie? How does the score stand? Even perhaps, are you playing stroke-play or match-play?

In a similar way, our own immediate preoccupations have to do with the suitability of an utterance to one particular situation; whether it would 'do' anywhere else is of secondary importance, and it is in any case a sufficient validation of the utterance even from the point of view of the first kind of question that we satisfy ourselves that it will do here.[3]

[2] Cf. Paper 11, pp. 187–8.

[3] Of course, some very odd utterances indeed, such as are unlikely ever to recur, may be expected in a very unusual situation. Cf. James Thurber, 'Midnight at Tim's Place', *Lanterns and Lances*, London 1961, pp. 19–20:

'Ah thought you-all was Bing Crosby,' said the windlestraw in a fake Dixie that was not too bad for one in her cups . . .

Suddenly we all had a fresh drink. 'How are you, Bing?' asked Kirkfield, clinking his glass against mine.

'*Non sum qualis eram sub regno bony Sinatra*,' I said quickly, having waited for years to wedge that line in somewhere.

'You finally made it,' my wife said, for she knows all my lines, wedged and unwedged.

(*continued*)

We need only fall back on the first question if we suspect that the un-suitability of an utterance in a particular situation has something to do with its not according with the rules of the language as a whole. This is perhaps the point to discuss more closely what we mean when we speak of an utterance being in one way or another 'suitable'.

2

Most people are aware, in one capacity or another, of difficulties en-countered in the use of language which are connected with finding the most fitting linguistic means of achieving certain goals or ends. Yet it is often insisted that, from the standpoint of linguistics, one should merely observe (and analyse) linguistic events; the suitability of such an event to the situation in which it takes place is usually taken for granted. I believe that there are good reasons for thus counting on its suitability, taking this word in either of two senses which I propose shortly to distinguish. But this is often done as if it were an act of faith rather than because of any reasoned consideration of the implications.

Not all examples of linguistic events, of course, are taken completely for granted. For it is recognized that users of language may, for instance, make slips of the tongue or pen. And also that people who are in process of learning a language may fail to conform, to a lesser or greater extent, with the accepted conventions of that language. But for the most part any piece of text under linguistic scrutiny is normally taken as being in some sense suitable to some known or else some imagined situation. In what follows I wish to make a distinction between *appropriacy* and *adequacy*, and thereafter use these terms rather than the vaguer word suitability.

I imply by appropriacy something like this: that there must always be *some* explanation (whether we can find it or not) of a particular piece of linguistic activity, however unexpected it may have been in the situation where it occurred. To qualify as genuinely linguistic it must first of all conform to certain rules which have to do with current conventions about the grammar and lexis of the language in question.[4] Given this,

---

[4] An utterance made by a learner of the language will of course not necessarily conform fully to the rules, and we make special allowances in such cases. There is no precise level of competence 'below' which we can say that what we have is no longer an authentic linguistic event.

I should add that sufficient contextual justification for using Horatian Latin at all on this rather odd occasion and for therefore being able at the appropriate point to *mis*-use it, is carefully provided at the beginning of the story, p. 19.

we might say that the quality of appropriacy is a further necessary condition for its so qualifying. If these two conditions are not both ful-filled, then what we are dealing with is, for one reason or another, not truly a linguistic event at all. We should note that this is by no means to say that it will therefore be totally without meaning.

Our admission of the appropriacy of a really bizarre utterance—bizarre, that is, in the situation where it occurred, involves of course the perception and taking into account of circumstances in this situation which we would not normally be in the habit of considering at all. In such matters, we tend for excellent reasons to assign relevance only to certain aspects of situations; but this tendency must not be allowed to control our assessment of appropriacy in *this* situation. For it is precisely when the linguistic requirements or expectations of one situation are assessed in such stereotype fashion that it may prove very difficult to see how some utterance made in it can then possibly be held to accord with it at all.

Yet I should wish to claim that it could be a perfectly appropriate utterance, however injudicious or unfortunate, for me to exclaim, in the middle of an important interview for some key job: 'I wish to goodness I could get out of this wretched place and go and have a nice glass of beer!' For if we examine the total situation, it will become clear (let us suppose) that I am an impulsive forthright sort of fellow, disinclined at all times to hide his feelings or his thirsts. It is then a relevant ingredient of the whole situation (of which my peculiar *temperament* is a part) that I, in the role of the person being interviewed, am unlikely (and should certainly not be expected) to conform linguistically to any pattern normally manifested by people being interviewed. There will be no doubt, of course, that my non-conformity has complicated psychological origins, lying below the linguistic activity itself; but so, for that matter, would conformity.

Utterances of this wayward or perverse kind are at the disposal of anyone who has a reasonable command of the language; for the rest, all the speaker needs is a strong enough disposition or inclination to give voice to them. But in ordinary life there are all kinds of restraints and curbs associated with situations. For language activity being directed to certain goals or objectives, however vague they may sometimes be, it is these ingredients in the situation (or perhaps we might say the situation assessed from the point of view of these objectives) which usually exert the decisive influence on what is actually said. There is no need here to go into the institutional nature of many of the conventions which play their part here; it is comparable, for example, to that of others which affect dress or table manners. So far as language is concerned, such influences assert themselves in one way or another whether a man is writing a play for the London stage or chatting with a friend. And in any kind of linguistic activity where one has a goal in mind, one can be motivated by its attainment with various degrees of single-mindedness; among other things, it will be this degree of single-mindedness, the degree of preoccupation with some goal, that will have an effect on what one finally writes or says.

Two factors come in here. First there is the extent to which a person is aware of the conventions, and of precisely how he *should* conform linguistically in order to have the best chance of attaining his goal; he may be extremely keen to attain an objective in a given situation without knowing the conventions to follow. But secondly, even if he does know them in principle, he may still not have the necessary linguistic skill or experience to follow them when it comes to the point.

The linguistic decisions that are made in connection with the attainment of a certain goal are in some sense the outcome or the concomitant of decisions about the *persona* which a man judges it to be proper to assume on a given occasion. But of course though there will be some sort of vaguely understood norm in these matters, each individual will handle the matter to some extent differently from every other individual. In the nature of things, it will be the case in most situations that different people will most successfully attain their goal by adopting approaches which are at least slightly idiosyncratic. Indeed it might be said that we take this for granted; that in many situations part of goal-attainment consists of 'putting oneself across' in a way that is *expected* to differ from person to person. This comes very much into literature and art; I think less, not more, of a writer or painter or musician if there is not something special about his work, in means as well as ends, something that I find in no one else.

I turn now to the distinction I wish to make between appropriacy and adequacy. I have suggested that 'appropriacy' serves as one criterion for what constitutes a linguistic event: linguistic activity that is not appropriate, in the sense in which I use the word, is scarcely linguistic activity at all. For the rest the term has rather limited value. And when we single out certain aspects of a situation and decide that the accompanying linguistic activity must, for certain purposes, be judged according to these, then it becomes necessary to talk in terms of 'adequacy'. In this way we reserve the word 'adequacy' for the way in which a piece of linguistic activity 'works' in specific connection with those aspects of a situation that are relevant to the achievement of some sort of objective. Hence what is appropriate may not be adequate, but what is adequate can always be regarded as appropriate.

Since linguistic activity *is* normally geared to the achievement of certain objectives, the criterion of adequacy is one of some importance. But though it is a useful (and indeed highly familiar) concept, it is not an easy one to handle, and we must now discuss some of the difficulties.

3

There is to begin with the question of a possible conflict between the views of writer and reader, or speaker and hearer. And then, between one reader, or hearer, and another. Is not this kind of thing, from the very start, in danger of reducing everything to something uselessly vague and intangible? The danger must simply be faced; it will at least be lessened if we understand the nature of the factors involved. And we may take comfort from the fact that we are after all by no means totally removed either from the author or from each other in terms of familiarity with the conventions of the medium. So those who are involved are like golfers who are either playing or else observing a game being played by another. And though there is room for a certain amount of disagreement about tactics, there are many things about which there is no such room whatsoever.

But, someone may say, supposing we cannot assess the author because we cannot decide what he is up to? Is he playing pelota or is he playing fives? Or worse still, something that is not exactly either, which we don't know about? This is a problem I shall touch on later.

A more practical difficulty, which we need not despair of sorting out a little, has to do with that diverse array of considerations or factors which we tend to conglomerate in trying to come to a decision about adequacy. Even if we begin by trying to confine ourselves to those which seem to be of a tangibly linguistic kind, we do not always have a clear enough notion of what should be taken into account and what not; and to what extent our assessment should be made on a grammatical or on a lexical basis, to say nothing of various refinements of this broad main distinction. In any case we often become spellbound by yet other factors which seem to take us beyond language altogether; factors such as are reflected in criticisms like 'Why did the fellow have to write such disgusting filth?' or 'So-and-so seems to have nothing really worth saying', criticisms which necessarily *involve* language but clearly involve much else beside. I shall return briefly later to difficulties of these kinds.

Another problem arises from our tending to look at the whole business of adequacy as if we habitually knew exactly what utterance *should* ideally occur in a given situation, and as if all we therefore had to do was somehow to measure the utterance actually encountered against this imagined perfect one. Apart from this not normally being possible, it would be fallacious to suppose that without taking account of the utterance itself we can be sure of knowing the situation perfectly; in fact the utterance is something which contributes to, which is part of, the total situation. It is therefore at once the thing we are wishing to measure and part of the yardstick wherewith we are proposing to measure it.[5] This is more obviously true and more obviously a difficulty in some cases than others. But how, for example, can we begin to say what such and such a poem *should have been*, even on the basis of the entire situational and kindred information usually at our disposal? And difficulties may be present even in quite simple everyday situations. Often, when I hear something said, I may need to 'establish' situation from utterance rather than anything the other way round. Thus I cannot always ask: 'What would have been the *right* utterance in this present situation?' What I shall often do is to assume that the actual utterance is 'right' and ask rather: 'What exactly is this situation in which it is so?' To lesser or greater degrees it can therefore be text which 'keynotes' situation rather than the reverse.

It tends to be precisely in those cases where we most feel the need for some kind of high-powered method of stylistic evaluation that we find that the extra-textual elements in the total situation offer us the least orientation and guidance. It may be, for instance, that someone publishes a poem in a journal, someone whose name I do not even recognize and of whose background I know virtually nothing. So I have only the vaguest preliminary idea of what he is likely to be driving at. And of course it is good that this *should* be so, for it is an absolutely vital part of the relative freedom in literature to say what one will, compared for example with what one can pull off in conversations with ticket collectors. Indeed this is an aspect of the general problem of 'freedom of speech' which is gravely neglected in what is usually said about the liberty of the artist to say what he will, and much more might be said about it.

[5] See Angus McIntosh, 'Saying', *Review of English Literature*, Vol. vi, No. 2, 1965, p. 11.

So when I sit down to read this poem, I must rely very largely on the text by itself in order to make out what my poet *is* trying to 'say'. And if the retort be made: 'Of course you must', I should still wish to note that the extreme degree to which I am forced here to rely on the text makes this problem for me very different from one where, far better oriented situationally, I am listening to my mother talking or going over a menu with a head waiter or taking in a boxing commentary on television. It is perhaps not irrelevant here to point out that the situation I have described—a man reading a lone printed poem by an unknown and absent author—is a rather odd linguistic event, and one which would be totally unfamiliar in some cultures. And to stress that many of the difficulties spring directly from the fact that such a heavy burden, in strictly informational terms, is placed on the utterance itself. These difficulties are of course intimately tied up with the freedom which the artist has in compensation, the freedom to give shape to the situation by the very things he writes rather than to have his every sentence dictated, or at least powerfully controlled, by some kind of highly restricted expectation on the part of those who are likely to read him.

4

I turn to a brief consideration of the confusions which arise from our finding it hard to disengage our judgement of the language from other judgements, for example, our opinion as to the triviality or worthwhileness of what the writer or speaker 'has to say'. Indeed, when we get to the higher realms of stylistic evaluation, we tend to deny any possibility of a distinction and we take refuge in such phrases as 'le style c'est l'homme même.' I should not be at all disposed to dismiss such denials lightly; all the same I do not like axioms which tend to be cited simply to save us the bother of really examining some problem on which they merely supply a comment and leave quite unexplained. And I feel that if we accept this one blindly, it cannot but obscure some important issues.

For there is a quite reasonable sense in which it is possible to separate (though not to dissociate) the intrinsic triviality or worthwhileness of an utterance from the language in which it is couched. Worthwhileness would seem to have to do with the propriety of putting across something, even if it is apparently trivial in itself, like the conversation of Nancy Steele in *Sense and Sensibility*, so long as this plays its part in some perhaps wider scheme which we judge to be itself admirable. The adequacy with which something is put across, linguistically, must in some way be assessed on this deeper basis; above all, it must not be confused with some kind of 'immediate' worthwhileness as judged in isolation. Always supposing that we know enough from all the sources available to us to have a reasonably clear impression of Jane Austen's intentions in this matter (and it would be idle to pretend that we are entirely without clues), we can say that the utterances of Nancy Steele would be less adequate if they failed to point up these intentions. There is, then, on the one hand the intention or purpose or aim, call it what one will. On the other there is the matter of the degree to which the author has succeeded, and what it is about the language of the utterance which helps to make the attempt a success or a failure or something in between. And we may say that linguistic adequacy is a necessary condition of the attainment of worthwhile literary ends.

Confronted with problems like this, the linguist is inclined to be rather cagey. He will often say that since we have no objective means of 'getting into the author's mind' (and therefore knowing what his aims really are) we must just take the language as we find it. One sometimes suspects indeed that some contemporary linguists would be happiest if all their textual material came from non-random *tours de force* of monkeys hammering away on typewriters; adequacy would then simply consist of succeeding in typing English at all, and most situational complexities would be avoided. But in so far as it is right that linguists should be interested in the relation of specific linguistic events to specific situations they should face this kind of problem more squarely. For my part I find the word 'objective' something of a stumbling block in contexts like the present one; in the last resort I doubt whether I have truly objective means of 'getting into' anything, even straight text, let alone author's minds. The most I can see is greater and lesser degrees of objectivity.

What is important and significant to me is that I am aware that people who speak and write have intentions and attitudes and so forth; and also that different people, or for that matter the same people at different times, achieve varying degrees of success in putting across, linguistically, something they are trying to communicate. I am not hereby asserting that we *can* get into other people's minds, but merely that when we use language we habitually behave as if we could count—at least up to a point —on so doing. And the study of style relates to some aspects of that very behaviour, in so far as it has a linguistic reflection.

On the specifically linguistic side, I should be inclined to regard the approach to all questions of adequacy of utterance to situation, however subtle, as involving the same basic procedures as those whereby we should evaluate the sentence about buying the spanner or the one about my getting cracking. And I should advocate that one start with simple cases offering a wealth of formal characteristics which lend themselves readily to linguistic analysis. For instance, the formal differences between a lecture delivered lucidly on a good day and the 'same' lecture confusingly delivered on an off day. Or the linguistic characteristics of some highly unsatisfactory eye-witness account of a traffic accident, presented with good will but little else. Or those of a good after-dinner speech as against those of a bad one made on the same occasion. Or the effects on grammar and lexis of speaking or writing under pressure, say too fast, or in conditions of alarm or fatigue, or after an intolerable deal of sack.

In considering such matters we should not allow ourselves to think in terms of the misleadingly metaphorical injunction 'let your language alone' as if 'one's' language were a kind of independent and all-efficient genie which did exactly what was required of it in all situations at the mere signal to get cracking. And if you object by demanding who is to decide which of the lectures or after-dinner speeches was good, and so forth, I can only answer that if this sort of question be pressed with just a little further pertinacity, it is quite easy to demolish the entire 'objective' foundations of the whole of science. I recognize of course that at the higher levels we can never in any absolute way measure the success or worth of an utterance. But that is a very different thing from maintaining that we can therefore say nothing illuminating whatever about it.

5

I have been considering one trend in contemporary linguistics which tends to prevent the systematic study of factors of linguistic adequacy: an unwillingness in some quarters to admit that it is the business of the linguist to meddle with such things at all. I should now like to mention one or two others of a different kind. One is a rather exclusive preoccupation on the part of grammarians with small units of utterance; this is largely the result, of course, of there being considerable difficulties about handling units larger than the sentence. The result is that we lack a wholly adequate frame of reference for handling many important linguistic features relevant to the matters we are considering, which often have to do with subtle interrelations *between* one sentence and another, and indeed between still larger units. The importance of this kind of thing is well brought out by Sir Roy Harrod in a passage about the Oxford philosopher H. W. B. Joseph[6]:

> These philosophers were careful also to keep their sentences, in so far as the subject allowed, crisp and clear. Thus, if one listened to one sentence, one had the idea that this was a most beautifully lucid exposition and expressed a thought that commended itself to plain common sense. But Joseph had a certain cleverness, which prevented his remaining quite in the austere Cook Wilson tradition. He was very fluent; and he had learnt the trick, which was truly a remarkable one, of running his sentences together into a discourse of interminable length. Thus, although each sentence seemed all right by itself, it was exceedingly difficult to grasp the meaning of the totality. He achieved what was almost an acrobatic trick. He rushed on and on; one could not complain that any single word was of obscure meaning, or even that any single clause was. None the less the whole was difficult to follow, and sometimes one could not help having the feeling, as sentence succeeded sentence, that he had cheated somehow in the process of leading us up to his clear and well-defined conclusion.

The disadvantages, from the point of view of stylistic analysis, of a preoccupation with rather short units should be associated with another characteristic of contemporary linguistic studies: the tendency for linguists to be more interested in grammar than in lexis. The comparative neglect of lexical matters is to be deplored even from a linguistic point of view: I have elsewhere pointed out that a merely grammatical description is no more a complete *linguistic* description than is a merely lexical one.[7] The actual grammatical patterns selected in an utterance are of course highly important from the point of view of style, but they are only part of the story and should be studied in close association with the selection from lexis and with various collocational phenomena. Needless to say, lexical features ‘carrying’ over large stretches of text, far beyond the dimensions of the sentence, are often of great stylistic significance. I do not propose here to go into the further point that the customary ordering of lexical descriptions of a language also does comparatively little to illuminate problems of style: for they do not normally bring together in one focus those things which *need* to be focused for this purpose.

[6] Sir Roy Harrod, *The Prof*, London, 1959, p. 23.
[7] See Paper 11, p. 187.

In any case, quite apart from a certain neglect of a really disciplined approach to lexical problems, grammar itself tends to be studied from certain angles only. The main preoccupation is with the various structures displayed in different *sentences* and it is one which generally considers 'potential' adequacy; in other words the peculiar suitability of one rather than another grammatical pattern to a particular situation is less commonly considered, and then for the most part in only a somewhat crude way in which many questions are begged. The subtle interaction of grammar and lexis has as yet received little attention.

6

I shall add a further word, in conclusion, about the separation of linguistic and non-linguistic factors. It sometimes happens that those utterances which are in one sense the most admirably *appropriate* are criticized—either openly or by implication—for the very clarity and transparency with which they reveal to the observer some characteristic of the author. Conversely it can happen that a certain linguistic muddiness may disarm criticism because it succeeds in concealing what one of my foreign students once called a whited elephant. But to go back to transparency: if I want to paint a woman looking like a gnarled artichoke root, and if I then make a real success of this, you are hardly entitled to blame my technique if your real complaint is that the painting should have been more like a Rubens; you can only blame my *intention*, on the grounds that it was not, in your opinion, a sufficiently worthwhile one. Indeed you should really have nothing but admiration and gratitude for my technical ability which has, after all, put the very minimum of obstruction in the way of your getting right down to the main business of assessing me as an artist, and deciding whether as such I have anything worth putting across.

Let me take an illustration from the world of letters. In a recent article[8] Kathleen Knott has taken C. P. Snow (now Lord Snow) to task for writing such passages as the following (from *The Affair*) about 'the new Mrs Eliot' who

> even after marrying me, and meeting my colleagues, and getting a
> spectator's view of the snakes and ladders of power . . . could not

[8] 'The Type to Which the Whole Creation Moves', *Encounter*, February 1962, p. 87.

quite credit it. Her grandfather and great-uncle had resigned fellow-
ships over the Thirty-Nine Articles . . . they had both been men of
independent means . . . She could not sympathise with the shifts, the
calculations, the self-seeking of men making their way.

What I should wish to maintain here is that the prose *as such* is
excellent of its kind, and that it is so precisely because—taken of course
along with much else in the novel—it provides the reader in an admirably diaphanous manner with an extremely informative picture of
Eliot's *Weltanschauung*. Whether this dead-pan portrayal of Eliot ('or
Sir Charles' as Kathleen Knott wryly observes) is of high literary value
is another matter, and one which I am glad to leave to others. My
concern here is to suggest that this question can be the more readily and
realistically debated precisely because the language, in this respect like
my hypothetical painting technique, leaves the very minimum of doubt
about what Sir Charles is wanting to put across. One might learn a good
deal by making a detailed comparison, from such points of view, of the
language of *The Affair* and of *The Old Men at the Zoo*.

To sum up: I have suggested that it is important for us to get to grips
with the problems relating to linguistic adequacy, and that this involves
strict attention to linguistic phenomena in specific situations. I have also
suggested something of the width of array of linguistic equipment that
this requires to deal satisfactorily with it, and that current linguistic
approaches and techniques at best do but somewhat coldly furnish forth
what we need. But I have also implied that a good deal of the theory at
present available to us can, with a little effort, be brought to bear directly
and profitably on these problems. I have said something further about
the difficulties we encounter through being torn between an evaluation
of the language from the point of view of whether it 'comes off' and a
scrutiny of the objective itself (this not necessarily being deduced
entirely from linguistic evidence) from the point of view of whether it is
a worthy one anyhow.

Sometimes I feel it would be easier if we lived in a differently adjust-
able world where we felt it our business to look at things the other way
round; would it not be rather a relief to scrutinize the extra-textual
situation from the point of view of its suitability to the utterance, and
criticize or even make appropriate adjustments to this *situation* where
necessary? This brings to my mind a story by Peter de Vries in the *New
Yorker* in which the narrator evidently thought as I do, for he went to
great pains to modify, and accommodate himself to, a large number of

things in the Connecticut cosmos in order to achieve the perfect con-
textualization, the truly ideal situation, for a sentence he felt to be
specially worthy of this effort. And the sentence? For the last words of a
paper on stylistic problems it has at least rarity value: 'Where was
Moses when the light went out?'

Six

'Graphology' and meaning[1] (1961)

I propose in this paper to do no more than consider a few aspects of a single problem: the exploration of possible parallels between the meanings of units like words and the meanings of units like letters. In dealing with words I shall be using the word *meaning* in a familiar way; in dealing with letters I shall be using it in relation to signals about something phonic, that is to say to signals which might be described as clues to pronunciation.

This provision of clues to pronunciation is not of course the only function of written symbols. For they have, from the point of view of ordinary meaning, the other role of serving as sub-morphemic units, the units whereby a distinction is made in writing between *bat* and *cat* for example, or between *pan* and *pad*. They are bits, so to speak, out of which morphemes (or what American linguists would call morphs) are built up; as such they have themselves no meaning in the ordinary sense but they do have what we can call distinctive value. And we may note

---

[1] This paper is not primarily concerned with terminology, but I should note that I have used the word 'graphology' in a sense which is intended to answer, in the realm of written language, to that of 'phonology' in the realm of spoken language. This makes it possible to reserve the word 'graphemics' for use in a way that answers to 'phonemics', which designates no more than one branch of phonology. This use of 'graphology' therefore underlines the fact that the grapheme, despite my emphasis on it in this paper, is not the only unit required for the analysis of written or printed language, cf. footnote 7, p. 102. But those who prefer may read 'the study of orthographic system⟨s⟩' for 'graphology' and 'orthographic' for 'graphological' throughout.

I employ the following symbols: ⟨. . .⟩ enclose grapheme symbols, as in ⟨b⟩ or ⟨bat⟩; /. . ./ enclose phoneme symbols, as in /k/ or /lamp/; italics are used to cite letters or words when no special graphemic implications are involved.

I should like here to record my indebtedness to Professor William Haas and to Professor M. A. K. Halliday for the help I have had, in discussion with them, on some of the problems touched on in this paper.

that by virtue of this role alone their existence could perfectly well be justified in some situation where there was no question whatever of any relationship between written language and spoken language. They could, for example, serve as the bits out of which morphemes were made in a written language used as the only form of language by a community all members of which were deaf and dumb.[2]

Quite apart from any such situation, I should maintain that an organized written system of language has a status equivalent to any spoken 'opposite number' it may have; it simply manifests *language* in another substance—one which appeals to the eye rather than to the ear. In other words it is not a mere second-degree system in the way implied by Aristotle in *De Interpretatione* when he says that spoken words are the symbols of mental experience and written words are the symbols of spoken words.[3] Without attempting to be too precise here, I should prefer to say (if I were to stick to Aristotle's terminology) that written language and spoken language *both* symbolize mental experience[4] but

139703

[2] If this happened, the written symbols would no doubt turn out to have an organization which ultimately 'derived', in some sense, from a phonological state of affairs in spoken language at some earlier date. But this organization would no longer relate directly to spoken language and at most the symbols would be visual derivatives from an old sound system (or perhaps more than one) rather than simple visual equivalents of units in an existing sound system. One might profitably envisage, in any case, an alternative situation to that suggested above, in which an entirely autonomous written language took shape, and where it was only subsequently that people discovered that they could utilize appropriate physiological etc. mechanisms to render it phonically.

[3] Cf. Angus McIntosh, 'The Analysis of Written Middle English', *Transactions of the Philological Society*, 1965, p. 40, footnote. References to other works on graphological problems are given at the end of the same footnote.

Additional note. See now also Sture Allén, *Grafematisk Analys som Grundval för Textedering*, Gothenburg 1965, which contains numerous further references.

[4] I should further maintain (at least in the case of fully institutionalized written systems) that it does this directly and so to speak in its own right and *not* via some circuit that leads to the goal only through spoken language. In other words it does not have to be 'converted' or 'decoded' into spoken language on the way.

Additional note. The earliest reference I know to this double role of written language is in the *Grammaire générale et raisonnée de Port Royal*, the first edition of which appeared in 1660. I cite from the 1845 reprint of the 1676 edition, Première Partie, Chapitre v, p. 29: 'Mais quoique ces figures ou caractères, selon leur première institution, ne signifient immédiatement que les sons, néanmoins les hommes portent souvent leurs pensées des caractères à la chose même signifieé par les sons: ce qui fait que les caractères peuvent être considérés en ces deux manières, ou comme signifiant simplement le son, ou comme nous aidant à concevoir ce que le son signifie.' This passage (which I owe indirectly to Professor Noam Chomsky) should be added to similar statements made slightly later by Wallis and Wilkins which are cited in the paper referred to in footnote 3 above.

that written language, by virtue of its graphological system, *also* symbolizes spoken language.

It is with this second function that I shall be concerned more directly here. For it is in the symbolization of what is spoken that I seek the parallels to things which, on the linguistic plane, are equally present in both written and in spoken language. Now in this role of symbolizing phonic phenomena, the 'bits' we spoke of earlier are units in a graphological system. From this point of view they are therefore in a very real sense not sub-morphemic at all. It may be true that in its other role the grapheme ⟨b⟩ in ⟨bat⟩ has no more than distinctive value; it is only ⟨bat⟩ itself (and not the bits out of which it is made) that has meaning. But from the standpoint of 'phonic reference' the matter is different. In the basically alphabetic system of English ⟨b⟩ carries what we may call phonic implications; in other words it *means* something within its own little world of reference, just as the morpheme *cat* means something in the wider world in which language as a whole operates.

If we approach matters from this point of view we are led to maintain that a written text normally carries a sort of double semantic load. First of all it carries meaning (to those who know the system) in the familiar sense that it can be a receptacle for the rules of the game of golf, or convey what happened in some road accident, or be the means of trying to persuade somebody to make one a loan. The smallest unit relevant to the system whereby all this is achieved is the morpheme. This kind of meaning, or something very close to it, can, we may note, be carried over into another language by the ordinary processes of translation. Secondly, however, this same written text bears another load of information which is transmitted by another system; this load is what enables us (if we know the system) to read our text aloud should we wish to. And the two systems are so far distinct that one may do this with reasonable adequacy without necessarily understanding the text (in the ordinary sense) at all,[5] just as—conversely—one may be able to understand a written language with little or no knowledge of how it is pronounced.

The smallest unit relevant to this second system, the system whereby conversion to spoken language is possible, is the grapheme. We may say

[5] Nor will some progress in understanding necessarily produce an improvement in our ability to interpret the text in phonic terms. The kind of situation discussed above is touched upon by Ludwig Wittgenstein, *Philosophical Investigations* Vol. i, Oxford, 1953, pp. 156 ff.: 'First I need to remark that I am not counting the understanding of what is read as part of "reading" for purposes of this investigation: reading is here the activity of rendering out loud what is written or printed . . .' Cf. footnote 19, p. 109.

therefore that in *this* system the grapheme has a status which might be described as morphemic. For example, any instance of the letter *b*, once it is identified by the reader as an instance of the grapheme ⟨b⟩, becomes meaningful, because he is then in a position to draw certain conclusions about its equivalent or equivalents in the system of the spoken language. This is what I mean by saying that ⟨b⟩, for example, has morphemic status in the graphological system. It does not matter for the moment that a grapheme may have two or more radically different equivalents in the spoken language. As we shall see, this is very like the problem of 'ordinary' morphemes which happen to be homonymous in the conventional linguistic sense.

It may be asked: what about a situation of the kind in which *b* seems to have no such morphemic status because it has in fact no 'phonic referent', for example in *lamb*? Are we justified in regarding the *b* here as an instance of the grapheme ⟨b⟩ at all? My answer would be that we are, because in the system of written language it has distinctive value whether it 'stands for' a phoneme or not. It does for ⟨lamb⟩ vis-à-vis ⟨lam⟩ precisely what (for example) /p/ does for /lamp/ vis-à-vis /lam/ in the system of spoken language. Since ⟨b⟩ has in this way a distinctive value parallel to that of /p/, and since this property of /p/ is quite central to the definition of it as a phoneme, there are very good reasons for a definition of 'grapheme' wherein distinctive value is also central. The question whether ⟨b⟩ in ⟨lamb⟩ has what from the point of view of our 'second' system I have called morphemic status is then irrelevant to the definition. In other words, a definition of the grapheme which seeks to march parallel with a definition of the phoneme can only do so by making strictly secondary any correlation there may be between a given grapheme and a given phoneme.

It follows from my insistence on this point that my concept of the grapheme differs considerably from that of most American linguists who have written on the subject. For they tend to start with a previously constructed (phonological) system of the spoken language. With this point of departure and with a definition of the grapheme in some such terms as 'that which renders a phoneme', they proceed to set up their 'corresponding' grapheme system accordingly. This is of some ideological interest. For if my own view is acceptable, namely that (though this is secondary in a definition) ⟨b⟩ is a morpheme in the graphological system and that /b/ is its meaning (or, to be safe, one of its meanings), then there is something remarkable about the procedure of these linguists. It is one which begins by ordering the phonic referents of graphemes into a system and then goes on, in effect, to derive the 'morphological' system directly from this system of referents.[6] This is so astonishingly contrary to the usual American approach to anything that has to do with meaning that it deserves to be noted.

My own approach, which is much more in line with the glossematic point of view as it was presented by John Uldall and with the work of the Czech scholar Josef Vachek, is to establish the grapheme system on the basis of visual criteria in combination with distinctiveness of value.[7] The theoretical basis for the establishment of the graphological and of the phonological system then becomes the same. If, as a result, the graphological system which we set up has an interest in its own right and a status other than merely derivative, this is to be regarded as a merit of the underlying theory and not a shortcoming.

I want now to ask: what is the nature of the load of phonic information carried by a written text which enables us, as we scan it, to read it aloud? I propose to go on using the word 'meaning' in this context as well as in connection with the normal semantic load carried by any text, written or spoken. But to keep these two uses apart I shall where necessary speak of:

1. Linguistic meaning: that which is involved when we understand or translate a text in the ordinary sense.
2. Phonic meaning: that which is involved in interpreting visual graphic material in phonic terms, for example in reading loud.

I retain the word 'meaning' in both cases because I wish to explore the similarities between the ways in which the two 'loads' are carried by the respective systems; to retain it helps to focus one's thoughts accordingly. My main reason for such an exploration is this: that the problems connected with meaning in the ordinary sense are notoriously complicated and it seems to me that in this other (graphological) realm we have

---

[6] Cf. footnote 17, p. 109.

[7] For references to the work of these scholars see footnote 3, p. 99. There are of course problems here which can hardly be explored in this paper but which I have attempted to deal with in a monograph which has not yet been published. There is for example the question of graphological units which carry 'meaning' but which are very different in visual form from what we would generally agree to describe as 'letters'. I do not want, for instance, anything in the nature of a suprasegmental grapheme of italicization, or a juncture-grapheme of hyphenization. It is not that such devices as italics and hyphens are unimportant, but rather that there are good reasons for not treating all *graphological* units as *grapheme units*, cf. footnote 1, p. 98. The parallels here with phonology and with morphology in the ordinary sense are sufficiently clear.

a somewhat similar system operating in a much simpler fashion. It might therefore serve to suggest ways in which we could approach the more complicated problems of meaning that we encounter in studying language as a whole. We must of course be on our guard against making fallacious deductions or predictions about the latter on the basis of our analysis of the former. The points at which the two systems fail to 'match' is therefore a matter of importance; these can best be discovered however under the stimulus and discipline of exploring parallels and similarities.[8]

In approaching these matters we should not be put off, or too strongly object, merely because of a feeling that the first kind of meaning involves us far more in things altogether outside language than the other does. Let us simply start with this position: that just as the word *cat* (written or spoken) has some sort of referent outside *language*, so has the grapheme ⟨t⟩ some sort of referent outside *written language*.[9] In this respect then the difference is in the nature of the relevant universe which may be said to lie outside in each case. The second is of course a much less complicated one because the scope of reference in question is only to certain phonic phenomena and to certain rather simple relationships between them.

I venture at this point to introduce two qualifying words of which I feel the need in speaking of either linguistic or phonic meaning. One is naturally diffident about suggesting additions to linguistic terminology; I am however here concerned more with the concepts which suggest the need for some such qualifiers than with the labels themselves. The two terms I propose are 'potential' and 'actual'; they are intended to correspond roughly (but, as we shall see, only roughly) to the more familiar terms 'lexical' and 'contextual' as these are habitually used to

---

[8] In this connection, I wonder how far those working on machine translation have perceived the similarities between the problem of 'translating' written language into spoken and the larger problem of translation in the everyday sense. I know of course that work has been done on the conversion of written language into spoken (and vice versa) but I do not know whether it is seen to be related to the other in the way I imply.
Additional note. The converse problem has recently been given some attention; see Garvin, L. and Trager, E. C., 'The conversion of phonetic into orthographic English: a machine-translation approach to the problem', *Phonetica* (Basle), 11, 1, 1964, pp. 1–18.

[9] It is not essential that a grapheme should in all instances have such a referent, nor that, where it has, it should in all cases function in this way by itself. The presence of ⟨b⟩ in ⟨lamb⟩, see p. 101, is an example where a grapheme has no referent in this sense. The use of ⟨sh⟩ to designate a single phoneme is an instance of the second kind of case; this I discuss more fully on pages 108–9.

qualify the word 'meaning'. For reasons which I shall bring up, I wish
to avoid these for the purposes I have in mind. Using those I propose, I
am in a position to speak of *potential linguistic meaning* and *actual
linguistic meaning* on the one hand, and of *potential phonic meaning* and
actual phonic meaning on the other.

By potential meaning I mean something that can perhaps best be
described negatively. Let us consider it, to begin with, in reference to
what I have called linguistic (that is ordinary) meaning. Let us think of
any word, say the word *cat*. Now there are many things which the word
cat cannot mean, and another way of saying this is that it is only appropriate in certain places in a piece of English text and only appropriate
even there in certain situational contexts. In one way or another it
cannot, if it is to fulfil these conditions, substitute for *elephant* or
grapheme or (though for different reasons) *tomorrow* or *big*.[10] We can
therefore say that it has only a certain range of eligibility, just as these
other words have theirs. So for one reason or another, *cat* is a form which
is only occasionally appropriate, and in the very large number of cases
where it is not, some other form or forms must be used.

The potential meaning of *cat* is then that which is conventionally
invested in it as against all other forms in the language; this, as I have
suggested, may be described if not defined as its restricted appropriacy
to certain places in a text in certain situational contexts. It will be seen
that this is something like what is often understood by 'lexical' meaning.
But the difficulty with this term is that it often seems to designate
nothing more than some vague mystical summation of the totality of
so-called contextual meanings.[11]

By my use of the term 'actual' I intend nothing subtle. Instance by
instance, in the various allowed places in a text in the appropriate
situational contexts, a form (for example *cat*) would appear to be

---

[10] I do not attempt in this paper to distinguish between the merely collocational criteria which define the appropriacy of *cat* or *elephant* or *grapheme* and the
grammatical criteria which are also involved when one comes to consider the
appropriacy of *cat* as against *tomorrow* or either of these as against *big*. Some
aspects of this problem are dealt with in Paper 11, p. 183.

[11] The term 'potential meaning' is intended to cover both the eligibility of a
form to occupy one or more places in grammatical structure and its collocational
eligibility (see previous footnote). It therefore involves statements both about the
grammatical role or roles of *cat* (e.g. as against *tomorrow*) and about the lexical
role or roles of *cat* (e.g. as against other nouns). We may therefore usefully speak
of a word as having 'grammatical meaning' and 'lexical meaning'. To use
'lexical' in this way rescues the term from the vagueness which at present often
vitiates its use.

capable of a variety of differing meanings, perhaps in the last resort as many such as there are instances. This variety can have nothing to do with the form *per se* except in the trivial sense that forms have, and are recognized to have, precisely this kind of variability of reference, which amounts to no more than saying that we are aware that any form is eligible to appear in a variety of contexts, linguistic and situational. Because the meaning appropriate to a given instance is specifically associated with this *actual* living manifestation of a form in its context, I apply the term 'actual meaning' to such cases.

The actual meaning depends on the actual context, taking this latter term in as wide a sense as circumstances may render necessary. Hence the somewhat similar implications of the phrase 'contextual meaning' as it is often used. But the two terms are not synonymous, for 'contextual meaning' is not tied to reference to a single instance; sometimes it is applied to a whole cluster or 'family' of instances which for one reason or another the investigator has chosen to associate as 'like' at a certain level of abstraction. If thus operates on a different axis from 'actual meaning'.[12]

If, turning from the linguistic to the graphological plane, we apply here the terms 'potential' and 'actual', this may help us to perceive some of the parallels between the system which conveys linguistic meaning and that which conveys phonic meaning. We may say, for example, that the grapheme ⟨c⟩ has potential phonic meaning on the graphological plane in the same sense as *cat* has on the linguistic plane; both have a range, but a severely restricted range, of eligibility. Thus ⟨c⟩ can never substitute (in the sense implied in the discussion of *cat*) for shall we say ⟨b⟩ or ⟨o⟩; it has—to put it crudely—the wrong phonic meaning for this to be possible. So just as any morpheme in isolation may be said to have potential linguistic meaning, so may a grapheme be said to have potential phonic meaning; in each case it is a question of severely restricted appropriacy. And when we speak of the potential phonic meaning of a grapheme our reference is to a level of abstraction parallel to that at which we are considering a morpheme when we speak of its potential linguistic meaning.

[12] On contextual meaning cf. M. A. K. Halliday, 'Categories of the Theory of Grammar', section 1.9, *Word*, 17.3, 1961. Where we wish to speak explicitly of a cluster of instances, we may speak of this as a 'use', cf. footnote 16, p. 108 below and Paper 11, p. 195.

Additional note. Since the above was written, some linguists (e.g. Dr J. O. Ellis) have proposed and used the term 'instantial' in place of the term 'actual'.

What then about the actual phonic meaning of a grapheme? Here, as on the other plane, we are concerned with the specific interpretation we give to a grapheme in a particular instance, for example when we set about pronouncing the first consonant in this sentence. This kind of thing involves getting to the point when we can produce the appropriate exponent of shall we say an /l/ in a given instance, endowed with the 'right' degree (within tolerated limits) of length, voicedness, velarity and so forth for the context.

As with the actual meaning of *cat* on the linguistic plane, this specific interpretation and rendering will inevitably depend on the context. Inevitably, because a ⟨c⟩ is a ⟨c⟩ is a ⟨c⟩, and if we are to render it differently (however grossly or slightly) at different times, it must be because we deduce from its environment its particular or actual meaning in a given instance. In just what ways our deductions are made from an observation of the context is an absorbing question, the more so because it is similar in many ways to the problem of how we arrive at the actual linguistic meaning of the form *cat* in a given instance.

This cannot be pursued very far here, but we may note that there are often two stages in our progress towards a final interpretation, in phonetic terms, of grapheme symbols. The first confronts us from time to time because of a feature of the grapheme system which is however in no sense a necessary characteristic thereof, a feature which is paralleled on the other plane. For there, after we have identified some sequence, for example *pen*, as a particular form as against all other forms, we quite often face an initial dilemma. Thus having identified the form *pen*, we still do not know without help from the context whether (among other things) it is to be interpreted as what my dictionary calls 'pen *sb*[1]' or as 'pen *sb*[2]'. Nothing within the form itself will resolve our dilemma; there is no simple answer to the question 'What does *pen* mean?'. I am therefore disposed to regard the potential meaning of the form *pen* as embracing what my dictionary concerns itself with under both entries.[13] When we have resolved our preliminary dilemma about *pen*, we have already made a selection without potential meaning and to do so we have

[13] For the sake of simplicity I am supposing that we are faced in this case with a merely binary choice, which of course is not the case.

Additional note. I should now describe 'unassigned' *pen* not as a 'form' but as an 'expression', and use form only in relation to a grammatically or lexically identified item such as 'pen *sb*[1]' or 'pen *sb*[2]'. But I should continue to speak of 'the' grapheme ⟨c⟩, despite the ambiguity of its phonological reference, because this ambiguity has no relevance to my criteria for establishing units in the grapheme system (see pp. 100–101).

had to use information from outside the form itself. Thereafter we are in a position to move on to the second stage and seek to interpret our actual instance.

In such cases we are confronted with the familiar problem of homonymity. I am suggesting that essentially the same problem is encountered when we consider graphemes. Thus the grapheme $\langle c \rangle$ confronts us with a similar preliminary hurdle. For till we see it in a sufficiency of context, we have no way of knowing whether it is (among other things) what we might label '$\langle c \rangle^1$' or '$\langle c \rangle^2$', that is to say whether it is 'the' $\langle c \rangle$ which stands for /k/, and therefore corresponds shall we say to the 'pen sb^1' which stands for *calamus*, or whether it is the $\langle c \rangle$ which stands for /s/, and corresponds to the 'pen sb^2' which stands for *ovile*.[14] Its potential phonic meaning would therefore have to be indicated by a full statement on the lines of: 'possibly /k/, possibly /s/ etc., but certainly not /b/, /i/ etc.'; this would then answer to what we might say about the potential linguistic meaning of *pen* on the lines of: 'possibly *calamus*, possibly *ovile* etc., but certainly not *elephant, tomorrow* etc.'

But if we can examine our instance of $\langle c \rangle$ in context, it normally becomes possible for us to resolve this problem of homophany and to say, for example: 'this instance of $\langle c \rangle$ stands for /k/', just as we would similarly be able to resolve our initial dilemma in the case of *pen*. This however is by no means the end of our quest. For merely to know, as we do at this stage, that our contextualized instance of a $\langle c \rangle$ means or stands for /k/ does not solve all our problems. Once again, the situation resembles that which we face when we encounter *pen* or *cat*. We may indeed have got to the point when we know, for example, that we are dealing with an instance of *cat* which refers to some member of the genus *Felis* and not to an instrument of punishment. But we are likely to need to know, as we tackle some particular piece of text, rather more than this. Is the author referring to the prowling leopard of the previous sentence, or has he switched and is it now kitty who has just strolled off into the jungle behind the house? It is only when we have some sort of an answer to this kind of question, instance by instance, that we may be said to have arrived at the actual meaning.

---

[14] The grapheme $\langle c \rangle$ may therefore be termed a *homophane* or be said to be *homophanous*. I have not coined these words. Alexander Graham Bell used *homophene* in 1883, and A. J. Ellis used this and the adjective *homophenous* in 1884; see *OED*, which points out that the forms with *a* would be more correct. The adjectives are of course much less useful in spoken than in written English because in normal speech *homophanous* and *homophonous* are homophonous!

And so similarly with the /k/ phoneme which we have inferred from our contextualized instance of ⟨c⟩: our goal has not been reached when, in such an instance, we have established no more than the correct *phonological* reference.[15] We need this information, to be sure, but what we also want to know is how to render the phoneme phonetically in the context in question, how to choose the particular exponent of the phoneme which is appropriate to that context. The information required for this has not necessarily been given to us at the stage when we have decided that ⟨c⟩ in this instance stands for /k/ and not /s/. The *phonetic* question 'What kind of /k/?' still remains, just as the question 'Which (or what kind of a) cat?' remained before. The answer to this phonetic question, like the answer to the question '/k/ or /s/?', derives from an observation of the context. The final correct interpretation, leading to a satisfactory rendering of the sound, corresponds to actual linguistic meaning on the other plane.[16]

I should like at this point to consider briefly the problem of a single grapheme which has, in certain situations, no very obvious phonological referent at all. How can we suggest that anything so used has properties which can be compared with those of a morpheme? What are we to do, for example, with the individual letters *s* and *h* in the collocation *sh* as in *ship* or *rush*? This question merits consideration because it may be cited as yet another example of close similarity between the two systems we are dealing with. For there is an interesting parallel here to the problem of two such morphemes (for so they would generally be labelled without question) as the *under*(-) and the (-)*stand* which make up the word *understand*. There are indeed two parallels. First, that in each case the meaning of the whole, that is the linguistic or ordinary meaning of *understand* and the phonic meaning of *sh*, could not be deduced or predicted from a knowledge of instances of the alleged components in other collocations, e.g. *underwear, bystander*; *st, wh*. Secondly, just as most people would agree despite this that *understand* is made up of two morphemes *under*(-) and (-)*stand*, so would they agree that *sh* is made

---

[15] It is not implied of course, here or earlier, that there is necessarily a *procedural* order whereby a phonological ambiguity is in fact resolved by the reader before any attention has been paid to a specific phonetic interpretation.

[16] It may be noted that within the kind of framework I have outlined we are at liberty, as on the other plane, to employ the term 'use', cf. footnote 12, p. 105. We may wish for example to associate in this way a number of similar actual meanings of ⟨l⟩ derived from the observation of a number of particular instances, e.g. a use where ⟨l⟩ implies a consonant with more than a certain degree of velarity.

up of two graphemes ⟨s⟩ and ⟨h⟩.[17] A full exploration of the implications of these parallels would be well worth while, but it is beyond the scope of this paper.

But if we are right in stressing various parallels on the two planes, there is one further question which it might be profitable to touch upon. So far we have explored in the main various similarities which might be described as belonging to the realm of lexis rather than to that of grammar. We may now ask, in conclusion, whether the graphological system can be said to involve a hierarchical ordering of units in any way similar to that characteristic of grammar in the ordinary sense, and whether it is possible, again in grammatical terms, to make statements about allowed and prohibited patterns of grapheme sequence.[18] Could we perhaps usefully regard the written word, bounded by spaces, as the 'sentence' of the graphological system? And if so, what is the grammar of such sentences? And are there intermediate units between the morpheme at one end and the sentence at the other?

These questions cannot easily be pursued very far here for they demand an exposition and scrutiny of the whole graphological system. But we can at least say that certain sequences of graphemes seem to satisfy rules of structure, whereas others do not. Of those which do, we have:

1. A class of sentences which are familiar in the sense that they are in recognized use, and as such have morphemic status as words in the other system. E.g. *tinkle, chough, at, predestination, a, when.*

2. A class of sentences which are not in recognized use but which are acceptable in pattern, and as such are eligible at any time (should the need arise) for morphemic status in the other system. E.g. *histle, geed, incontravite, bumplers, ig, splander.*[19]

---

[17] This is of course not true of those who regard a grapheme as 'that which renders a phoneme' see pp. 101-2. To them *sh* or *kn* or even *ough* would, when they 'render' a single phoneme, be regarded as single graphemes. But this leads to almost impossible complexities scarcely less absurd than those which would be involved by regarding (*a*) *thing for taking stones out of horses' hooves with* as a single morpheme because it 'rendered' a single instrument.

[18] On 'graphotactics', see Eric Hamp, *Studies in Linguistics*, Vol. xiv, 1959, p. 105 ff.

[19] Cf. Paper 11. Forms of this second type raise a point of some philosophical interest. Objections to claims for any fundamental parallelism between the linguistic and the phonic planes have been made on the ground that whereas a written system *may* operate without any reference to a spoken equivalent (cf. p. 100) it *must* always carry meaning in the ordinary sense. It is therefore argued that its phonic 'load' is merely contingent, whereas its semantic (in the ordinary sense) load is not. I am not sure how cogent this argument would be even if the

3. A class of nonsentences, i.e. sequences which are not acceptable in pattern and are thereby ineligible for morphemic status in the other system. E.g. *rsmi, uaogsl, abvgnerttho, trlifg, b, jlibf.*

Our ability to assign certain sentences to class 2 would suggest that having established (even if perhaps only intuitively) a graphological grammar from a corpus of text, we may thereafter assess the grammaticality of sentences which have not cropped up in the corpus itself. In other words, just as on the linguistic plane we are able to generate new sentences which obey the pattern-rules of ordinary grammar, so on this other plane we are able to generate new sentences from a knowledge which rests on the observation and analysis of a sufficiency of old sentences. We are also able, on the same lines, to establish a category of non-sentences (3). We need not be unduly disturbed if we encounter marginal cases, especially between 2 and 3. For this, together with the basic contrast between 2 and 3, is very similar to a problem we encounter in ordinary grammar relating to degrees of grammaticalness.[20]

In considering this problem on either plane we should try to keep grammatical and collocational criteria as distinct as the facts permit. For 'mere' grammatical acceptability, though a prerequisite, is not enough in itself. Nor should we forget that we are always at some stage forced to take account of context in various ways. And to the extent that situational context comes in, our assessment of the acceptability of sentences in the ordinary sense seems to depend partly on the universe outside and our conceptualizing of it, and partly, given all this, on the conventional procedures by which we operate with a set of signs and a grammar. In some parallel fashion rather similar 'external' and 'internal' considerations would seem to be relevant when we undertake to assess the acceptability of sequences of graphemes. Here, once again, interesting lines of exploration suggest themselves.

[20] See the discussion by Noam Chomsky, *Syntactic Structures*, The Hague, 1957, p. 15. Cf. paper 11, footnote 1, p. 183 for further references.

---

facts were there to back it up. But it should be pointed out that the reverse state of affairs is not only theoretically possible, but familiar; in other words there are situations where the written system *may* operate without any linguistic reference but *must* carry meaning on the phonic plane. The commonest context where this arises is in 'drill' exercises and the like in text books which set out to provide material for pronunciation practice which consists of shorter and longer sequences of letters characteristic of the graphological system of the language in question. These sequences do not necessarily have any meaning other than on the phonic plane. Cf. footnote 5, p. 100.

Seven

Intonation systems in English (1963)

I found some difficulty in choosing a title for this paper, a title which, while being reasonably brief, would yet give some indication of what the subject matter was to be. What I was hoping to indicate was that, while the paper is concerned with the intonation of English, it is not my purpose to add to the description and classification of the range of *phonetic* data that is covered by the term 'intonation'. This has been examined, and continues to be examined in ever-increasing detail, by phoneticians in this country and abroad, and I have in no way extended the scope and delicacy of their observations. What I propose to discuss here is the role of the contrasts that are recognized under this heading of 'intonation' in conveying meaning in English.

The reason for choosing the word 'systems' as a means of at least hinting that this was to be the topic was twofold. The term 'system' itself was meant to suggest that the contrasts in meaning which are carried by intonation in English can be regarded as finite, as choices from among a limited number of possibilities; while the use of the plural, 'systems', was intended to convey the fact that, as it seems to me, there is not just one set of such choices but a number of such sets. The use of a given pattern, such as a particular pitch contour, will mean one thing under certain circumstances and another thing under other circumstances; moreover these circumstances are definable in such a way that we can say in a given instance which of its possible meanings the contour in question will have.

If I were asked to put forward a thesis to summarize the burden of the paper, it would be this: that the most useful way of explaining the role of intonation in conveying meaning in English is by regarding the contrasts concerned as part of English grammar. In other words, if we admit that

||1 where are you / <u>go</u>ing // and

||2 <u>where</u> are you / going //[1]

are different in meaning, as I think we must, then this distinction is as much a part of English grammar as that between, say, 'I'm going' and 'I'm not going', or between 'I'm going' and 'I shall be going'. Nor is the former distinction, that carried by intonation, necessarily more delicate than the latter: we should not assume that we can describe the rest of our grammar first and leave the contrasts carried by intonation to be added as a kind of appendix at the end. The question: 'Where, in a description of English grammar, do we bring in our account of the contrasts carried by intonation?' is to be answered I think purely grammatically: they will come in in their appropriate place in the grammar, alongside the other contrasts to which they are related and with which they interact. And some of them will come very early on: not only are they of considerable importance in spoken English, but also in many cases some more delicate distinctions, not necessarily only ones expounded by intonation, are dependent on them. For example, it is difficult clearly to separate ||2 <u>where</u> are you / going // from ||2 ˄ you're / going / <u>where</u> // until after one has distinguished ||2 <u>where</u> are you / going // from ||1 where are you / <u>go</u>ing //.

In suggesting that the meaning of intonation contrasts would be accounted for in grammatical terms, and integrated into the description of English grammar together with other contrasts that have always been treated as grammatical, I do not mean to imply that the categories and labels that have been used to designate the meaning of the various contours in informant reactions studies, such as 'calm/excited', or 'interested/bored', are to be dismissed as irrelevant. These represent the informant's interpretation of the grammatical meaning of a contour within the scales on which he is asked to identify it; and they provide a valuable clue to the contrastiveness of sets of contours and to the place of such contrasts in the language. Indeed in some cases there is little

---

[1] In the examples, tone group boundary is shown by //, foot boundary by /; tonic syllables are underlined. Tones are numbered 1–5, compound tones 13 and 53 ('one three', and 'five three'). A caret (˄) following the tone number indicates a 'silent beat' in the first foot. In tone <u>2</u>, the syllable on which the rise begins is shown by the underlining of the first letter (except where the fall and rise takes place on a single syllable).

more that the grammarian can say; although if he merely recognizes a grammatical system called 'temper of speaker', with a fixed number of contrastive possibilities, say the two terms 'calm' and 'excited', and defines where in the total framework of the grammar this choice is made, he has done something. But in other cases we can see that the informant is interpreting what is in fact a more specific choice; and, more important, we can show perhaps that the specific meaning of a given contrast depends on other grammatical factors. This after all is probably one of the main reasons for the uncertainty or disagreement of the informants in placing a contour on a given scale or even in deciding which scales are relevant to it at all. Both types of doubt occur: in some cases the informant is not sure whether the scale 'interested/bored' is applicable to a given contour or not; and in other cases even if he thinks it is he is not sure how to rate it, whether it should be 'very bored' or 'slightly bored' or 'mildly interested'.

Of course there is nothing new in the suggestion that intonation is related to grammar. This was clearly recognized by Armstrong and Ward;[2] and, to take only recent studies, in the works of Dr Lee[3] and Dr Maria Schubiger,[4] and in Messrs O'Connor and Arnold's *Intonation of colloquial English*[5] intonation is described and explained with reference to categories such as 'statement', 'question', '*if* clauses' and so on. The work of Professor Quirk and his team, the first results of which appeared as 'Studies in the correspondence of prosodic to grammatical features in English',[6] is showing in great detail how the choice of pitch movement and other intonation features is linked to other grammatical choices. The point I am making here is not in any way in conflict with these views; on the contrary it is indeed dependent on them. But it is an additional point: namely that the intonation contrasts are not merely *related* to *other* grammatical choices but are themselves at the same time

[2] Armstrong, Lilian E. and Ward, Ida C., *A Handbook of English intonation*, 2nd edition, Cambridge: Heffer, 1931.

[3] Lee, W. R., 'English intonation: a new approach', *Lingua*, 4, 1956; *An English intonation reader*, London: Macmillan, 1960.

[4] Schubiger, Maria, *English intonation: its form and function*, Tübingen: Niemeyer, 1958.

[5] O'Connor, J. D. and Arnold, G. F., *Intonation of colloquial English*, London: Longmans, 1961.

[6] Quirk, Randolph *et al.* 'Studies in the correspondence of prosodic to grammatical features in English', *Proceedings of the Ninth International Congress of Linguists*. The Hague: Mouton, 1964. See also Crystal, David and Quirk, Randolph, *Systems of prosodic and paralinguistic features in English*, The Hague: Mouton (Janua Linguarum Series Minor 39), 1964.

distinct and still grammatical choices in their own right. Thus //1 ˄ I'm / going // and //4 ˄ I'm / going // represent terms in a grammatical system just as much as do 'I'm going' and 'I'm not going'.

In discussing these aspects of English grammar it is helpful if we first distinguish, in phonological terms, the three different *kinds* of choice that are usually subsumed under the single heading 'intonation'. These need names, and with some apology I propose to use the terms 'tonality', 'tonicity' and 'tone'. By tonality I mean the division of an utterance into tone groups. This is a variable in English: that is to say, we can have two utterances which are alike in every respect except in that one consists of one tone group and the other of, say, two. For example:

//1 ˄ there's a/nother one / in the / office //
//1 ˄ there's a/nother one //1 in the / office //

These two utterances can be said to 'differ in tonality'. Another example would be:

//–2 ˄ was he / here when you / came //
//2 ˄ was he / here when you //2 came //

Or the two utterances might both consist of two tone groups but divided at different places:

//1 this of course de/pends on what you //1 mean by / criticism //
//1 this of course de/pends on what you / mean by //1 criticism //
and more subtly

//1 this of course de/pends on / what you mean by //1 criticism //
//1 this of course de/pends on //1 what you mean by / criticism //

Tonicity refers to the placing of the tonic, or nucleus. In each tone group (with an exception to be mentioned later) one and only one of the strong syllables carries the major part of the pitch movement—or rather, more accurately, carries the part of the pitch movement by which the tone group can be identified for tone. This may I think be usefully referred to as the 'tonic syllable'. Keeping all else constant, we can vary the position of the tonic:

//1 ˄ he / obviously be/lieved he could / do it //
//1 ˄ he / obviously be/lieved he could / do it //
//1 ˄ he / obviously be/lieved he could / do it //

If we regard the tone group in English as made up of one or more

rhythmic units or 'feet', following Professor Abercrombie's account of
the nature of the foot,[7] each foot beginning with a beat which may be
either strong syllable or silence, then if we keep the rhythm constant
there are as many possible places for the tonic to fall as there are complete feet in the tone group: three, in the last example. If the rhythm is
allowed to vary, strong and weak syllables thus being redistributed, then
other possibilities arise for the choice of the tonic syllable, for example:

//1 ˄ he / obviously be/lieved he / could do it //

//1 ˄ he / obviously be/lieved / he could / do it //

Tonicity helps us to see more clearly the structure of the tone group.
There are two different places in the tone group where meaningful
choices are made (I know that there are in fact more, but we need I think
to recognize two in the first instance): the tonic, already mentioned,
which is present in every tone group, and the part before the tonic *if it
has at least one strong syllable in it*. This we can call the 'pretonic'. If I
give one more example, showing contrasts made in these two different
places, this will lead in to the third of the three types of choice, that of
tone. If we replace

//1 ˄ he / obviously be/lieved he could / do it //   by

//4 ˄ he / obviously be/lieved he could / do it //

we have kept the tonic in the same place, but changed its tone: tone 1
replaced by tone 4. If on the other hand we replace the same

//1 ˄ he / obviously be/lieved he could / do it //   by

//-1 ˄ he / obviously be/lieved he could / do it //

we have kept the tonic in the same place, *and* left its tone unchanged, but
changed the tone in the pretonic. There are thus the two possible places
in the tone group where we can choose for tone: the tonic, always
present, and the pretonic, present in some but not in all tone groups. If
for the moment we say that no further choices are made after the tonic
syllable, we can use the term 'tonic' to refer to the whole of the rest of
the tone group from the tonic syllable right to the end. Then each tone
group consists either of a tonic only or of a tonic preceded by a pretonic.
The question whether or not it is possible to make pretonic choices in a

[7] Abercrombie, David, 'Syllable quantity and enclitics in English', *In
Honour of Daniel Jones*, London: Longmans, 1964; 'A Phonetician's view of
verse structure', *Linguistics* 6, 1964 (both reprinted in Abercrombie, David,
Studies in phonetics and linguistics, London: Oxford University Press (Language
and Language Learning 10), 1965).

given tone group is determined quite automatically by the rhythm: if there is at least one strong syllable before the tonic begins, then a pretonic choice is made and the tone group is said to contain a pretonic; if there is no strong syllable before the tonic begins, then that tone group has no pretonic.

Now the third choice, that of tone. This concerns the actual pitch movement of the tone group: falling, rising and so on. I am using 'tone' here to refer to the choice of pitch movement, reserving 'tone group' as the name of the unit that carries this choice; thus departing slightly from O'Connor and Arnold's usage. Where they refer to 'tone group 1' and so on, I shall say simply 'tone 1' and so on, because I need to distinguish between the tone group, meaning the unit, and the tone, meaning the term in the choice.

How many tones are there in English? The answer to this question depends on two variables: whether we are going to regard the decision as a purely phonological one or as partly determined by the grammar; and, whichever we decide, on how delicate our analysis is going to be. If we start from the grammar, and ask how many different grammatical choices are made by tone, we find without going to any very great degree of delicacy at least two dozen such choices, each representing a choice among two or three or four possibilities; if all these are regarded as different tones we should have to say that there are at least fifty or sixty tones in English. But in fact all these grammatical choices are made by selecting one or other of a very small number of contrastive pitch movements, so that if we ask instead 'What are the phonological resources of tone that are exploited in the grammar of English?' the number is very much smaller. It seems simpler, in other words, to start, as most writers on the subject have done from Armstrong and Ward onwards, from a purely phonological concept of tone; as is done also in the study of languages like Chinese where tone expounds lexical rather than grammatical meaning.

If we decide to answer the question phonologically we still of course have to decide how delicate we want to be. O'Connor and Arnold's first division into ten represents a more delicate analysis as a first step than Kingdon's[8] into five. The important point is to allow for varying—that is for increasing—delicacy, the decision to subdivide resting in each case on the observation that there is a meaningful contrast between the varieties recognized as distinct. We can start by making the minimum

[8] Kingdon, Roger, *The Groundwork of English intonation*. London: Longmans, 1958.

distinctions that are necessary for showing how the choices in meaning are made, and then subdivide to account for the more subtle choices. From this point of view I find it simplest to begin with a set of five tones for English. With these we can take into account the vast majority of utterances in RP: in the samples of conversation studied in the course of the work on which this paper is based, one hundred per cent. With an initial set of five tones we can describe many of the grammatical contrasts carried by the choice of tone; we then need to subdivide them in order to account for the remainder. There may still be some utterances which lie altogether outside the system, for which we should need to make further provision in the analysis; at present, however, I am not convinced that there are.

There has so far been no agreed convention as regards the numbering of the English tones; I have adopted a numbering representing as far as I could the most general usage, beginning from Armstrong and Ward's use of 1 for falling and 2 for rising. The five tones would then be as follows:

//1 yes //   //1 John does //
//2 yes //   //2 John does //   or   //2 yes //   //2 John does //
//3 yes //   //3 John does //
//4 yes //   //4 John does //
//5 yes //   //5 John does //

The two varieties of tone 2, rise and sharp fall-rise, are brought together at this stage as variants of a single tone; the distinction between them is regarded as more delicate than that separating the others and is left to be accounted for at the next step.

To these five must be added two compound tones, and this explains the exception, referred to earlier, to the generalization that each tone group has only one tonic. In compound tones there are two tonics in the tone group, and therefore there must here be at least two complete feet each with its strong syllable. There are only two of these compound tones, 13 and 53:

//13 John / does //
//53 John / does //

There are thus, as Professor Sharp described in his paper on the subject,[9]

[9] Sharp, Alan E., ' Falling-rising intonation patterns in English', *Phonetica*, 2, 1958. See also the same author's 'The analysis of stress and juncture in English', *Transactions of the Philological Society*, 1960.

a number of different tones that have phonetically some form of fall and rise: 2, //2 haven't / you //, 4, //4 possibly //, and the 'fall plus rise' 13, //13 ‿ I'm / off / now //. Fall-rise also appears as a sandhi form (a modification due to the phonetic environment) of tone 1 when followed by another tone 1 (or other tone group starting high); the first often has an anticipatory rising pitch at the end which is not however the exponent of a rising tone, as in

   //1 ‿ he / told me but I've for//1 gotten //

This primary, least 'delicate', system of five (or seven) tones concerns only the tonic contrasts. More delicately we can recognize, for each tone, either subvarieties of these at the tonic or pretonic contrasts. I do not propose to go into these here, because I should like to pass on to the grammar; but those which I think should perhaps be recognized as the next step in delicacy are shown in the following table; they yield a set of nineteen in all.

TABLE I

TONE (PRIMARY; PITCH MOVEMENT ON TONIC)

1	fall
2	rise; sharp fall-rise
3	low rise
4	fall-rise
5	rise-fall
13	fall plus low rise
53	rise-fall plus low rise

TONE (SECONDARY)

	Pretonic		Tonic	
1	1 even (level, falling, rising)	⎫	1+	high fall
	−1 uneven (low 'spiky')	⎬ × ⎨ 1	mid fall
	. . . 1 suspended ('listing')	⎭	1−	low fall

2	2 high (level, falling, rising)	⎱ × ⎰	2	rise
	−2 low (level, rising)	⎰	2̲	sharp fall-rise

3	3 mid (level)		
	−3 low (level)		

4		4	high fall-rise
		4̲	low fall-rise

5		5	high rise-fall
		5̲	low rise-fall

The secondary tones may be exemplified from tone 1. On the one hand, within the tonic, we need to recognize the different ranges of fall: three at least (wide, medium and narrow) and possibly a fourth (very wide):

$$//\mathrm{I} - \underline{\text{yes}} //   //\mathrm{I} - \, {}_{\wedge} \text{ it's im}/\underline{\text{possible}} //$$
$$//\mathrm{I} \, \underline{\text{yes}} //   //\mathrm{I} \, {}_{\wedge} \text{ it's im}/\underline{\text{possible}} //$$
$$//\mathrm{I} + \underline{\text{yes}} //   //\mathrm{I} + \, {}_{\wedge} \text{ it's im}/\underline{\text{possible}} //$$

These are clearly distinguishable when anything precedes the tonic, as the tonic will then begin either at a higher pitch than the preceding syllable, or on the same pitch, or at a lower pitch. On the other hand, as pretonics to tone 1, we can distinguish the high (in fact very variable, with many further subdivisions) from the 'spiky' variety, the latter I think particularly characteristic of London speech:

$$//\mathrm{I} \, {}_{\wedge} \, \mathrm{I} \, / \text{ just } / \text{ don't be}/\underline{\text{lieve}} \text{ it } //$$
$$//{-\mathrm{I}} \, {}_{\wedge} \, \mathrm{I} \, / \text{ just } / \text{ don't be}/\underline{\text{lieve}} \text{ it } //$$

This 'spiky' variety of pretonic is very useful for observing the rhythm of English speech, since here it is the foot that determines the pitch movement: each foot begins low and rises sharply, so that the strong syllables stand out very prominently. Apart from one or two references to these more delicate, or 'secondary', tones I shall refer now in general only to the primary set of five, with the two compound ones making these up to seven.

So much then for the resources, the phonological patterns to which the grammar is to be related. For the rest of the paper I should like to go on to consider briefly how these resources are exploited in English grammar.

The meaning of tonality and tonicity can be summarized quite shortly. First it must be said that it is *not* the case, in my opinion, that the tone group can be used to define any unit in English grammar. In a slight majority of cases, if my own samples are representative, the tone group corresponds in extent to the grammatical clause; but it is also frequently, and under fairly clearly definable conditions, either more than one clause or less than one clause. Indeed it is this range of possibility that makes tonality meaningful: the tone group can be thought of as representing a unit of information, and the speaker is free to choose how many units of information he is conveying and where he divides them; this decision is not imposed by the grammar (that is, by non-intonational features of the grammar) except within rather wide limits. In other words tonality is an independent grammatical choice.

For the sake of brevity I shall consider here only those cases where one tone group is co-extensive with one clause. This can be regarded as the unmarked or neutral state of affairs, since it is easiest to describe all other possibilities as being in contrast with this one. That is to say, where you have, say, two tone groups in one clause this is most easily explained by reference to the difference between this and the 'one clause —one tone group' situation.

Within each information unit there will be one, or in compound tones two, of what we may, following Lee Hultzén,[10] call 'information points'. These are represented by tonicity, the placement of the tonic. Here again we can recognize an unmarked state: this is that the tonic, or more strictly the beginning of the tonic, will fall on the last *lexical* item in the tone group. Since we are considering here only those cases where the tone group is one clause, this means that it will fall on the last element of clause structure that contains a lexical item:

//1 ⌃ I / saw / John / <u>yes</u>terday //   but

//1 ⌃ I / saw / <u>John</u> / there //

//1 ⌃ I / saw / <u>John</u> //   but

//1 ⌃ I / <u>saw</u> him //

//1 John's re/<u>signed</u> //   but

//1 <u>John</u> has //   or   //1 <u>John</u> / has done //

By contrast, of course, the tonic can start anywhere: certainly on any word, and probably, with enough ingenuity, on any morpheme; if it falls on a lexical item that is not clause-final, or a final item that is not lexical, or an item that is neither final nor lexical, this can be regarded as marked tonicity, giving contrastive information—an information point has been chosen in contrast to what the structure would lead us to expect:

//1 <u>John's</u> re/signed //

//1 ⌃ I / saw / <u>him</u> //

//1 ⌃ I / saw / <u>him</u> / yesterday //   or   //1 <u>I</u> / saw him //

Compound tones can be regarded as having one major and one minor information point, in that order:

//13 ⌃ there's a/<u>no</u>ther one / in the / <u>off</u>ice //

---

[10] Hultzén, Lee S., 'Information points in intonation', *Phonetica*, 4, 1959.

It is in the choice of tone, however, that the possibilities are widest and most varied. With tonality and tonicity we are as it were locating the units and main points of the message; whereas with tone we are contributing positive grammatical meaning, closed-system information like that of tense or number or polarity. The grammatical meanings of the tones can perhaps be most easily understood if we observe the high probability correlation between the use of a given tone and other grammatical features. For example, we tend to use tone 3 for a clause that is non-final in a sentence if it is co-ordinate with the following clause, and tone 4 for a non-final clause that is subordinate to the following clause:

//3 ⌃ I'll have / one more ciga/rette and //1 then I must / go //

//4 ⌃ if you / want to be / certain you'd //1 better look it / up //

But there is no exact correlation: the choice of tone is not *determined* by the sentence structure. We can recognize tone 3 followed by tone 1 and tone 4 followed by tone 1 as regular sequences: tones 3 and 4 thus occur in contrast in non-final position preceding tone 1, and this choice can be regarded as a grammatical system. We find a clue to its meaning by noting the partial dependence between this system and a system in sentence structure; but the two choices are distinct, and in our grammar we need to show both the similarity and the difference between them.

But probably the main set of choices for which tone is used, and certainly the main set if we limit ourselves to cases where the tone group is co-extensive with one clause and the clause is a complete sentence on its own, are those which are linked to the grammatical system of 'mood', and it is these that I should like to exemplify for the remainder of this paper. By 'mood' I mean the choice among affirmative, interrogative, imperative and none of these—the latter I may perhaps be allowed to refer to as 'moodless'.

The close relation between the meaning of the different tones and the choice of mood is clearly shown for example in O'Connor and Arnold's discussion of the use of the different tones in their book *Intonation of colloquial English*. Here however I want to approach this relation by defining the categories of mood formally: an affirmative clause is one in which (a) there is no interrogative ('WH—') element, and (b) the subject precedes the predicator (that is, the verbal element) with no other nominal element in between: 'John's resigned'; an interrogative clause is one in which (a) the subject follows the first word of the predicator or (b) there is an interrogative element (or both): 'when did

John resign'; an imperative clause is one which has a predicator, in the appropriate form of the verbal group, but no subject: 'resign'; and a moodless clause is one which has no predicator: 'John' or 'yesterday'.

These are thus not the same things as the contextually defined sentence functions of statement, question, command, and answer or exclamation; there is a high correlation between the two (for example between interrogative mood and the sentence function of 'question'), but it is not absolute. Thus 'John's resigned', in any tone, is an affirmative clause, whether it is a statement or not; 'has John resigned' is an interrogative clause, likewise whatever its tone and whether or not it is a question; and so on.

Affirmative clauses have tone 1 as their neutral tone. This does not necessarily mean that tone 1 is the most frequent, but that it is easiest to explain the choice of tone in affirmative clauses by regarding all other possibilities as being in marked contrast to tone 1. Affirmative clauses usually have the sentence function of statement, in which case an affirmative clause on tone 1 can be regarded as an unmarked statement. There are people, no doubt familiar to most of us, who cause confusion—at least to me—by asking questions with tone 1 affirmative clauses; for them

//1 John's re/signed //

could be a question. Such people might perhaps not mind being left temporarily outside the system. This tone 1 in affirmative clauses can then be regarded as entering into a number of different contrasts:

1 against 4 low
1 against −3 with low pretonic against 5
1 against 3 with mid pretonic against 2
1 against 13

If tone 1 means simply 'statement', then tone 4 means 'statement with reservation'. This is a familiar tone which we feel we can explain by saying 'there's a "but" about it':

//4 ⌃ it's / not / going to be / easy //   (but still, I'll try)

This reservation generally refers, especially if the tonic is in a marked position, to the information point:

//4 I wouldn't / buy that / ancient / car //

means 'even if you or someone else would', while

//4 ⌃ I / wouldn't / buy that / ancient / car //

means 'but I might try and get away with borrowing it'.

Secondly, if tone 1 means simply 'statement', tones 3 and 5 mean respectively perhaps 'uncommitted statement' and 'committed statement'. This is tone 3 with the low pretonic (-3), and the great majority of such instances, as indeed also of those with tone 5, seem to be rather short clauses which are generally also complete utterances. 'Uncommitted' usually implies uncertainty or lack of interest:

//-3 ˄ he / <u>might</u> do //
//-3 if you / really / <u>want</u> //
//-3 ˄ it's / quite / <u>possible</u> //

By contrast tone 5 is at the opposite extreme: 'committed' may imply superiority, assertiveness, rejection of any doubt expressed or felt:

//5 ˄ of / <u>course</u> he / will //
//5 ˄ he / <u>wasn't</u> / satisfied //
//5 ˄ I'm / not ac/<u>cepting</u> it //

Thirdly, by contrast again with tone 1 but on another dimension, tones 3 and 2 tend to register respectively agreement and disagreement with a preceding utterance. This is tone 3 with the mid pretonic, the same variety as is used for non-final clauses in a compound sentence; these confirmatory clauses often begin with a 'yes' or 'no' signalling agreement:

//3 yes I'll be / back to/<u>morrow</u> //
//3 no you / needn't / <u>worry</u> about it //
//3 ˄ it's / my / <u>fault</u> //

Often the agreement is to a request; hence the note of reassurance felt with this tone:

//3 I'll / <u>do</u> it / for you //

Tone 2 on the other hand is contradictory: likewise often introduced by 'yes' or 'no' but this time in disagreement:

//2 ˄ I / don't think he / <u>will</u> //
//2 ˄ no I / <u>didn't</u> //

The contradiction is not necessarily direct, of course; what is being contradicted may not have been spoken: in

//2 ˄ it's not / <u>my</u> fault //

no accusation may actually have been made, but the choice of tone

indicates that the speaker is defending himself. This incidentally illustrates one of the basic principles of these intonation contrasts, namely
that each tone is used both in that verbal context which gives the clue to
its meaning (e.g. tone 4, //4 ⌄ I'd / like / to but I //1 daren't //) and
alone, not in that context (e.g. //4 ⌄ I'd / like / to //), in which case it
gets its meaning precisely by implying that context—the hearer knows
that if something had preceded or followed it would have been something of this kind.

Occasionally tone 2 affirmatives are questions; but this seems to be
much rarer—at least in RP; it is I think much more frequent in American English—than is often assumed, and there are no examples in my
texts. Such clauses probably tend to be rather short clauses:

//2 ⌄ he / has //

It may be, and I think this has been suggested, that there is a difference
between 'he has' as contradiction and 'he has' as question. I am not
convinced that there is any difference in my speech, but I have unfortunately found no textual examples of affirmative questions with
which to test this out.

Fourthly, where tone 1 is simply a statement, tone 13 is a statement
with supplementary information point, the latter being particularly
common on final adjuncts and on lexical items following a marked non-
final tonic:

//13 ⌄ there's a / parcel on the / doorstep //

//13 John might / know //

//13 ⌄ we / ought to / finish it to/day //

To summarize these contrasts, the clause written 'they were here
first' might represent seven distinct clauses contrasting as follows:

//1 they were here / first //
//4 they were here / first //

//1 they were here / first //
//-3 they were here / first //
//5 they were here / first //

//1 they were here / first //
//3 they were here / first //
//2 they were here / first //

//1 they were here / <u>first</u> //
//13 <u>they</u> were here / <u>first</u> //

With interrogative clauses the pattern of choices is rather different. Here we have to begin by distinguishing the two types of interrogative, the 'yes/no' interrogatives, those which demand an answer in terms of polarity, and the 'WH—' interrogatives, those which do not raise the question of 'whether or not' but demand an answer to 'who', 'where' 'what' etc. The 'WH—' interrogatives are like affirmatives in having tone 1 as their unmarked or neutral tone, whereas yes/no interrogatives have tone 2. This by the way gives the clue to the basic general meanings of tones 1 and 2: tone 1 means 'I know the polarity—that is, I know whether it is negative or positive', whereas tone 2 means that the polarity is unknown. 'WH—' interrogatives on tone 1 can then be regarded as simply questions; their tonic remains on the normal place on the final lexical item:

//1 who are you / <u>looking</u> for //
//1 why should you / <u>worry</u> a/bout all / that //

This is in contrast with tone 2, but tone 2 here means two different things according to the placing of the tonic. If the tonic remains in its normal place, as in

//2 who are you / <u>looking</u> for //,

the clause is a question accompanied by a request, as it were, for permission to ask: 'may I, or may I not, know the answer?' This variable, the strength or degree of purposefulness of the utterance, operates with all moods, though with different tones carrying the different degrees; I have labelled it, perhaps rather unsatisfactorily, the 'key', and distinguished the degrees of 'strong', 'moderate' and 'mild'. Tone 2 here thus represents the 'mild key'; it is felt to be a tentative enquiry, often described as polite, hesitant or diffident. If on the other hand the tonic is on the 'WH—' element, the clause becomes the familiar 'echo' question, meaning something like 'I didn't hear', 'I've forgotten' or 'I don't believe you'—'will you kindly remind or reassure me?':

//2 <u>who</u> are you / looking for //

Here again are the two contrasts into which these 'WH—' interrogatives enter:

//1 whose / <u>turn</u> is it //
//2 whose / <u>turn</u> is it //

//1 whose / <u>turn</u> is it //
//2 <u>whose</u> / turn is it //

All tones other than 1 and 2 are rather rare with 'wh—' interrogatives.

Yes/no interrogatives are somewhat different; perhaps the English speaker feels that asking someone whether or not is a very different kind of question from asking them the why and the wherefore. The neutral tone for yes/no is tone 2, meaning simply a question:

//2 ˄ is it / <u>my</u> turn //
//2 are you / feeling / <u>better</u> / now //

There are four varieties of this tone, giving subtle variations which I will not try to account for here, but which I might perhaps illustrate:

//2 are you / feeling / <u>better</u> / now //
//<u>2</u> are you / feeling / <u>better</u> / <u>now</u> //
//–2 are you / feeling / <u>better</u> / now //
//–<u>2</u> are you / feeling / <u>better</u> / <u>now</u> //

In contrast to tone 2, yes/no questions may have on the one hand tone 1, meaning strong question, question with demand for answer (and sometimes even for a satisfactory answer):

//1 ˄ have you / <u>finished</u> it / yet //
//1 are you / feeling / <u>better</u> / now //

and on the other hand, more often with fairly short clauses, tones 3 or 5, with meanings not unlike their meanings in affirmative clauses, tone 3 non-involvement and tone 5 positive involvement:

//3 ˄ would it / <u>matter</u> //
//5 ˄ would you / <u>pay</u> for it / though //

Tag questions, as in //2 ˄ you've / <u>seen</u> him //2 <u>haven't</u> you //, are a special kind of yes/no interrogative, rather complicated as regards their intonation possibilities; I propose to omit them here. There is room for some individual variety in the use of tag questions, and perhaps those people whom I referred to earlier as using tone 1 affirmative for asking questions could best be regarded as having zero tag at the end of them.

Finally, alternative questions normally take tone 2 followed by tone 1:

//2 ˄ is it / <u>mine</u> or //1 <u>yours</u> //
//2 will you bring it / <u>over</u> or //1 shall I come and / <u>fetch</u> it //

Sometimes with short clauses alternative questions occur on a single tone group with tone 1, and it is this that allows the humorist to treat them as simple yes/no questions:

//1 ⌄ d'you want / tea or / <u>coffee</u> //   (answer: //1 <u>yes</u> //)

Imperative clauses take a wide range of tones; there are of course many ways, linguistically at any rate, of getting someone to do what you want him to do—and of stopping him from doing something you want him not to do. There is in fact some variation in tendency between positive and negative imperatives, at least as regards their 'key' as I have called it: prohibitions seem to require a gentler approach. We can take together, I think, tones 1, 3 and 13:

//1 wait for the / <u>chairman</u> //
//3 wait for the / <u>chairman</u> //
//13 <u>wait</u> for the / <u>chairman</u> //

It is difficult to identify any of these as the neutral form; usage varies greatly between different situation types. But in positive imperatives tone 1 is fairly frequent: it expects compliance, as it were, but without being too peremptory; in the negative, however, it is less frequent and much more peremptory, and a situation in which tone 1 is appropriate in the positive may demand tone 3 in the negative. I am told by my Scots-speaking friends that it is these tone 3 commands more than anything else in our speech which reveal the smoothness and hypocrisy of the English character: we mean

//1 don't be / <u>late</u> //

but we say

//3 don't be / <u>late</u> //

We might perhaps best describe the difference between positive and negative imperatives by regarding tone 1 as neutral for the positive, tone 3 being a milder variant; and tone 3 as neutral in the negative, with tone 1 marked as strong. For both types, however, the mildest is tone 13, especially when accompanied by that creaky voice modulation which turns it into a plea:

//13 <u>don't</u> be / <u>late</u> //

There is another closely related system in the imperative, which I have called 'force': this makes use of tone 4 in its low variety (<u>4</u>) and tone 5. I have called 4 'compromising' and 5 'insistent'; the point is I think that in tone 4 imperatives the speaker is willing to give ground (there is often an 'at least' in such clauses), while in tone 5 he is specifically not willing to give ground, and there is a feeling that some external authority, that of duty or reason perhaps, is being invoked. Examples of tone 4, 'compromising':

//<u>4</u> ⌃ at / least / try to ex/<u>plain</u> it //
//<u>4</u> ⌃ well / don't just / run a/<u>way</u> //

and of tone 5, 'insistent':

//5 ⌃ well / <u>tell</u> him / then //
//5 ⌃ in / that <u>case</u> / don't / <u>give</u> it to them //

Finally, as a separate choice, tone 2 with an imperative clause simply turns it into a question: 'is this what you want me to do?', for example

//2 ⌃ re/<u>sign</u> //
//2 don't / <u>give</u> it to them //

It would take too long to give examples of the word 'please' with all these imperatives, but it is interesting to note that it occurs regularly with tones 1, 3 and 13, both initially and finally, and, more often initially than finally, with tones 4 and 5. Foreign students, with whom one's sympathies grow daily, really need to learn about 'please'; it can make or mar their relations with the English. The many faces of 'please' can be demonstrated if it is tried out on different tones, as in the following summary of imperative contrasts:

//1 don't for/<u>get</u> please //
//3 don't for/<u>get</u> //
//13 <u>please</u> don't for/<u>get</u> //

//1 please do the / best you / <u>can</u> //
//<u>4</u> please do the / best you / <u>can</u> //
//5 please do the / best you / <u>can</u> //

//1 go a/<u>way</u> //
//2 go a/<u>way</u> //

Finally, in the mood system, moodless clauses: those without any verbal element in them. These resemble affirmatives in their range of choice, but with one or two additional possibilities that I have grouped together, rather arbitrarily, under the name of 'function'. First, a mood-less clause on tone 2, unlike an affirmative clause, regularly is a question:

//2 yesterday //

In moodless clauses consisting merely of a 'WH—' form, such as

//2 who //

the opposition between 'mild question' and 'echo question',

//2 who are you / looking for //   and

//2 who are you / looking for //

is of course neutralized, and the question may be of either type. Secondly, tone 3 (–3 if pretonic is present) with moodless clauses is often as with short imperatives, a warning:

//3 careful //

though it may also be, as with affirmatives, uncommitted:

//3 ⌃ per/haps //

Thirdly, moodless clauses (and also some imperatives) display the low, exclamatory variety of tone 5:

//5 what a / joy //

and, I hope not too appropriately,

//5 look at the / time //

Tone 3 in some moodless clauses, specifically in vocatives, and also in some short imperatives, raises an interesting problem. I mean here the type

//3 John //

//3 hurry //

where mid level is followed by a low rise on a single foot or even a single syllable. I have been treating this tone, for example in //3 don't be / late //, in the way that seems to me in general most appropriate, namely as a normal tone 3 tonic //3 late // preceded by a pretonic in which the mid level, as in //3 don't be / late //, contrasts with a low level as in //–3 ⌃ we / shan't be / late //. Now the presence of a pretonic implies the existence of a separate, secondary choice; it is therefore true in all tones that one cannot have both pretonic and tonic on one syllable—in fact not on one foot, since it is a strong syllable that each such choice requires. There is however this one exception: if we analyse tone 3 in this way, then when we come to //3 John // and //3 hurry // we appear to have both pretonic and tonic choices on a single syllable, which is also in each case one morpheme. Short of setting up a sixth tone to account for these, which I think would be a pity in view of the similarity between them and tone 3

//3 John //3 don't be / late for / dinner //

we must probably just state that in tone 3 vocatives and imperatives, if there is only one foot in the tone group, pretonic and tonic are realized as a single element.

This then represents the sort of account which we may perhaps be able to give about the place of intonation in English grammar. I would like just to make a few concluding remarks. I have confined myself largely to intonation within the mood system, and where the tone group coincides with one clause which is also a complete sentence; this may perhaps be the most important aspect of the grammatical meaning of intonation, but it is far from being the whole story. Secondly I have concentrated on a primary system of five tones, with only a little reference to the more delicate distinctions; there is a great deal to be said about these, and indeed a great deal still to be found out, as current work by Professor Quirk and his associates is already showing. The 19 possible secondary tones that I have shown in Table I represent my view of the next step in delicacy, but certainly not the final step. Thirdly, I have not touched on the tendency for particular items in the language to be associated with particular intonation patterns: I mean such items as 'in any case', normally separate tone group, tone 1:

//1 ˄ in / any / case it's //1 not his / business //

'mind you', pretonic in tone group having tone 4 or tone 53:

//4 mind / you it's / difficult //
//53 mind / you I / never in/tended to / do it //

'far from it', separate tone group, tone 5:

//5 far / from it //

'come to think of it', separate tone group, tone 4, if initial; tonic of tone 3 in tone group of tone 13 or 53 if final:

//4 come to / think of it I //1 gave it / back to / you //
//13 ˄ I / gave it / back to you / come to / think of it //

and so on.

It is tempting to try and generalize, out of this mesh of detail. We should like to ask what can be abstracted from this; whether there is such a thing as 'the general meaning' of intonation, or of a particular tone, in English. I think we ought to fall for the temptation: at least there is a mnemonic value in such generalizations, for example in English teaching, given of course that they have some validity. On tonality and tonicity I did generalize, since the more specific observations on these depend on looking beyond or within the clause: tonality representing the apportionment of continuous speech into units of information and tonicity the assignment of a principal information point in each such unit.

With regard to tone, I think we can see some sort of basic significance behind the falling and rising movements. We go down when we know whether something is positive or negative, and we go up when we don't know. Thus tone 1 means, as noted earlier, 'polarity known and stated'; tone 2, 'polarity unknown'; the fall-rise variant of tone 2 means 'I do not know whether the answer is yes or no, but this is the specific point about which I should like to be informed'. Tone 4, which falls and then rises, means that we know, but then there is some doubt or reservation present; tone 5, which is the exact contrary, means that we first raise the doubt, or note it, in order then to dismiss it. So with tone 4, 'you may think it's cut and dried, but it isn't'; with tone 5, 'you may think it isn't cut and dried, but it is'. This leaves tone 3, the low rise; and here we are not quite sure; we think we know, but only in a dependent sort of way: the fact, or at least the significance of the fact, is conditional on something else. It may be that a formulation of this kind is so vague, and leaves so much to be supplied in the explanation of particular cases, that it is of little help. But I am not sure that we can go very much further than this in seeking to ascribe a single overall meaning to the patterns of English intonation.

Perhaps I might end up with a little imaginary dialogue constructed to bring out this bare minimum that may be thought of as common to the various uses of each tone:

//2 does he / know //

//3 ˄ he / may know //

//1 ˄ he / knows //

//4 ˄ he / says he / knows //

//1− ˄ he / knows //

//1+ ˄ he / must know //

//4 ˄ if he / <u>knows</u> //
//2 <u>does</u> he / <u>know</u> //
//5 ˄ he / <u>does</u> know //

TABLE II

Summary of grammatical systems carried by intonation as referred to in the text

Tonality: distribution into 'units of information'
    tone group = clause (neutral)
    tone group greater than clause (especially main followed by or including subordinate)
    tone group less than clause (especially thematic adjunct or complement)

Tonicity: location of 'information point'
    tonic = final lexical item (neutral)
    tonic = pre-final item or final grammatical item (contrastive)

Tone (assuming tonality neutral):
    Place of clause in sentence structure: final main 1, non-final co-ordinate 3, non-final subordinate 4.
    Affirmative clauses
      reservation: 1 unreserved, 4 reserved
      commitment: 1 neutral, -3 uncommitted, 5 committed
      agreement: 1 neutral, 3 confirmatory, 2 contradictory
      information: 1 one information point, 13 two information points
      'key': 1 neutral, 1 + strong, 1 − mild
    Interrogative clauses, 'WH-' type
      'key': 1 neutral, 2 (with final tonic) mild
      relation to previous utterance: 1 unrelated, 2 (with 'WH-' tonic) echo
    Interrogative clauses, yes/no type
      'key': 2 neutral, 1 strong
      involvement: 2 neutral, -3 uninvolved, 5 involved
      place in alternative question: 2 first alternative, 1 second alternative
      specification of point of query: 2 unspecified, 2 specified
    Imperative clauses
      'key' (positive): 1 neutral, 3 moderate, 13 mild
      'key' (negative): 3 neutral, 1 strong, 13 mild
      force: 1 neutral, 4 compromising, 5 insistent
      function: 1 etc. command, 2 question
    'Moodless' clauses (also as affirmative)
      function: 1 answer etc., 2 question, -3 warning, 5 exclamation

In the section under 'tone', the headings (e.g. 'reservation') indicate the nature of the choice, the entries under each heading representing the terms in the choice with their appropriate tone. Thus ' 1 unreserved, 4 reserved ' means 'in this choice tone 4 indicates reservation, by contrast with tone 1 which indicates no reservation'. Secondary tones are indicated where relevant.

Eight

Linguistics and machine translation (1960)

One of the questions that can be asked in relation to many subjects today is what effect the computer has had, or is coming to have, on the development of the subject as a whole. Broadly speaking the computer is most immediately momentous in two ways: it makes available new modes of operation, and it vastly increases the number of facts, and of factors, that can be taken into account. But at the same time it imposes the need to think explicitly, to specify the steps in a process in such a way that a computer could carry them out; and it is perhaps in the combination of this with the other two aspects that its potential effect lies.

Linguistics is in no way out of range of the computer, and we can now look back on some ten years' work in the use of computers for operating on linguistic data. The relevance of a computer to linguistics is by no means limited to machine translation; but machine translation is perhaps the most widely popularized branch of computational linguistics, and has already produced its fund of comic stories many of which though undoubtedly apocryphal give a fair idea of the kinds of problem involved. It has also produced some anxiety on the part of those who imagined that an attempt to render Shakespeare into Icelandic by computer was already imminent; whereas in fact those working in MT (to adopt the familiar abbreviation by which machine translation has come to be known) have a much more immediate and realistic aim, that of providing adequate renderings of scientific papers, of which the number is now so great that it exhausts the available resources of human translators.

It is convenient to date MT from the famous 1947 memorandum on the subject by Warren Weaver; but its origins include such sources as wartime work on code-breaking, the theoretical study of communication and the development of information theory, and the design and construction of the electronic digital computer itself.[1] It was probably these origins that gave to the early work on MT its particular slant: most of the effort was directed towards problems in electronic engineering and in the coding and transmission of information. This in turn determined the approach of many of those working in the field.

The solution of the relevant engineering and mathematical problems is of course a prerequisite of success in any MT project. But there is another side to the subject, as recognized already in the discussion at the VIIth International Congress of Linguists in London in 1952. MT is a problem in applied linguistics, a problem requiring the application of those parts of general linguistic theory which deal with the systematic description and comparison of languages: descriptive linguistics, and comparative descriptive or 'contrastive' linguistics. To say this is to imply that it is not enough to approach the problem with 'just common-sense' (that is, uninformed) ideas about language; these are no more adequate than such ideas would be in mathematics and engineering. This does not mean that MT demands no new thinking about language. But such thinking has its point of departure in existing knowledge about language and in the training of the professional linguist. If MT is linguistic engineering, and there has to be a new profession, that of 'linguistic engineer', both linguistics and engineering will figure in the training of its members.

A hint of what this implies may be provided by the number two. This is a fundamental concept in electronic engineering; all operations must be ultimately representable in binary form, and this applies to operations on language as well as to numerical calculations. It is important therefore to know what kinds of linguistic elements are representable in this way; and since any finite system can be encoded, or recoded, in binary form, a piece of language text can be represented in a computer simply by using binary numbers to replace letters of the alphabet. But this is not a fact about language, except in a very abstract and indirect sense; it is a fact about any communication system—in this case English orthography—that makes use of a limited set of symbols.

[1] See Émile Delavenay, *An Introduction to machine translation*, London: Thames and Hudson, 1960; W. J. Locke and A. D. Booth, *Machine translation of languages*, New York: M.I.T. Technology Press and Wiley (London: Chapman and Hall), 1955; and article by A. D. Booth in *Aspects of translation*, London: Secker and Warburg (Studies in Communication 2), 1958.

One cannot argue from this that linguistic organization is inherently binary. Thus, it may be necessary to represent in the computer not merely text in a given language but also some facts relating to the language in which it is written: for example, that a certain verb is in the past tense. The number of tenses in any language is limited; let us suppose here a language which has three tenses, past, present and future. This set of three can be represented in binary code; but the apparent cut into two which this involves is simply a way of coding the information, no more meaningful than the fact that in the coding of the letters of the alphabet N equals twice G.

It is natural to want to introduce some general meaning into the binary mode of representation, since it would clearly be an advantage if it could be made to carry linguistic information. But there is no generalizable significance to the number two in linguistics, and the question of the underlying contrasts that are inherent in a grammatical choice is not always easy to solve. It does not necessarily depend on the more tangible features of the language: it might be, for example, that the present tense was distinct from the past and the future in that the former was a simple form while the latter two were compound, but this would not necessarily reflect their function in the language. An example will bring this out. Both English and Chinese show an opposition between singular and plural in the noun (it is restricted to one class of nouns in Chinese, but this does not affect the point at issue), in which the plural is formed by the addition of an element to the singular: English *student / students*, Chinese *xuesheng / xueshengmen*. This might seem a simple opposition in each case. But in fact the two contrasts are far from identical, since in English both terms are 'contextually marked', singular meaning one and plural more than one, whereas in Chinese the so-called 'singular' is actually an unmarked term in the opposition: the plural means more than one but the 'singular' means any number. The conditions determining the choice of one form or the other are quite different in Chinese from those relevant to the choice in English.

The linguist involved in MT can reasonably be asked to display the facts of a language in a form most suited to this particular operation, but he cannot simplify facts out of existence. Perhaps one reason for the somewhat oversimplified view of language that has sometimes been assumed in connection with computational research has been the readiness to assert that 'language is a code' and then to interpret this assertion in a rather superficial way. The metaphor is an unfortunate one, in many ways, since a code implies the existence of some pre-coded message and a single coding operation; whereas if language is a code then it is a product of multiple encoding with complex relations obtaining at each level, and the only evidence for any message is the code itself. It is doubtful whether the analogy is of much relevance to work in MT.

The view of translation as a coding process has certainly very different implications; here the 'message' is a text in one language and the coded message is the translation of that text in another language. There are perhaps parallels here, although again the relation of translation is far more complex than any code. It might be of interest to set up a linguistic model of the translation process, starting not from any preconceived notions from outside the field of language study, but on the basis of linguistic concepts such as are relevant to the description of languages as modes of activity in their own right. There are many possible ways of regarding translation; the outline suggested here makes use of the general notion of linguistic 'levels' as the different types of pattern found in language, recognizing 'grammar' and 'lexis' (vocabulary) as the levels of linguistic 'form'; and 'context' (in the sense of 'context of situation') as the network of relations between linguistic items and categories and non-linguistic phenomena, rather like 'meaning' in the non-technical sense. 'Meaning' is used here in a technical sense to refer to both the internal and the external relations of language; the 'meaning' of a linguistic item or category is its relation both to other linguistic features and to features of the non-linguistic environment—in this case, since we are considering translation, to features in another language.

Linguistic form is related to spoken substance by 'phonology' and to written substance by 'graphology'. Within linguistic form, grammar refers to the relations of items and of categories in 'closed system' contrast, characterized by the very complex interaction of small sets of possibilities; lexis to the relations of items in 'open set' contrast, involving relatively few dimensions but with a wide range of choice within each. Grammatical relations thus permit a greater degree of abstraction, so that in addition to 'items' of the language such as *the* and *it* we can talk in terms of 'categories' such as 'systems' (tense, number), 'structures' (co-ordination, modification), 'classes' (noun, relative (clause)) and 'units' (sentence, clause); the various units are said to be related on scale of 'rank'. Let us now look at translation in the light of some of these general concepts.[2]

[2] For a fuller discussion of these concepts see Paper 1 above; cf. also Papers 6 and 11.

Translation, as a process, is unidirectional; but a translation, which is the end-product of such a process, is in mutual relation with the original: either of the two texts could replace the other as the language component, one might say, of a given total situation. Taken together the two texts constitute a type of comparative description of the two languages, in which the two languages impinge on each other at a number of different levels. We can leave aside phonology and graphology, since these relate the form of a language to its spoken or written substance and are only incidentally relevant to translation within certain pairs of languages. For translation the important levels are those of form, namely grammar. and lexis, and that of context.[3] At these levels we have as it were two types of evidence, or two bodies of source material, for the comparison— that is, for the bringing into relation with one another—of the two languages.

On the one hand, there are actual translations; texts in the two languages, the one being translated from the other. These yield probabilities of equivalence between items occurring in them. Such probabilities may be stated as simple, unconditioned probabilities, or as conditioned either in sequence or in combination. So one can ask, for example, 'What is the most probable tense of the English verbal group in translation of the Russian past tense?'; or 'What is the most probable tense of the English verbal group in translation of the Russian past tense if the latter is (a) in a clause preceded by a clause in which the verbal group also had past sense, or (b) combined with perfective aspect?' The study of texts will reveal, for any feature, a limited set of equivalents which can be ranged in order of frequency; and evidence concerning the probability that, in a given environment, any given equivalent will occur.

On the other hand, there is the material furnished by a comparative analysis of the two languages, in which their formal and contextual features are described by means of a single set of categories. Since descriptive categories are not universals, so that if we find something we want to call a 'verb' in one language this does not necessarily mean we shall find such a thing in another language, categories used for the comparison of two languages are derived from the separate description of each. Once these can be shown to be comparable, degrees of likeness can be stated and measured. By stating the formal and contextual equivalents of grammatical structures and items, and of lexical items, within similar categories, the comparison brings out the likeness and unlikeness

[3] Cf. J. C. Catford, *A Linguistic theory of translation*, London: Oxford University Press (Language and Language Learning 8), 1965.

between the two languages. This may extend also to partial equivalence, where correspondence is not one to one but systematic statement is still possible.

For lexis the statement of equivalence between two languages is traditionally made by a bilingual dictionary. The aim of the ideal dictionary could be said to be to state under what circumstances a word in Ly is the contextual equivalent of a word in Lx. The bilingual dictionary faces, in the main, two difficulties. One is the nature of 'equivalence': the contextual equivalent is not necessarily the translation equivalent, since the latter is determined not only by contextual meaning but also by formal meaning, that is by the tendency to occur in collocation with other words. This difficulty can be met by extending the concept of a citation to cover not just *a word* in a given collocation but *a collocation* of words: the item for the statement of equivalence would not be 'to climb (mountains etc.)', since the contextual equivalent of 'climb' here might not in fact collocate with all the words that are the contextual equivalents of 'mountain' (still less with those of the 'etc.'), but would rather be 'to climb a mountain'.

The other difficulty is that the category of 'word' is not a universal constant. The term 'word' may here be rather misleading. In the first place, even within one language it is used to cover, and thus to conflate, two and sometimes three rather different categories, whose members only partially coincide. The name 'word' is given to one of the units in grammar; this unit is then taken as the unit for dictionary entry. But the dictionary attempts to state lexical, not grammatical, meaning; what the dictionary is really describing is the 'lexical item', which is not always co-extensive with the grammatical word. In those languages, such as English, which also have an orthographically defined 'word'—defined as 'that which occurs between two spaces in the script'—the word is now a unit on three levels and the probability that all three will yield exactly the same entities is far from certain. In the second place, even where the dictionary clearly recognizes and treats the lexical item as distinct from the grammatical 'word', the lexical item itself is not a constant across languages. Languages vary considerably in their organization of lexical meaning, in the sense that a given lexical item in one language will not always enter into the same relations of contrast and combination as its translation equivalent in another language. The basis of a comparative study of the vocabulary of two languages, of which a bilingual dictionary is an example, is the identification of the lexical items, and the statement of their meaning, in the language to which they belong. The thesaurus, with its systematic treatment of the lexis as a whole, may have some advantages over the dictionary for this purpose.

In grammar, relatively little work has been done in the comparative description of particular pairs of languages; here especially, perhaps, the approach must depend on the specific purpose in view. For certain purposes comparison is an important concept; one area to which it is clearly relevant is the teaching of foreign languages. Machine translation would seem to be another such area, although it is unlikely that comparison would mean exactly the same thing in the two cases. For MT the salient concept is the replaceability of items and categories of one language, in certain environments, by items and categories of the other, and it seems likely that statistical evidence has a place in the formulation of the statements underlying such comparison.[4]

Here perhaps a word of caution is needed. Counting is of no value in itself, and the laborious compilation of tables of occurrences of isolated and ill-defined sets of items is sadly unrewarding. Statistical investigation presupposes questions that the investigator wants to answer and an assurance that the figures relate to some entities that are relevant to these questions. But with this proviso it does not seem unreasonable to suggest that quantitative methods have a place in the comparison of texts for MT purposes. Translation itself is after all an approximation, and it is unlikely that MT can operate with a simple 'right or wrong' view of translation equivalence.

Grammatical equivalence between two languages for MT purposes may therefore rest to a certain extent on quantitative studies of the grammar of each. Such equivalence can be related to the concept of a 'rank scale': a scale of grammatical units, of which the 'word' is one. These units are the stretches into which language text is cut when grammatical statements are being made about it. Again they are not universals: they must be recognized afresh for each language. In comparing two languages it is not possible to relate the languages as a whole; we select for comparison items from within them—and not only items, of course, but abstract categories (classes, structures and so on) of which the items are 'exponents'. These items, and the categories set up in abstraction from them, can be related to the grammatical units as a starting-point for the study of their equivalence.

This implies a concept of 'equivalent units', the units of the two languages being related to each other on the basis of probability of

---

[4] See Paper 9 of this volume; also J. C. Catford, op. cit., chapter 12.

translation equivalence. If we can say, for example, that a clause in Lx can usually be translated by a clause in Ly, this being implied perhaps when the two units, one in each language, are called by the same name, then we can try to make a systematic statement to account for the occasions when this does not work. Suppose for illustration that we can describe Lx and Ly, separately, each with a system of five grammatical units, which we will call, in a descending hierarchy, 'sentence, clause, group, word, morpheme'. Then a clause, for example, in Lx will normally, but not always, be translated by a clause in Ly. Grammatical equivalence between any features would be relatable in the first instance to the appropriate unit or units, each of which is characterized by a network of structures and systems to which the items of the language are referable as 'exponents'; these would then serve to display the formal similarities and differences between the two languages. If Lx, for example, makes a class distinction at the rank of the group between verbal group and nominal group, does Ly make the same distinction? And if so are the items which are exponents of the verbal group in Lx always translated by items which are exponents of the verbal group in Ly?

Lexical equivalence would not relate exclusively to any one rank in the grammar. While the reason why one unit in the grammar of any language is called 'word' may be that that unit, more than any other, yields lexical items, what defines the lexical item is not the fact that it is grammatically a word—it may not be—but the fact that it cannot be fully described by the grammatical categories. The latter account for the 'closed systems' of language, and the items entering into them, this being the essential characteristic of grammar. One important consequence of the difference between grammar and lexis is that information theory, which is entirely appropriate to the statement of grammatical meaning, since information is a property of closed systems, is not of relevance in the study of lexis: there is no way of quantifying the information carried by an open set.

As an illustration of the translation process, below are given two sentences, each in both a Chinese and a Russian version. These sentences are shown segmented into their successive lower units: clauses, groups, words and morphemes, with each boundary implying all those below it (a group boundary must also be a word and morpheme boundary, and so on). The segmentation has been made to display maximum likeness, as in a comparative description of the two languages; it is also over-simplified in two ways: first, lineally discrete segments have been recognized throughout, though in fact grammatical units may not be segmental (e.g. the English word 'ran' consists of two morphemes, but this does not imply that it contains two segments), and second, 'rank-shifting' has been avoided where possible. 'Rankshift' is the operation of one unit in the structure of a unit of lower rank: e.g. a clause is defined as operating in sentence structure, but in 'the man who came to dinner', 'who came to dinner' is a rankshifted clause operating inside a nominal group.

Each sentence is then 'translated' at each rank into English: first each morpheme is taken separately, then each word, and so on. In each case the English equivalent *item* is one which might turn out—at a guess: the counting has not been done—to be the most frequent translation equivalent *at that rank*: the one which would be the first choice for entry in a bilingual 'dictionary' of morphemes, words, groups etc. Similarly the grammatical *pattern* chosen is that which might be the most frequent translation equivalent at the rank concerned. The concept 'the most frequent translation equivalent' for a *grammatical item* in isolation, such as English 'the' or '-ing', is however inapplicable; such items are here symbolized 'X' until their incorporation into higher units. If we start from the morpheme, we can follow the translation step by step up the rank scale, each equivalent being adjusted as it finds itself co-occurring with certain other items, in a certain grammatical relation, in the unit next above. So for example Chinese *tie*, as a morpheme, would most frequently be translated 'iron'; when it is taken as part of the word into which it enters, this translation is the one most likely to appear (as when it is a word on its own, or in the words *tieqi* 'ironware' or *shengtie* 'cast iron'); elsewhere other equivalents must be chosen (*gangtie* 'steel', *tielu* 'railway'). Each step can be regarded as a process in which the equivalent is retained unless positive contrary indications are found in the next unit.

It appears clearly that, while equivalence can be stated, in terms of probabilities, for all ranks, translation in the accepted sense does not occur below the rank of the clause, and a good translation needs to be based on the sentence as its unit. So-called 'literal' translation is, roughly, translation at group rank, or somewhere between group and word.

It has sometimes been thought possible for MT to proceed by means of a sentence dictionary, all possible sentences of L*x* being entered, together with their translation equivalents in L*y*. Since the number of possible sentences is unlimited and, at least in scientific registers, a sentence is hardly ever repeated in its lexico-grammatical entirety, this is a practical impossibility. With the distinction of grammar and lexis it becomes, with present day computer storage, perhaps conceivable. Sentences containing identical sequences of lexical items (but differing in grammar) might recur, and sentences with identical sequences in grammar (but differing lexically) certainly do: regularly in the sense of 'having the same primary grammatical *structure*', at least down to the rank of the word; even the same sequences of grammatical *items* probably turn up now and again. This might seem a possibility to be explored.

The illustration below shows, for one of the English sentences, the grammatical and lexical material separated out. I(a) is a linear statement of the grammatical structures at all ranks; I(b) shows the grammatical items which are the exponents of each of the elements of structure. II gives the sequence of lexical items. From the point of view of linguistic theory, such separation is justifiable: in a sense grammatical description and lexical description are partially independent, since different relations (and therefore different theories) are involved, although description is not complete until the two levels have been related. But the weakness of this from the point of view of MT is that in translation there has to be constant cross-reference between the grammar and the lexis, since in all languages some grammatical items can only be identified by reference to lexical ones, and vice versa. For example, only the grammar of the English sentence shows which of a number of lexical items 'part' is; conversely only the lexical identification of 'part' allows us to say whether it is singular noun or plural verb.

In general therefore the unit selected as the basis for MT has been much lower on the rank scale, well below the sentence: usually the word or the morpheme, or a combination of both (especially where the source language is Russian). The use of the word or morpheme yields, by comparison with the sentence or clause, inventories of manageable size. At the same time it involves complex programmes for the selection among possible equivalents, usually based on items in the immediate environment (though where grammar is involved structures would be more powerful, because more general), plus routines for reordering the components of the units above the translation unit. So for example the morpheme/word *chang* must be identified both lexically, as translatable by 'long'—e.g. by collocation with *gong-li* 'kilometre'; and grammatically, as a finite intransitive verb 'is/are long'—which can be shown by its association with the item *gong* 'altogether', a member of a small class of words which can only precede a finite verb, but is more usefully shown (since this will cover a much greater number of instances) by the identification of the clause structure.

In fact there is no reason why any one unit should be taken as the sole basic unit for translation. In describing a language we give no special priority either to the morpheme or to the sentence: all units are equally 'basic'. In translation too we operate with all the units, and 'shunt' from one to another, taking account of the particular systems and structures through which the units are interrelated.

If we analyse the translation process with 'translation equivalence' regarded as linked to the grammatical rank scale, we can distinguish three stages in it. These are not of course discrete steps taken one after the other, but rather abstractions useful to the understanding of the translation process and of 'a translation' as its end-product. First, there is the selection of the 'most probable translation equivalent' for each item at each rank, based on simple frequency. Second, there is the conditioning effect of the surrounding text in the source language on these probabilities: here grammatical and lexical features of the unit next above are taken into account and may (or may not) lead to the choice of an item other than the one with highest overall probability. Third, there is the internal structure of the target language, which may (or may not) lead to the choice of yet another item as a result of grammatical and lexical relations particular to that language: these can be viewed as brought into operation similarly by step-by-step progression up the rank scale. Stage three is distinct in that the source language no longer plays any part here. The weighting of these (descriptive) factors from the structure of the target language against the (comparative) factors drawn from the source language is one of the major theoretical problems; in effect one is asking what part is played by the original in determining the form of the translation.

As an example, consider the translation of the item *duo* in the Chinese version of the first sentence below. As a morpheme it is most likely to require, in written English, the rendering 'many', though there are a number of other possible equivalents. When it turns out, by reference to the unit next above, that *duo* is here a complete word, not part of a word, it becomes more likely that it is a verb, to be rendered 'are many'. This version is clearly unlikely to survive for long, and in many examples would be replaced at clause rank by 'there are many', on internal grounds: English would transform 'the problems are many' into 'there are many problems'. In this example, however, when we go one further up the rank scale, the place of *duo* in group structure shows that it stands to the numeral in a relationship rendered in English by the addition of 'than': 'many than 23,000'. The rules of English require that in the structure of which this is an example the comparative form (which has no *item* equivalent in Chinese) should be selected: 'more than'. A more sophisticated translation might alter this at clause rank to 'over', but this could not be generalized to all such occurrences of *duo*: 'over three o'clock' is not acceptable. The question of what is left over to stage three will in any case depend on the comparison of the target language with the source language: if one was translating *trois jours* from (written) French, the English plural form 'days' could be arrived at by translation from *jours*, whereas in the translation of the Chinese equivalent *san tian* the use of the plural form 'days' in concord with the numeral form 'three' would appear as an internal feature of English.

The human translator performs all stages of the operation at all ranks in a single process. A computer programme, if it is to achieve a reasonable degree of generality even in one pair of languages in one direction, might take these steps separately. In whatever way the translation process is broken down, the focus of attention cannot be restricted to any one grammatical unit; and the notion of a gradual advance towards the final choice of an equivalent, each step being achieved by the placing of the item in a wider context so that it enters into a new network of grammatical relations, may not be altogether fanciful. It is here that the concept of a grammatical 'unit' is relevant, in that each unit is simply a unique complex of such relations and thus defines a specific and distinct environment within which a translation equivalent is being sought.

Whatever model of the translation process may be relevant to MT, it seems inevitable that description must precede translation; and it might be pointed out that the computer has a place here too. Indeed one major contribution of the computer to MT in the first instance may well be its role in the detailed description of the languages concerned. Among the information required of such a description are statistics, especially grammatical—e.g. occurrences of classes, and of sequences of classes, of each unit, but also lexical—occurrences of lexical items *in collocation* (most linguistic statistics to date has been lexical and has ignored sequences); and statements linking the actual occurrences to the contextual meanings of the forms concerned: contextual meaning itself cannot be stated in quantitative terms, but for MT purposes it probably needs to be related to statistical analysis in grammar and lexis. Subsequent comparative descriptions, of pairs or groups of languages, might include direct comparison, suitable for a programme concerned with only one pair of languages such as Russian-English, and indirect comparison via a machine interlingua, for a general programme to be adapted, with insertion of appropriate dictionaries, to an increasing number of different languages. The machine interlingua would be not a natural language nor an artificial language but a mathematical construct serving as intermediary between any pair of natural languages. It would of course have no output, and would reduce the total number of programmes very considerably—for example from 90 to 20 if it was desired to translate each way between each pair from among ten different languages. The interlingua approach, though not generally favoured in the past, has much to recommend it for long-term application, giving as it does more scope for exploiting the power of linguistic theory. It is also likely to be of great interest to linguistics, since it could yield, not universal descriptive categories, which would be too vague to be interesting, but a general frame of reference for the comparative categories which have to be set up when two languages are formally compared. It is not only MT which needs comparative descriptions; they have a place in other applications of linguistics, and nowhere more than in foreign language teaching. But for the sort of comparison for which computational studies are needed, work in machine translation provides both the incentive and the opportunities required.

Appendix

A. 'Rank by rank' English translation of Chinese and Russian sentences.

Conventions:

///	sentence boundary
//	clause boundary
/	group boundary
(space)	word boundary
–	morpheme boundary
[[ ]]	boundary of rankshifted clause
[ ]	boundary of rankshifted group
1	morpheme equivalents
2	word equivalents
3	group equivalents
4	clause equivalents
5	sentence equivalents
X	grammatical item
(PN)	proper name

(1) Chinese

///[Zhong-guo	di]	tie-lu	/	gong	chang	/
1 (PN)| country	X	iron | way		altogether	long	
2 China	X	railway		altogether	is are + long	
3 of China		railway		is are altogether long		

4 the railways of China are altogether more than 23,000 kilometres in length

5 The railways of China are altogether more than 23,000 kilometres in length, of which the greater part is in the Northeast Provinces

2	wan	3	qian	duo	gong-li	//
2	ten + thousand	3	thousand	many	metric | mile	
	20 + thousand		3 + thousand	are + many	kilometre	

more than 23,000 kilometres

qi	da	bu-fen	/	shi/	zai	dong-bei	///
thereof	great	part | share		X	at	east | north	
thereof	is are + great	part		X	is are + at	northeast	
the greater part thereof				X	is are in the northeast		

the greater part thereof is/are in the northeast

(1) Russian

/// Obšč-aja		dlin-a /	železn-ych dorog	/	Kita-ja	/
1 general | X	long | X	iron | X	way	(PN) | X		
2 general	length	of + iron	of + ways	of + China		
3 the overall length		of railways		of China		

4 the overall length of the railways of China is over 23,000 kilometres

5 The overall length of the railways of China is over 23,000 kilometres, of which the greater part is in the Northeast Provinces

ravn-a	/	23	[	s	ličn-im	]	tysjač-am	/
equal	X	23		with	extra	X	thousand	X
is + equal		23		with	with + extra		to + thousand	
is equal		to 23		over			thousand	

kilometr-ov	//	bol'š-aja ich		čast'	/	na-chod-it-sja	/
kilometre	X	great	X	their	part	X	on go come	X	X
of + kilometres		great		their	part		is + found	
kilometres		the greater part of them					is found	
		the greater part of them is in the Northeast Provinces						

v	provinci-jach	/	Sever-o-vostok-a	///
in	province	X	north	X	east	X
in	provinces		of + northeast	
in the provinces			of the Northeast	

(2) Chinese

/// Wo-men /	suo kan-jian di //	bi-jiao /
1 I	X	X	look	see	X	compare	compare
2 we		X	see		X	compare	
3 we		what which	see			compare with	
4 what we see						compared with what we	
5 What we saw was even more interesting than what we had heard before							

wo-men	/	yi-qian		/	suo	ting-jian		di //
I	X	X	before		X	listen	see	X
we		before			X	hear		X
we		before			what which	hear		
heard before								

geng	you	/	yi-si	///
X	have		mean	think
still + more	have		significance	
have even more			significance	
is are even more interesting				

(2) Russian

/// vs-jo		to	[[č-to	/	my	u-vid-el-i	]]
1 all	X	that	what	X	we	by | see | X | X
2 all		that	what		we	saw
3 all that			what		we saw	
4 all that			what we saw			
5 All that we saw was far more interesting than what we had heard before						

gorazd-o		interesn-eje	/	to-go	
good + at	X	interesting	X	that	X
far		more + interesting		of + that	
is are far more interesting				of that	
is are far more interesting than that					

[[č-to	/	my	slyš-al-i	/	ran-še	]]///
what	X	we	hear	X | X	early	X
what		we	heard		earlier	
what		we heard			earlier	
what we heard before						

B. Grammatical and lexical features of an English sentence.

///The railway-s [of [China]] are / altogether /
more [than [23,000 kilo-metre-s [in [length]]]] //
[of [which]] the great-er part / is / in [the North-east Province-s] ///

I (a): Linear statement of sentence, clause and group structure

///α /S dhq (/pc (/h)) /P h /A h /C e = hq (/pc
(/ohq (/pc (/h)))) //β /B = S q (/pb = c (/d = h)) deh
/P h /A = C pc (/dnh) ///

I (b): Sequence of grammatical items

the ( )s of ( ) are ( ) more + than (numeral) ( )s in ( )
of which the ( )er ( ) is in the ( ) ( ) ( )s

II: Sequence of lexical items

railway China altogether 23,000 kilometre length great
    part northeast province

Nine

A four-letter word in 'Lady Chatterley's Lover' (1960)

In *Lady Chatterley's Lover*[1] I have noted 293 instances of the verb *know*.[2] Of these, apart from 11 special cases,[3] all but 40 could be translated into French by some form of the verb *savoir*; the rest by *connaître*. I shall consider here how a computer might be instructed to examine the linguistic environments (i.e. co-texts) in which these instances occur, in such a way as to arrive at a satisfactory dichotomy of them into what I shall call S-instances and C-instances[4]; we may regard this as part of the more general problem of translating the book into French. The main purpose of this paper is to examine the extent to which grammatical as

---

[1] *Lady Chatterley's Lover*, Penguin edition, 1960. All references are to the pages of that edition. I am indebted to my former colleague Dr R. D. Huddleston for a careful examination of relevant points in the text of *L'amant de Lady Chatterley* (translation by F. Roger-Cornaz), Editions Gallimard, 1932.

[2] My list is probably not exhaustive, but I have not intentionally omitted any examples. Instances involving dialect have been included. I have ignored compounds of the verb.

[3] See Appendix 5. This is not to say that the French translator in fact chooses in all but 11 instances to use *savoir* or *connaître*; there are for instance occasions when he does not because stylistic considerations lead him to modify the structure of a whole sentence, with consequent departures from the 'expected' treatment of *know* itself. Nor is it suggested that *savoir* or *connaître* would always (outside the 11 instances) be wholly satisfying stylistically without any such structural modifications. At the same time, it is reasonable to speak of the 'correct' choice, instance by instance, of one of these two verbs, since such a choice is in almost all cases very much more nearly satisfying than the 'wrong' one. Machine translation must, it is clear, operate for some considerable time with grades or degrees of satisfactoriness in this way and be content often to *approach*, without attaining, stylistic perfection.

[4] S-instance, C-instance: instance requiring translation by (appropriate form of) *savoir*, *connaître* respectively.

distinct from collocational[5] (lexical) criteria are adequate for the solution of problems of this kind.

A very crude translation procedure which simply operated with one French equivalent of *know* would obviously do much better to have *savoir* only rather than *connaître* only. Furthermore, if we cannot avoid making less than something like three dozen mistakes by following some more complicated procedure, we shall be well advised to stick to the crude one.

The steps outlined below whereby, it is suggested, all but a very small number of errors might be avoided, are probably not the most economical from a procedural point of view. A final streamlined scheme might well concentrate on the identification of the comparatively small number of C-instances on the basis of certain grammatically distinctive environments which will be discussed in the course of the present paper. The approach outlined below is somewhat more cumbersome but it has the advantage of calling attention to a considerable number of important problems as they arise, and it furnishes a basis upon which a simpler procedure could probably be established without much difficulty. This approach may also suggest a way of coming to grips with comparable translation problems.

An examination of the material from the novel reveals that there are two almost infallible grammatical indications that we are dealing with an S-instance:

1. If *know* has a clause object. There are 136 instances.[6]
2. If *know* has no object. There are 60 instances.[7]

This means that 196 of our 282 S/C-instances will be no problem at all to a computer which can identify instances of *know* as being in either of these two syntactic situations; the question of collocations does not arise here at all.

It might be suggested, then, that our first instructions to the computer should be:

1. Check whether *know* has a clause object. If so, take as an S-instance. If not, proceed to 2.
2. Check whether *know* has no object. If so, take as an S-instance. If not, proceed to 3 (see p. 154).

---

[5] For 'collocation' see Paper 11, p. 183 (and footnote 3); cf. also Paper 1, p. 19.
[6] For an analysis of the types of clause used, see Appendix 1.
[7] For notes on these instances, see Appendix 2. For four special cases which are not included among the above 60, see page 158.

We are now left with only 86 cases still in doubt, of which about 46 per cent are in fact going to be C-instances. In this collection of material still unaccounted for, there is a fairly common situation, characteristic indeed of about half of our remaining instances, in which *know* has one of a quite small set of pronominal objects; it may be advisable, at any rate from a procedural point of view, to consider these separately. There are 42 cases, and we may notice in advance that 28 of these are in fact S-instances and 14 are C-instances. The solution of the problem of discrimination here would not, as far as one can see, be greatly furthered by recourse to purely collocational criteria (except perhaps of such a sophisticated and involved kind as would be hardly practicable for the present purpose); once again it would seem rather to depend in the main on grammatical factors.

Ideally, as we shall see, the assembly of such evidence calls (at least in some cases) for scrutiny of a certain amount of text outside (and usually before) the clause in which *know* itself occurs; and it would sometimes be desirable to investigate the relationship of *know* to items in the preceding sentence. We shall return to this matter later.[8] To make any such investigation by means of a computer would be a complicated business and should therefore be avoided if possible. So we shall consider how far we can get simply by using grammatical criteria derived from observation of the above-mentioned pronominal objects as such, without attempting to associate them (in terms of any kind of anaphoric reference) with any noun, phrase, clause, sentence etc., somewhere in the co-text.

The pronominal objects which we shall group tentatively into a set are presented, with frequency of occurrence, below[9] (see next page). It will be seen that if we subdivide this set into A and B and simply regard members of sub-set A as S-instance objects and members of sub-set B as C-instance objects,[10] then we shall make a correct determination in a very high proportion of cases. In fact our computer, working on this principle, would make only two errors in 42 problems; it would identify 28 genuine S-instances and 12 genuine C-instances and would

---

[8] See footnote 12, and pp. 155–6, 159, 162.

[9] For a discussion of the first two members of this set, with examples, see Appendix 3.

[10] With more material, we should no doubt be able to add *whom* (*who*), *you*, *us* and perhaps other pronouns to this sub-set. There are certain other pronouns, not attested in the appropriate situation in our material, which need further investigation e.g. *this*, *these*, *those*.

		PRONOUNS	S-INST.	C-INST.	TOTAL
S E T	SUBSET A	1 it	17	2	19
		2 that	5	0	5
		3 what (what all)	4	0	4
		4 which	2	0	2
	SUBSET B	5 him	0	3	3
		6 her	0	1	1
		7 me	0	3	3
		8 them ('em)	0	5	5
		Total	28	14	42

err only in interpreting the two remaining C-instances (both involving *it*[11]) as S-instances.[12]

Following steps 1 and 2 therefore, further straightforward (albeit somewhat crude) steps in our series of instructions to the computer might be:

3. Examine whether *know* has a pronominal object from among the set listed. If so, proceed to 4. If not, proceed to 5 (see p. 155).

4. If the object belongs to sub-set A, take as an S-instance. If not, take as a C-instance.

The value for our purposes of the distinction between sub-sets A and B rests on two facts:

i. That B-pronouns will in all cases except *them* ('*em*)[13] invariably 'stand for' animate objects, whereas A-pronouns will in most cases 'stand for' inanimate objects[14].

[11] See Appendix 3.

[12] We are of course ignoring here the fact that the actual practical problem of identifying a preceding *what* or *which* as the object of *know* may present considerable difficulties. The same kind of difficulty crops up, though comparatively rarely, elsewhere:

(a) With *how much*. For two instances, see Appendix 4.

(b) Where *know* is in a relative clause and has as its object a word or phrase outside that clause. E.g. 23: *all the things* (not followed by a relative pronoun); 103: *all* (*that*). Cf. also the C-instance (215) quoted in footnote 17, and 291: *the only home* she had ever known.

[13] Even with this word as object of *know* there is (in our material) a probability of 4:1 in favour of an animate referent. Cf. footnote 18.

[14] In this text the probability of *it* being 'inanimate' as object of *know* is 17:2.

ii. That these two types of objects correlate with C- and S-instances; closely (it turns out) in the case of animate object/C, less closely in the case of inanimate object/S.

In view of this, and leaving for the moment the shortcomings of step 4, a clearly profitable step 5 would be one which attempted to exploit the fact that an animate *nominal* object almost invariably implies a C-instance. We may also utilize in step 5 the fact that a proper-name object, whether animate or not, has the same implication[15]. If we wish at this stage to avoid errors arising from the fact that the complementary correlation inanimate noun object or non-proper-name object/S is not very close, our step 5 can be formulated thus:

5. Examine whether the object is animate[16] or a proper-name. In either case, if so, take as a C-instance. If not, proceed to Step 6 (see p. 158).

This, in fact, in our material, would correctly identify another 12 C-instances, bringing our total of correctly identified C-instances up to 24.[17]

The main crudity of our procedure so far lies in step 4, and it rests on two facts:

i. Any pronoun object from our set which has anaphoric reference to an animate noun or to a proper-name will certainly be a very strong indication of a C-instance. But we cannot be sure in certain cases (e.g. *it* and sometimes *them*) whether our pronoun *has* this reference; not, at least, unless it can be associated specifically with some previous referent which will decide the issue. Hence the need,

---

[15] A proper-name object, once it has been identified (by whatever means) as an object at all, can be identified simply by its initial capital except in the very rare cases where the object occurs in sentence-initial position.

[16] This of course makes the assumption that the computer could be provided with usually reliable information about whether a given noun was 'animate' or not. Clearly this might in some cases be difficult, though it would hardly present serious problems in the instances found in *Lady Chatterley's Lover*.

[17] The instances are:

(a) Two personal names: 135: *Lady Chatterley*; 313: *Richards*.
(b) Three pronoun objects: 55: *anybody* (twice; once in preceding clause); *nob'dy* 93.
(c) Seven 'animate' nouns or nominal phrases: 51: *the people*; 59: *any woman*; 134: *your Ladyship*; 170: *men*; 215: (in preceding clause) like *all the men I've ever known*; 270: *dozens of people*; 285 *the man*.

ideally, for the scrutiny of text outside (and usually just before) the clause in which *know* itself occurs.

ii. Some *inanimate* objects other than proper-names occur after *know* in C-instances. So a way of identifying these instances must be found. And not only they, but pronoun objects like *it* and *them* in anaphoric reference to such objects, must be interpreted accordingly[18].

So far we have not come to grips with the difficulties arising out of ii above, and we followed a somewhat makeshift procedure to get round i. The result is that, having by now identified all instances of animate or proper-name objects, we have still only got our total of correctly identified C-instances up to 24; another 16 C-instances of various kinds remain unidentified. We have of course lost two cases where the object *it* was involved, by assuming that this was valid evidence for these being S-instances[19]. And we have as yet done nothing about those seven remaining nominal objects which, though neither animate nouns nor proper-names, should in fact be taken as evidence for C-instances.

At this point we may pause to examine how far we have got with our 282 instances on the basis of the steps so far carried out:

1. Yields 136 correct S-instances.

2. Yields 60 correct S-instances.

3, 4. Yield 28 correct S-instances, 12 correct C-instances and two incorrect S-instances.

5. Yields 12 correct C-instances.

Our haul so far is thus 224 correct S-instances and 24 correct C-instances. We are therefore left with 34 still problematic cases in our total corpus of S/C instances: there are 32 not as yet tackled and two in need, if possible, of revision. 18 S-instances remain to be correctly identified, and 16 C-instances. For the sake of clarity we may list this remainder as follows:

---

[18] It may be noted that, in assuming that all cases of an object *them* (*'em*) were animate, we went wrong in one case. But it happened to be a case where, though its reference was to inanimate nouns, we were still in the presence of a C-instance, so we obtained the correct answer anyhow. The case is 264: 'you have never known either real tenderness or real sensuality: and if you do know them, . . . it makes a great difference.'

[19] The two cases lost by this assumption are:

287: His hand lay as she knew it, . . .

267: 'Yes! The Villa Esmeralda! Yes! I know it! . . .'

These are in fact both translated by C in the Roger-Cornaz version.

A. Outstanding S-instances:

    i. Involving objects so far not treated   14

    ii. Special cases where no object is involved but in which the
        computer might have had difficulty in recognizing that this
        was so, and which were therefore not listed among the 60
        instances of *know* without an object   4

                                                Total   18

B. Outstanding C-instances:

    i. Involving objects so far not treated   7

    ii. Where the participle *known* in non-finite constructions is
        involved   7

    iii. Where the pronoun object *it* was wrongly interpreted   2

                                                  Total   16

It is clear that Ai and Bi comprise a fairly small but still quite important group of cases. If we can set up a procedure for sorting them out, we
shall have solved quite a high proportion of our instances. The information available from the material collected from the novel is not abundant
enough to permit a full treatment of the underlying problem, but we
may tentatively state the position as follows:

    i. That cases of *know* with noun (or noun phrase) objects even *other*
    than animates and proper-names are likely to be C-instances; and
    similarly with pronoun objects referring anaphorically to such noun
    objects (as distinct from clauses, sentences, etc.).

    ii. That the exceptions are what may tentatively be called 'inanimate
    indefinites' of the type *nothing, nothing at all, anything, very little,
    how much, all, all the things, a thing or two, even less.*[20]

It is reasonable to suppose that a computer could be programmed to

---

[20] For the passages containing these, see Appendix 4. The list is of course by
no means exhaustive, and besides certain qualification, it requires such additions
as: (*a*) *little, much, everything, a bit, a (whole) lot, a great deal.* In groups like *a lot
of people* (which would of course be ineligible) the animacy of the object must be
established from *people*; so with phrases like *a lot of, a number of, a group of,* just
as with adjectives like *many, several, certain, numerous, (a) few,* it is the following
noun which is crucial. It should be noted that not only 'inanimate indefinites'
but also pronouns referring anaphorically to these will indicate S-instances. Such
pronouns will usually belong to sub-set A, but *them* (from sub-set B) may be
expected from time to time with this kind of reference.

identify instances of *know* which had objects belonging to this set of 'inanimate indefinites', and our sixth step might therefore be:

6. Check whether the object is one of the 'inanimate indefinite' group.[21] If so, take as an S-instance. If not, take as a C-instance.

The result of applying this step is to give us 21 more correct identifications, 14 of S-instances and seven of C-instances. This leaves only four S-instances and nine C-instances unidentified; we may now consider these in turn. The four S-instances are:

   i. 98: The phrase sounded queer, she didn't know why.

   ii. 312: '. . . I must say good-bye to you, Mrs. Bolton, you know why. . . .'

   iii. 242: 'Anyone would think I'd been I don't know where! . . .'

   iv. 282: (*in a letter*) The woman has gone away: we don't know where to: . . .

There are obvious difficulties about such cases. They were not treated as objectless instances under step 2, partly because of possible procedural complications but also partly because there are theoretical grammatical difficulties. Are they in fact objectless instances at all? For if so they are certainly different from constructions like 'I know now'. On the whole (though there is a case for treating them as clause-objects) it seems best from both points of view to treat the above and similar cases along with the 'inanimate indefinites', enlarging our list to include *why, where, when, how* and prepositional phrases such as *for what reason, in what way*. 'I know now' would of course have to be treated as (in itself) a truly objectless instance.

Finally there are nine C-instances. Of these, seven involve the participle *known* in non-finite constructions.[22] We should not perhaps make too much of the fact that all such instances of *known* in the novel are C-instances, though clearly it is of importance and value, and suggests an extremely simple and perhaps generally reliable procedure for handling them. Anything more sophisticated might best perhaps involve some kind of transformational approach; for if they were con-

---

[21] For a suggestion about the slight extension of this group, see below.

[22] (a) 22 (three cases): Connie wondered a little over Clifford's blind, imperious instinct to become *known*: *known*, that is, to the vast amorphous world he did not himself know, . . . *known* as a writer, as a first-class modern writer.

(b) 85: he was just part of a phenomenon, the phenomenon of the high-classfolks, so far unknown to her, but now to be *known*.

(c) 141: She did not want it, it was *known* and barren.

(d) 160: and of shapes not before *known* to man.

(e) 299: 'Clifford is too well *known*.'

verted into the active, the object in all but one of the instances recorded from our text would identify them as C-instances; this single case would still remain in doubt without broader co-textual scrutiny and identification of the anaphoric reference.

There is not much we can do, by simple methods, with the two outstanding C-instances involving *it*. Our mistake here could of course have been avoided if we had refused to divide our set of object pronouns so sharply into sub-sets A and B. But we should then have had to be prepared in the case of *it* (and the same would apply to *them* and perhaps some of the others) to evolve some quite complicated procedure for establishing the nature of the anaphoric reference; only thereafter could we be sure of arriving at a correct conclusion. We must leave this problem at this point, noting only that it has been possible throughout to side-track any such procedure with a remarkably small amount of resultant error. There may well, however, be many other translation problems where a more subtle and involved grammatical approach cannot so easily be avoided. I say 'grammatical approach' because it seems likely that elaborations of fundamentally *syntactic* procedures will be more powerful in such cases than anything based on merely collocational criteria.

These notes at least suggest the vital relevance of grammatical relationships in problems of this kind, even though it may turn out that this S/C problem itself is not entirely typical. It is obviously desirable that investigations of numerous other translation-problems should be made. I have been aware of singularly few purely collocational clues in this particular study. I have also been surprised both at the rather small number of relevant grammatical clues required to establish most S- and C-instances, and at how much can be achieved without extending our scrutiny beyond the clause in which *know* itself occurs. Since we well know that many clues (especially in relation to anaphoric reference) do lie outside, this has some interest from the point of view of information theory. It will also be noted that the subject of the verb *know* appears to have no relevance. If therefore (for 'total' translation purposes) one were to evolve a generalized procedure for the examination of verbs, and if this provides (as it almost certainly will have to) for the scrutiny of their subjects, then it will be necessary, in the case of *know*, to save needless work by having an instruction: 'bypass all routines for examining subjects'.

The highly significant distinction between clause-objects and non-clause-objects in the present problem illustrates the importance of a scheme of grammatical analysis which makes this procedurally as simple as possible to recognize, prior to the classification of instances on this basis. This paper makes little or no useful contribution in such directions except perhaps in pointing out the fundamental importance of grammatical analysis for problems of translation.

Appendices

APPENDIX I. 'KNOW' WITH CLAUSE OBJECT

Instances of *know* with what would conventionally be called a clause object number 125. Along with these I have grouped 11 instances of clause-like constructions involving an infinitive instead of a finite verb. The cases are:

1. 85: and she soon knew how to have him in her power.
2. 120: Yet the hand knew, too, how to unclothe her where it wanted.
3. 239: She never knew how to answer him when he . . .
4. 63: Connie did not know what to say.
5. 90: She did not know what to say.
6. 126: She didn't know what to think.
7. 147: For he did not know what to do with himself.
8. 147: He did not know what to do with himself.
9. 220: '. . . An' sometimes I don' know what ter do wi' him . . .'
10. 284: She did not know what to do . . .
11. 54: . . . and he had not known where to find her.

It will be noted that these only occur after *how* (3), *what* (7) and *where* (1). In all the 136 cases except three (219: 'You must *never* insult him, you know . . .' 243: What he thought in his under-consciousness he would never know. 290: '. . . But what it really amounts to, I don't know') the clause follows *know*, and in all but nine of these 133 instances, it follows immediately. These nine cases are:

1. 25: Michaelis knew at once he had made an impression on her.
2. 121: And she knew, if she gave herself to the man, it was real.
3. 204: '. . . I know beforehand I don't care for his sort . . .'
4. 302: Inwardly, he had known for a long time she was leaving him.
5. 120: Yet the hand knew, too, how to unclothe her where it wanted.
6. 21: Vaguely she knew herself that she was going to pieces . . .
7. 123: For he knew by experience what it meant.
8. 132: . . . and she knew, more or less, where they were.
9. 235: 'And we *shall* know better where we are when I come back shan't we?'

The situation may be presented diagrammatically thus:

		contact	what	where	that	how (much)	if	why	when	at what time	TOTAL
											TYPE OF OBJECT CLAUSE
Position	immediately following	52	39	11	10	6	3	1	1	1	124
	following, but separated	4	1	2	1	1	0	0	0	0	9
	preceding	1	2	0	0	0	0	0	0	0	3
	Total	57	42	13	11	7	3	1	1	1	136

NOTES:

1. In all cases where the clause follows immediately after *know*, it is without any separation by punctuation except for *she knew, partly,* for which see 2a below.

2a. In the 52 instances of contact clauses immediately following *know*, there are only 14 gambits: *he* (14); *it* (9); *I* (8); *she* (7); *there* (4); *you* (2); *they* (1); *we* (1); five nouns or noun phrases each used once: *Luke*; *the people*; *another part*; *his leaving*; *his wife*; one adverb: *partly* (130: And she knew, *partly* it was her own fault). In the five instances of separated contact clauses the opening words are *it* (2); *I* (1); *he* (1); *she* (1).

2b. In the 72 cases of other clauses immediately following *know*, there is only one instance where the 'head' word (*what, where, that* etc.) does not itself begin the clause:

25. He knew just where he was with Clifford.

APPENDIX 2. 'KNOW' WITHOUT OBJECT

Of the 60 instances, no less than 50 have the characteristic that *know* is followed by some mark of punctuation. The 10 exceptions are:

1. 32: Perhaps if he'd known he might even have wished to get her and Michaelis together again.
2. 32: But, as she knew by foreboding, that would come to an end.
3. 103: (second case) . . . the peculiar passion of *knowing*, knowing as he knew.
4. 177: 'Yes,' he said. 'You know without asking.'
5. 204: 'Nay, you know better than I do . . .'

6. 235: '. . . But you don't really know yourself . . .'
7. 259: She knew now.
8. 273: She knew now.
9. 294: '. . . You'd know if you saw him . . .'
10. 310: So he had really inwardly known all the time.

It will be noted that most of these have an adverb or a prepositional phrase immediately after *know* and that these do not belong to the small group we finally (p. 158) incorporated in step 6. The comma after *foreboding* in the second example is important. 1 and 6 pose problems and it is not easy to see how 6 could be solved with certainty without a sophisticated analysis of the co-text.

APPENDIX 3. 'IT' and 'THAT' AS OBJECTS

There are 22 S-instances in the text—17 with *it* and five with *that*. In all cases but one there is anaphoric reference to a clause, sometimes in the same sentence as *know*, sometimes in the preceding one (but never further back). The single exception is cataphoric:

160: But as a matter of fact, though even Connie did not know it, downhill half a mile below the 'hotel' was old Stacks Gate . . .

In all cases but one, *it* and *that* follow immediately after *know* and are themselves followed by some mark of punctuation. The exception is:

150: But which room she was in, the woman who held the other end of the frail thread which drew him so mercilessly, that he did not know.

The two C-instances with an *it*-object (quoted in footnote 18) have anaphoric reference *not* to a clause but to a previous noun or noun phrase. Most *it*-objects with noun reference will probably turn out to be C-instances but S-instances are possible, e.g. (not in our text):

A. 'I'm going to give you some remarkable news about Ethel.'
B. 'I know it already.'

APPENDIX 4. RESULTS OF APPLICATION OF STEP 6

Identification of 14 S-instances:

1. 28: 'Me!' he said, almost fiercely; 'he'll know *nothing* from me! . . .'
2. 139: And they lay and knew *nothing*, not even of each other, both lost.
3. 216: . . . looking at him from the unknown, knowing *nothing* any more.

4. 195: 'I'm afraid I know *nothing at all* about these mechanical things, Sir Clifford.'
5. 195: 'Do you know *anything* about motors?'
6. 202: She wanted him not to know *anything at all* about herself:
7. 202 (continuing from 6): and especially not to know *anything* about her feeling for the keeper.
8. 71: . . . but I know *very little* about him.
9. 308: *How much* did the rest of the servants know or suspect?
10. 308: '*How much* do the servants know?'
11. 103: She was coming bit by bit into possession of *all* that the gentry knew.
12. 266: The efficient, sometimes charming women knew *a thing or two* about the sensual realities.
13. 266: But they knew *even less* of tenderness.
14. 23: . . . about *all the things* Clifford wanted to know.

Identification of seven C-instances:

1. 22: to *the vast amorphous world* he did not himself know.
2. 58: '. . . I only know *my own case* . . .'
3. 101: And gradually her fingertips knew *his cheeks* and *lips*, his *jaw* and *chin* and *throat* perfectly.
4. 79: but he well knew *the tone of Scottish obstinacy* underneath.
5. 145 (quotation): 'Who knoweth *the mysteries of the will* . . .'
6. 264: '. . . you have never known either *real tenderness* or *real sensuality* . . .'
7. 291: She crept close against him, clinging fast to his thin, strong naked body, *the only home* she had ever known.

On the difficulty of handling some of these S- and C-instances (especially where the object precedes *know*) see footnote 11.

APPENDIX 5. INSTANCES OF 'KNOW' PRESENTING SPECIAL PROBLEMS OF TRANSLATION

It is not of course implied (cf. footnote 3) that all the 282 instances which we have labelled S- or C-instances are necessarily *best* translated by S or C, but merely that one or other of these verbs would be adequate. There are however 11 instances which probably require separate treatment. Of these, four involve the phrase *know about* with no object-word or phrase interposed:

1. 53: Of course she *knew about* it long ago.

2. 104: And it was marvellous, the things that happened and that she *knew about*.

3. 276: And she now dreaded the thought that anybody would *know about* herself and the keeper.

4. 276: If Clifford *knew about* her affair, how unspeakably humiliating.

These cases take us beyond *savoir* and *connaître* and it is suggested that *know about* would best be treated as a separate problem. That is to say that whenever they occur side by side it should be considered whether the two words are to be taken as a single lexical item 'know-about'. Here of course we should encounter the problem of distinguishing between 'he knows-about many languages' and 'he knows about twenty languages'.

There are seven other problematic cases. Of these, three involve the phrases *get to know* 'learn about' and *let . . . know* 'inform in due course'; these too might best be treated as single lexical items. The instances are: 233, 28, 312. For the four remaining instances I can suggest no obvious solution:

1. 'experience' 276: He had known all that sensuality even with a Bertha Coutts!

2. 'experience' 290: '. . . It's that all the way through. I knew it with the men . . .'

3. 'realize' 288: She never knew the fierce bitterness with which he resented insult.

4. (? 'recognize') 38: '. . . Ye shall know the tree by its fruit.'

APPENDIX 6. PROCEDURAL INSTRUCTIONS FOR A COMPUTER

1. Check whether *know* has a clause object. If so, take as an S-instance. If not, proceed to 2.

2. Check whether *know* has no object. If so, take as S-instance. If not, proceed to 3.

3. Check whether *know* has a pronominal object from among the set listed (p. 154). If so, proceed to 4. If not, proceed to 5.

4. If the object belongs to sub-set A, take as an S-instance. If not, take as a C-instance.

5. Examine whether the object is animate or a proper-name. If either, take as a C-instance. If neither, proceed to 6.

6. Examine whether the object is one of the 'inanimate indefinite' group listed on p. 157 (and added to on pp. 158). If so, take as an S-instance. If not, take as a C-instance.

Ten

Typology and the exotic (1959-60)

1

Language, which makes classification possible, at the same time makes it impossible to avoid classifying. Part of the process of learning our native language is learning to classify; and this we continue to do in all our language-centred activities, including of course the sciences. In the linguistic sciences we turn round and bring the classifying process to bear on language itself, which was our means of classification in the first place.

We do this in two ways: *intra*-linguistically and *inter*-linguistically. Intralinguistic classification is an essential part of the description of any language; it is here that, out of the progression of events that constitute a language, we abstract units—clause, word, syllable and so on—and classes of these units, such as 'dependent clause', 'verb (word)' and 'long syllable'. The nature of intralinguistic classes has been a central problem in linguistics for more than two thousand years, and is of considerable interest to scientific theory in general.[1]

In interlinguistic classification, by contrast, the aim is to classify not the items within a language but the languages themselves. This is a more recent pursuit, dating from the beginnings of historical linguistics at the end of the eighteenth century. Languages were classified into families and groups according to their line of descent by divergence from common originals. Perhaps the greatest achievement of nineteenth-century linguistics was the working out of the principles of genetic relationship, and of the detailed history and historical classification of languages of the Indo-European and some other families.

[1] See for example R. H. Robins, *Ancient and mediaeval grammatical theory in Europe*, London: Bell, 1951. See also the papers presented to the ASLIB Symposium on Classification in Linguistics, Cambridge, May 1963.

Relatively early in these studies it became clear that degree of genetic relationship did not correlate fully with degree of similarity between languages, at least on any intuitively recognizable criterion of similarity: it was by no means always true that the more closely related two languages were the more they seemed to work alike. Likeness among languages was to a certain extent independent of their history, and thus formed a distinct dimension of classification. This became the subject matter of a new branch of linguistics, linguistic typology.

In any scheme of classification there are likely to be things which do not seem to fit in, and this gives rise to the concept of the exotic. Historically, a language will be exotic if, like Basque, it has no known relatives. Typologically, if course, what is exotic will depend on the criteria of classification. If the cats in my neighbourhood are classified according to colour, the Siamese is exotic; but if according to length of tail, then the exotic one is the Manx.

In any case, there are two aspects to exoticism: the rare and the odd, and these are not necessarily congruent. The rare is simply rare, either as type or as token; in this sense the Manx might be exotic either (a) because there are very few species of tailless cats or (b) because such species have very few specimens. The odd, however, is a qualitative rather than a quantitative category: it is something that is somehow *very different* from the rest. It is true that this difference may be quantifiable; if the Manx is exotic in this sense because its tail is *very much shorter* than that of all the others this can be stated as a measurement. But the essence of oddness is that there is something unexpected: a feature that is unpredictable, in itself or in its environment, or a combination of features cutting across the predicted syndromes. It is easy to confuse the rare and the odd in the typological study of languages.

The first problem in linguistic typology is to decide what is being classified. Traditionally, the answer has been: languages. But this raises a difficulty. This is not primarily the difficulty of defining 'a language', since within limits any definition would suffice provided it was adhered to rigorously. Rather the difficulty is that if we want to say that two languages are alike, that Lx resembles Ly, then we must presuppose that Lx resembles itself.

Resemblance will be defined in terms of certain crucial properties. The choice of such properties is to some extent arbitrary; but each must be general enough to tell us something worth while about the languages concerned, and (if more than one is chosen) all must be interdependent enough to yield reasonably clearcut language types. But the more general a property, the less likely it is that it will be displayed consistently throughout a whole language; and there will be even less consistency if more than one property is taken into account. Whereas, to put it crudely, if an animal species suckles its young, all members of the species do so and this coincides with other features (as well as with evolutionary history) in marking such species off from those that do not, languages do not yield such clearly diagnostic yet still interesting properties. It would be relatively easy, for example, though with doubtful cases, to classify languages according to whether they had free-standing personal pronouns or not and, if so, how many; but this would be neither general enough, nor in correlation with enough other features, to make it of interest as a crucial dimension. On the other hand, to a truly general question such as 'is sequence used to show grammatical relations or not?' there are few languages where one can give even a reasonably straight answer.

In other words, when one looks at the most significant features of languages, the first conclusion is that no language seems to resemble even itself. It is difficult to find a set of characteristics in respect of which a language can be shown to be internally homogeneous. Yet this is what is needed if we are to classify languages as wholes.

The impulse to classify languages stems no doubt from the desire to find some pattern in the differences among them. Many of these differences were unexpected, in the sense that they were first observed when languages being described by linguists for the first time were found to display new features, or were found not to display features which had hitherto been supposed to be universal. Such features can of course be used as criteria of classification; but they tend to reflect the chance order in which the languages have been taken into consideration. If one looks first at English, French, German and Latin and then, with these as norms, at Modern Chinese, one can pick out certain features in which the first four resemble each other and Chinese differs from them all. This arrangement may be favoured because it is felt that the first four are *more likely* to resemble each other, whether because of genetic relationship, cultural or geographical affinity, or other less reputable assumptions; but it is not the only possible arrangement even on external grounds. One might point out that English, French, German and Chinese are spoken today whereas Latin was spoken 2,000 years ago; or that English, French and German are languages of highly industrialized communities; or that only English and Chinese have over two hundred million native speakers, and so on.

On internal, linguistic grounds, however, any grouping of these five languages into two types would find some justification, simply because the structure of language is complex and multifarious. If we wanted to group together English and Latin against Chinese, French and German, we could point out that the latter have front rounded vowels while the former have not. Not all such groupings would be equally powerful; some certainly account for more facts than others, and perhaps the most intuitively satisfying of the binary groupings would put English, French and Chinese into one class and German and Latin into the other. But at present there is no way of weighting the various criteria so as to suggest which should be regarded as crucial and which not.

This does not mean that we abandon typology until linguistics has developed a measure of likeness embracing all the relevant features suitably weighted; this may never happen. It means rather that we have to concentrate on particular features, one at a time, accepting different classifications for different dimensions of likeness and being prepared to classify parts of languages instead of languages as wholes.

2

It need not be feared that typological statements lose their interest or value if they remain, for the moment, tentative and partial. What is more important, if they are to be valid in theory and useful in application, is that they should be firmly dissociated from any value judgements. Value judgements on language, which are not to be confused with critical assessments of the appropriate and effective use of language, are so much a part of our ideology and have caused so much misunderstanding that it is perhaps worth while looking at those which are found in earlier typological studies in order to see how such views may arise. Probably no linguist today would question the axiom that no language is intrinsically superior or inferior to any other; but fifty years ago this view was still rather revolutionary.

Clearly, English is not adapted to the linguistic requirements of a Polynesian fishing expedition, or of the rituals of the pre-European peoples of Australia; nor are their languages adapted to electronics. But all are intrinsically capable of being adapted. The nature of language, because of the way in which we 'use language to live,'[2] is such that any

---

[2] J. R. Firth, 'A Synopsis of linguistic theory', *Studies in Linguistic Analysis*, Special Volume of the Philological Society, Oxford: Blackwell, 1957.

language will be capable of admitting the new elements needed for its adaptation to any new activity. Each language as it stands is adapted to the situation-types that the community is concerned with. Since totem magic universally precedes electronic magic, such *adaptive* changes in language are irreversible.

Some linguistic changes are clearly of the adaptive type; these are mainly changes in lexis, such as the addition of new items and the development of new patterns of existing items: *neutron* is a new item, *nucleus* an old item entering into new collocations such as with *atomic*. Other changes, however, especially in grammar and phonology, are internal to language, in the sense that they are not accountable for as adaptation to a changing environment: the only generalization that can be made is that the normal state of a language is one of constant change.

It seemed natural at first to assume that *all* linguistic change was irreversible and evolutionary: that language showed an innate tendency to improve, with the implications that, the English being considered further up the socio-economic scale than the original inhabitants of Australia, English was a better language for the English than was Worora for the people of North Kimberley. With English and Latin, both being regarded as languages of civilized communities although differentiated in time, the position was more complicated.

For a time the prevalent view was that an extensive range of inflexion represented the highest stage of linguistic evolution. This was no doubt mainly due to the prestige of the Indo-European classical languages. By contrast with these, English was held to represent a state of decadence; the concept of retrogressive evolution was ready to hand as an analogy in biological theory. Schleicher compared favourably the luxuriant Gothic form *habaidedeima* with its impoverished English relative *had*. At the bottom of the scale was Chinese, which was thought perhaps never to have grown up: it was regarded as a succession of unclassifiable monosyllables and was sometimes said to have 'no grammar' at all.[3]

Towards the end of the nineteenth century the linguistic horizon had become very much widened, and many more non-Indo-European languages had become known to linguists. Languages had usually been grouped typologically into three classes, according to the way in which they displayed the value of a word in the structure of a higher unit: inflexional (Latin, Sanskrit, Russian), agglutinative (Turkish, Hungarian) and isolating (Chinese). This dimension stands out as diagnostic if one

---

[3] See O. Jespersen, *Language: its nature, development and origin*, London: Allen & Unwin, 1922, especially pp. 76–80 and 319 ff.

starts from the classical Indo-European languages and observes differences, whether or not one wishes to impute special merit to any one type. The new horizons, however, encompassed a set of languages which seemed not to fit, particularly some North American Indian languages such as Paiute; they did seem however to fit a fourth class that had been suggested much earlier, that known as 'incorporating'.

But this fourth 'type' disturbed the scale of values. 'Incorporation' looked very much like inflexion run riot; yet it was associated with primitive societies. Moreover it was noticeable that in at least those Indo-European areas where the languages had an accessible history there were numerous instances of inflexion disappearing and being replaced by isolating structures, but very few traces of the opposite process: one of the rare examples of the latter is the inflected future tense of the Romance languages (Italian *prendero* from Late Latin *prendere habeo*). Jespersen thus suggested reversing the order of evolution, and advanced the view that languages progressed from polysynthesis (incorporation) through synthesis (inflexion and agglutination) to analysis (isolation). English now appeared as one of the most favoured Indo-European languages, while the highest stage of all was represented by Chinese and Vietnamese.[4]

Jespersen's view had the advantage that it accorded with more of the observed facts of linguistic history. But his scheme of classification was still based on the same criteria as had been used earlier, which related only to one specific aspect of linguistic patterning, although an important one; and it seems to call for three distinct assumptions, all of which need to be questioned. One is that typological variation results from linguistic change, in the sense that if different 'language types' are found one has evolved from the other; the second is that such change is irreversible, presumably because correlated with social evolution; and the third is that linguistic change, even if shown to be irreversible, is the same thing as progress.

These three assumptions are independent of each other. Even where typological variation *can* be shown to result from linguistic change, such change is not necessarily irreversible. Even where a given change *can* apparently be shown to be irreversible, in the sense that there are instances of *x* being replaced by *y* but none of *y* being replaced by *x*, this may have nothing to do with social evolution: it may merely mean that

---

[4] Jespersen, op cit., esp. pp. 323 ff., 422 ff. For a discussion of the principles of classification see Edward Sapir, *Language: an introduction to the study of speech*, New York: Harcourt Brace, 1921; Harvest Books, 1949, Chap. 6.

this is how languages change if they change at all, whereas a language is, as it were, free to choose whether it will change in respect of a given feature or not. Even if a change does take place, and it appears irreversible, and it seems to be associated with a certain stage of social development, this may still not represent progress *in language*: language might need to change in order to remain where it was, so to speak—in order to continue to operate effectively in a changing social environment.

But the premises on which these assumptions rest have not been demonstrated. There is no firm evidence that the East Asian languages proceeded through a stage of inflexion to reach their present isolating state, and Chinese, which has a known history of some three thousand years, appears more isolating in its earlier periods, having shown some agglutinative tendencies in the last millennium and a half. The number of languages with a known history is very small, but even among these the tendency to change in a particular direction appears only as a probability. The most that can be said is that if a language in a state x changes at all it may be more likely to change towards a state y than towards a state z.

More recently, therefore, most linguists have taken the view that, unless further evidence emerges, we cannot postulate either irreversibility or even a general tendency of linguistic change; and that there are no grounds for thinking of languages as 'progressing' or as developing typologically in a certain way in response to social development. Indeed, typological studies as a whole were for many years rather left out of consideration.[5] Not only was it realized that greater caution was needed in evaluating the existing evidence; more important, perhaps, was the need to accumulate more evidence, both by establishing the facts for a wider variety of languages and by examining these facts with the deeper understanding of language that resulted from advances in descriptive linguistic theory.

This does not mean that linguists ceased to be interested in typological problems as such, but rather that the traditional criteria of classification proved to presuppose too much, as well as being at once too partial and too vague. Even where they did, on the existing evidence, seem to lead to interesting questions—such as whether there was any significance in the fact that no 'polysynthetic' language (and no 'multiple classifying' language, as a 'type' found in Oceania had come to be called) had appeared in a community practising settled agriculture—the validity of

[5] An important recent study is C. E. Bazell: *Linguistic typology*, London: School of Oriental and African Studies, 1958.

these categories as objectively definable 'language types' is very doubtful: Bazell remarked of 'polysynthetic' that it 'deserved the self-
contradictory definition of the Oxford dictionary: "characterized by
combining several words of a sentence into one word"'.[6] The categories
of isolating, agglutinative and inflexional can, as Bazell has shown, be
redefined in such a way as to give a precise and objective foundation to
this original and very real typological dimension. But this still remains
only one of many possible lines of differentiation between languages, and
one moreover where relatively few languages fit squarely into one type.

There is indeed no reason why any one dimension of classification
should be taken as uniquely crucial for typology. This particular dimension is certainly relevant; but it is limited to grammar and centres
around the rank of the word. What the classification reflects, in fact, is
the variable status of the word as a grammatical unit in different languages. Many of the Indo-European languages, which were the
starting-point for this scheme of classification, make a very clear
grammatical distinction between the unit *word* and units of higher rank:
the word is in fact identifiable, in some of its classes at least, by virtue of
its being the unit which carries inflexion. In English and French the
distinction is blurred, which leads to complications in the orthography
(*qu'est-ce que c'est*; *soapdish, soap-dish* or *soap dish*?) which then blur it
still further; in Turkish the word is a phonological unit, as well as being
in general grammatically identifiable by agglutination; whereas in
Chinese the word is definable only by a complex process of grammatical
abstraction.

There is some uncertainty about how far the word has a special status
among the grammatical units. The fact that it is not a constant—that the
word is not 'the same thing' in different languages—does not confer
special status on it, since this is simply an aspect of a general truth
applicable to all units; the use of the same names merely implies that
there is something in common, and the term 'word' tends to be used as
the name for that grammatical unit which in the language concerned
most frequently also carries lexical meaning. But this is not a grammatical
criterion; and in some languages it is difficult to know to which, if any,
of the grammatical units the name 'word' should be applied. It is safe
to say that the word has not so clearly unique and dominant a status in
the grammar that it can be the sole concern even of a purely grammatical
typology; and there are other levels to be taken into account besides
grammar.

---

[6] Bazell, op. cit., p. 18; cf. Sapir, op. cit., p. 128.

Typological studies today, therefore, while, like all linguistic studies, they have developed out of the work of previous scholars in the field, have perhaps four important characteristics in which they differ from the earlier approach. First, the criteria of classification have become more rigorous, thanks to advances in descriptive linguistic theory and method. Second, typological statements are made purely descriptively, without any assumption of patterned change in language or of social causality and without judgements of progress and decay. Third, in addition to the original dimension of isolating-agglutinative-inflexional, other criteria, both within grammar and at other levels, are taken into account. Fourth, such criteria are applied not to whole languages but to parts of languages: one system in a language may be isolating and another system in the same language agglutinative, or a language may display one type of lexical patterning in its verbs and a different type in its nouns, and so on. In this way a picture can be built up which is both more useful in application, for example to language teaching and machine translation, and more accurate, and therefore able to suggest more interesting questions, in terms of linguistic theory.

Eventually, when enough languages have been described in comparative terms, it may be possible to return to the search for crucial 'type-determining' criteria; we do not know. The fact that a linguist, if he is told what part of the world a language unknown to him comes from, can make guesses about its grammar, lexis and phonology with a fair probability of being right means that he cannot help pursuing his own as it were private typology to explain and codify his 'intuitions', the deductions he makes from linguistic geography and history. It is idle to pretend that such correlations, which we all apply in practice, have no basis in fact, in the actual observations that linguists make of languages. But this does not necessarily mean that they can be generalized systematically. Such generalizations even when made will not of course provide us with 'causes'; but it is of little use speculating about causes until we know what it is that has to be 'explained'.

3

Typology is, so to speak, generalized comparative descriptive linguistics; or generalized 'contrastive' linguistics, to use a term that has come into use, particularly with reference to language teaching, for the comparative description of languages. Comparative description means the comparison of (parts of) two or more languages in respect of how they work, without any reference to the historical consideration of whether they are genetically related or not. It may be of interest here to suggest some of the features in respect of which languages can be compared from this purely descriptive point of view, before we return finally to their implications for typology and the question of exoticism.

If languages are to be compared, they must be described in the same terms according to a general framework for the description of language, or general linguistic theory. A number of different models, with of course a great deal in common, are current in modern linguistics, all of them being valid and useful for different purposes; the formulations adopted here, in those cases where a specific choice has to be made, are based on the theoretical work of J. R. Firth and others, with some modifications in the area of grammar.[7] Some of the ways in which the comparison of languages seems relevant to typology are sketched in the following paragraphs.

In grammar, how many units below the sentence do we require to give the most effective description of the language concerned? Where among these units do we find non-segmental relations (one item inside another, or one item fused with another)? Where do we find 'rankshift' (an item operating with the value of an item of lower rank, as when a clause enters into the structure of a clause or of a group instead of into that of a sentence)?

What elements of structure, and what structures, are displayed by each unit (is there, for example, a distinction between object and complement in the clause)? To what extent, and where, is sequence a structural feature? What recursive structures are there, and where are they found? How far does the language make use of simple (one-element) structures?

What classes of each unit (clause classes, word classes and so on) can be recognized syntactically (that is, according to the operation of the items in the structure of a higher unit)? How far do these syntactic classes correspond to morphological types (groupings of items which are alike in their own structures)? Is there a significant distinction between 'free' and 'bound' (capable, and not capable, of standing alone as a one-element structure of the unit above), and if so where?

---

[7] Cf. Paper 1 above. For an excellent summary of Firth's work see R. H. Robins, 'General linguistics in Great Britain 1930–1960', *Trends in Modern Linguistics*, ed. Christine Mohrmann et al., Utrecht: Spectrum, 1963, pp. 11–37.

Such questions can be asked about any language, and the answers for different languages compared. It is apparent that, to be of interest, comparison implies semantic, or 'contextual', identification. Let us suppose that two languages each display three primary classes operating in clause structure, referred to in the description of these languages as 'verbal group', 'nominal group' and 'adverbial group'; the significance of this formal likeness depends on the semantic equivalence, so that we need to know, for example, what the probability is that a nominal group in Lx will be translatable by a nominal group in Ly. Unless this probability is well above chance, there is no sense in which a single comparative class 'nominal group' can be identified as common to both languages.

Once such an identification is made numerous further questions follow; here by way of example is a set of questions, still within grammar, that might be asked about the (class) nominal (of the unit) group. Some will be special cases of the questions already asked: for example, what elements of structure does it display, and which (if any) occur recursively; what are the word classes operating in its structure, and which are closed and which open? Others will be formulated specifically for this class.

Is there a system, or are there systems, of secondary classes of the noun? If so, are such classes marked phonologically (e.g. nouns ending in --a)? Do they show, and are they shown by, grammatical selection or concord? Have they semantic significance, such as reference to animate, human, abstract; sex, function, shape? Are there any closed classes, such as personal pronouns?

Is there a system of number? If so, what are its terms; are there different number systems associated with different secondary classes of the noun? How is the number system displayed, and is there concord? What is the relation of the number system to numeration (for example, is a plural noun (a) obligatory, (b) optional or (c) excluded in a group containing the numeral 'three')?

What other systems are there in the nominal groups (such as case, possession, determination), and what are their terms? Are all such systems independent (is each term in one system combinable with each term in all the others); if not, what is the extent of dependence among them? Which systems also occur elsewhere than in the nominal group?

Questions of this kind show the importance of linguistic theory in the comparison and typology of languages. It is in the theory that a concept like that of 'system' is defined, and once it is defined anything that is identified as a system in a language has certain properties in respect of which it can vary. One can state the number of terms in the system, and whether or not there is an unmarked term; in a study of texts one can also ask statistical questions, such as the relative probabilities of the terms, and the conditioning of these probabilities either in sequence or in combination with terms in other systems. One can think perhaps of a general typology of language systems.

These are examples from grammar; comparison may refer also to other levels. In the relation of lexis to grammar, how far are the lexical items of the language co-extensive with one particular grammatical unit (are the 'words' of the grammar also the 'words' of the dictionary), and how far do the grammatical classes of this unit also define lexical sets (for example, do the items forming the lexical set of, say, colour terms also form a single grammatical class)? Within lexis: do the items forming a lexical set also form an ordered series (with structure and one element in common, as *oaktree, pinetree* and *beechtree* do but *yesterday, today* and *tomorrow* do not)? Conversely, does the ordered series also constitute a lexical set (as *oaktree, pinetree* and *beechtree* do but *oaktree, shoetree* and *axletree* do not)? In Chinese, for example, they regularly do, whereas in Malay they often do not. Does the lexical set contain an unmarked member? What types of compound lexical items are found?

In phonology, where the patterns have much in common with those of grammar (in the sense that related concepts will account for them), many of the same questions can be asked, *mutatis mutandis*: this includes for example those concerned with general system typology. Other questions are specific to phonology, and to the phonological realization of grammatical and lexical items and relations. What formal contrasts can be directly referred to their phonological exponents (for example, rising tone showing perfective aspect in Cantonese)? To what extent is the language a 'tone language', either in the sense that intonation is used to carry lexical meaning, or in the sense that the phonological unit associated with intonation contrasts is the syllable? In Yoruba, intonation carries both lexical and grammatical meaning; in Mandarin Chinese, intonation systems operate both at the syllable and at a higher unit. What phonetic features operate prosodically, and what is their patterning and extension (for example palatalization in Russian, extending into two syllables from a consonant nucleus)? Are any phonaesthetic series found (such as English *bump clump hump mump(s) rump* etc.)?

These questions illustrate some of the ways in which the apparently unlimited differences among languages might be classifiable. As Sapir wrote, 'if we take our examples freely from the vast storehouse of language ... we find that there is hardly a possibility that is not realized in actual usage'[8]; it is the range of this 'possibility' that linguists seek to define in their theoretical models of language. These provide both a framework within which languages can be compared and at the same time a range of variables any one of which will serve for typological statements. The latter are then partial and restricted: not 'this language is of such-and-such a type', but rather 'in this language this phonological system, or this grammatical structure, has these properties'. Of course not all the variables are wholly independent of each other, and one of the tasks of typology is to discover the areas of dependence.[9] But such dependence is not easy to demonstrate, and emerges most clearly if each language is first 'classified' on a number of distinct dimensions; in this way are displayed both its partial similarity to other languages and, no less important, its uniqueness.

4

Linguistic typology can thus perhaps be regarded as the typology of language features, rather than as the typology of languages. Such a 'feature typology' is relevant to the problem of the exotic in language. Exoticism is potentially a typological concept, although it is not necessarily so: it may not be defined in terms of linguistic features at all, and usage in this respect has varied. Sapir contrasted 'exotic' with 'familiar' languages,[10] this being a cultural rather than a linguistic classification— or rather, to the extent that 'languages familiar to the linguist' is a linguistic concept, it is institutional[11] (concerned with the use of language) rather than descriptive (concerned with the nature of language). Firth similarly used 'exotic' to refer to the language of a community whose culture differed to a marked degree from one's own[12]; here the point of reference may be 'a language in which linguistic studies are normally written', so that for example a Polynesian language will be exotic by reference to English. This can of course be a two-way relation: English and Kiriwinian are 'mutually exotic'. Exoticism in this

[8] Sapir, op. cit., p. 30.
[9] See for example Roman Jakobson, 'Typological studies and their contribution to historical comparative linguistics', *Proceedings of the Eighth International Congress of Linguists*, Oslo: University Press, 1958, pp. 17–25.
[10] Sapir, op. cit., p. 30.
[11] See Trevor Hill, 'Institutional linguistics', *Orbis*, 7, 1958, pp. 441–55.
[12] See e.g. J. R. Firth, 'Ethnographic analysis and language', *Man and culture: an evaluation of the work of Bronislaw Malinowski*, ed. Raymond Firth, London: Routledge & Kegan Paul, 1957, p. 118.

case is independent of whether or not there are marked linguistic differences correlating with the cultural ones: Chinese and Yoruba would be mutually exotic although there are some typological similarities between them, as also Chinese and English.

Another way of defining exoticism is to regard a feature as exotic if it is found only in a small number of languages. This is again an institutional linguistic criterion, depending on language community and not on the nature of language; but it substitutes 'rare' for 'unfamiliar'. The difficulty is that, however we define 'a language' here (presumably also institutionally, as 'what the language community regards as being "its language"'), there are, to quote Swadesh, 'probably far more than a thousand distinct Amerindian languages, and if classified into groups comparable to the Germanic or Slavic, there would probably be 200 or more—counting, of course, isolated languages not assignable to such families'.[13] We should need to count languages rather than language groups, since otherwise English and German would have to be treated as identical; so we are left with the figure of over a thousand. Now the point is not that Amerindian languages *ought to* be shown to be exotic, but that on this criterion no feature shared by even a quarter of them *could* be regarded as exotic, since even if it appeared nowhere else it would be found in nearly ten per cent of the world's languages. To take into account the number of speakers would be equally unsatisfactory, since Chinese is spoken by about one-sixth of the world's population and English by nearly one-tenth, so that any feature found *only* in Chinese or *only* in English would be excluded from appearing as rare. Neither of these criteria of rareness seems to define anything that is of any interest.

It would be worth considering whether exoticism could be defined descriptively, that is linguistically in the strict sense: by reference to the properties of the particular feature of language that is concerned. This may most easily be discussed through an illustration. A form cited from Classical Japanese is *kirashimeraru-bekarazaredomo*, translated 'though I should not have been caused to cut' and classified as 'oblique actual concessive passive causative negative potential'.[14] With this might be compared the verbal group in the English clause *he'll have been going to be taking over from me every day for a fortnight soon*: describable as

---

[13] Morris Swadesh, 'Perspectives and problems of Amerindian comparative linguistics', *Linguistics Today*, ed. André Martinet and Uriel Weinreich, New York: Linguistic Circle of New York, 1954, p. 186.

[14] Basil Hall Chamberlain, *A Simplified grammar of the Japanese language*, Chicago: University Press, 1924, p. 62.

'present in future in past in future finite non-modal non-contrastive positive active'. Both items are characterized by the selection, in one structure, of terms from a number of different systems, as reflected in the long string of labels. The same number of selections, apart from the recursive tense, is also made in the English *he took over*: 'past finite non-modal non-contrastive positive active'.

Here we have a descriptive feature which may, if objectively definable, be of typological interest. It could perhaps be formulated as 'number of independent systems from which selection is made by a given class'. The English (class) verbal (of the unit) group can be described as choosing for finiteness (and, if finite, for modality), tense (at least once, with the possibility of recursion), emphasis (contrastive/non-contrastive), polarity (positive/negative) and voice (active/passive); and all these choices are independent of each other. In comparing it with the Japanese form it is important to know whether the same is true of the latter: whether each label represents a grammatical (closed) choice and there is, for example, a non-causative form in contrast with this one. Given that such questions can be answered, it would be pertinent to ask what is the total range, that we find in language, in the number of grammatical systems from which a class makes independent selection at the same time.

The minimum is of course one; let us postulate that the maximum that we find, or the maximum that we find with a given class (since this may be significant), is eight. Put in terms of the number of forms displayed by the class, since each combination of choices implies a separate form, this would mean that, if all systems were binary (to cite the simplest case), classes could be found with up to 2^8 different forms. Classes with eight systems, or with six and above, might be regarded as 'exotic' simply because they represented the extreme of the range of possibilities known to occur. It is here, however, that the concept of the 'rare' should perhaps be introduced; if the distribution of classes among the eight possibilities is uneven, and those with seven and eight systems are very rare, then the fact that these values lie at the extreme is more likely to be significant. Exoticism might then perhaps be defined as the concurrence of the rare and the extreme.

Of the many cautions with which such a formulation should be hedged about, three in particular may be mentioned. First, it is all too easy to make practically anything look exotic simply by the way it is described and labelled; here, it would need to be ensured that the choices are truly contrastive and independent and that the forms implied actually exist. Second, there are many different ways of describing a feature, especially a complex one such as those illustrated, all of which may be correct, in the sense that they account for the facts[15]; it is important to ensure that the descriptions used are congruent and that, where alternatives are available, the simplest ones are chosen for comparison. Third, we must be aware that we have still not explained anything. We have merely postulated that features displaying extreme values in respect of certain properties may be worth noticing because this may lead to interesting further questions: for example, is there any difficulty in choosing, or in learning to choose, simultaneously within each of so many grammatical systems? is such a feature unstable, in the sense that it has less persistence through time than other grammatical features? is it more than usually subject to dialectal variation?

Only a limited range of linguistic features can be examined from the point of view suggested here; but these include many of those with which the search for the exotic is traditionally and intuitively associated. Examples from grammar are concord, range of choice, depth, and various forms of 'ambiguity' such as polysemism and polymorphism. Concord is the multiple exponence of grammatical categories, and we can ask how many times a single category may be discretely shown in the same structure: there are six occurrences of the noun-class prefix in Enindiljaugwa *ni-miebina nini-miigara nana-mamalja na-ŋaba ni-duruŋana niŋeeni-riŋga* 'What is the name of that big man I saw?',[16] and seven exponents of instrumental case in the nominal group in the Russian *oni prijechali s dvumja stami pjatjudesjatju tremja belymi lošad'mi* 'they came with 253 white horses'. Range of choice refers to the number of terms in a system, the number of contrastive possibilities among which a choice is made at a particular place in structure. Depth is the degree of recursion attained in a recursive structure, such as the piling up of qualifiers in the English *the towel at the back of the drawer in the cupboard behind the door into the passage*; here the interest lies not so much in the limit of depth tolerated, which is often (though not always) merely probabilistic and therefore measurable only in texts, but in the extent to which such recursive structures combine with others, recursive and non-recursive. Polysemism and polymorphism are familiar as features of inflexional systems, but extend beyond these: polysemism may be

[15] Barbara M. H. Strang, for example, describes the English verb phrase (=verbal group) in terms of eleven variables, excluding person and number; see her *Modern English structure*, London: Edward Arnold, 1962, Chap. 8.

[16] See A. Capell, 'Languages of Arnhem Land, North Australia', *Oceania* 12, 1941-42, pp. 364-392. The language is also known as Andiljaugwa.

applicable for example to the structure of English nominal compounds such as *paper chase*, *damp course*, *baby sitter*, *colour bar*, since ambiguity can arise as in *gas mask* (to allow, or to prevent, the inhalation of gas?).[17]

Each of these and other such features calls for its own cautions and reservations. In concord, for example, it is not always easy to decide how many discrete exponents of a given category occur, and whether or not what is being expounded is 'the same category'. Moreover concord is often associated with a high degree of polymorphism and polysemism, as in the nominal group in German and Old English, so that no single exponent may serve to identify the category concerned. In other words, statements such as 'in this language the nominal group can only select once for number and case, but it makes this selection in *n* different places' are rarely as clearcut as they seem. Similarly in assessing the number of terms in a system it needs to be ensured that they really are in choice relation, and not merely the members of a paradigm: how many of the sixteen cases of the Finnish noun can occur with one and the same value in structure? With regard to polymorphism, Russian can be shown to have nine different ways of marking genitive plural in the noun; but English, in one account, has fifty-three ways of showing past tense in the verb. Quite apart from the considerable reduction in polymorphism that can often be brought about by a prosodic analysis of the phonology, one needs to take into account the number of terms in the system: the Russian genitive plural would pass unnoticed if the noun had only two cases.

Finally, there is the general caution about value judgements. Recently there has been some tendency for these to creep back into statements about language under cover of information theory, with the concept of 'redundancy' that this involves. Redundancy in information theory has of course no evaluative connotations, and many linguists have been careful to point out that this is equally true when the concept is applied to language: redundancy is an inherent property of language structure—in fact it is presupposed by the very concept of structure. But unless the term is kept strictly to its mathematical sense, within information theory, where it is a measure of the non-equiprobability of terms in systems (and therefore applicable only in *textual* studies of language), its use may lead to misunderstanding.

To take an example: concord has sometimes been regarded as an

[17] See Robert B. Lees, *The grammar of English nominalizations*, Bloomington: Indiana University Research Center in Anthropology, Folklore and Linguistics, Publication 12, 1960; The Hague: Mouton, 1963.

instance of redundancy. This could not be justified by reference to information theory, and it ignores the fact that concord is itself potentially and variably meaningful: it may define the limits of a certain structure, or it may display, either alone or in combination with another feature, the relation between one element in a structure and another. It is difficult to find an objective criterion of such 'redundancy', and certainly impossible to measure it. But it is all too easy to read into the term an implication that something is unnecessary and expendable, and thus to suggest that the language is guilty of 'inefficiency'. Those concerned with language statistics need to be especially on their guard against turning very partial measurements into sweeping evaluations.

The basic problem is that language has too many variables. When a language is described, it appears as a complex of relations constraining, and in fact defining, a set of categories to which the items of the language are referable as exponents; since no single set of such relations is isolated from the total multidimensional continuum, the concept of 'a feature' is highly artificial. This does not matter in description, where the aim is to show how each language works and the model is devised precisely to account for the properties of language. But for typology it is necessary to postulate features, and the problem is then, when comparing them, to identify and give due weight to the relevant aspects of their environment. This explains the tone of hesitation which, it is hoped, pervades the present paper. If the general picture seems negative and inconclusive, this may serve to warn against too facile judgements on the divergencies and vagaries of language.

Eleven

Patterns and ranges (1961)

Grammarians tend to be occupied primarily with the establishment and description of allowed patterns and with the rejection of whatever falls outside these.[1] Some way of looking at language in which a distinction is made between grammar and lexis seems to be necessary if the patternings are to be economically stated or defined. For there is a difference between speaking about the eligibility of a particular *class of unit*[2] in some place or places in the grammatical structure of a language and about the eligibility of *exponents* of that class of unit in such a place or places in a particular sentence. And we can only preserve the simplicity of our grammatical description if we are prepared from the start to let it be understood that there are lexical factors, factors of collocational[3] eligibility, which (in different ways to be considered later) tend to rule out of actual use a large number of 'sentences' (and smaller units) even

[1] For criteria of 'grammaticalness', see especially Noam Chomsky, *Syntactic Structures*, The Hague, 1957, pp. 15 ff. *Additional note.* For subsequent discussion and further references see *The Structure of Language*, ed. Jerry A. Fodor and Jerrold J. Katz, New Jersey, 1964 especially p. 384 ff. and 400 ff.; Noam Chomsky, *Aspects of the Theory of Syntax*, M.I.T. Press, 1965; L. J. Cohen, 'On a concept of degree of grammaticalness', *Logique et Analyse* No. 30, June 1965, p. 141.

[2] See M. A. K. Halliday, 'Categories of the Theory of Grammar' sections 3.1 and 5.1, *Word* 17.3, 1961. The present paper owes much to the stimulus of Dr Halliday's remarks on grammar and lexis, especially in sections 2.1, 6.3, 7.3–4, 8.1, and in private discussion. I take this opportunity of expressing my thanks also to two other colleagues, J. M. Sinclair and J. P. Thorne, for helpful comments on an earlier draft of this paper, which was presented in February 1961 at a staff seminar at the School (now Department) of Applied Linguistics, Edinburgh University.

[3] For the term 'collocation', see J. R. Firth, *Papers in Linguistics 1934–51*, Oxford, 1957, 194 ff., and *Studies in Linguistic Analysis*, Oxford, 1957, p. 11. The distinction between collocational and grammatical criteria is considered in paper 9 of this volume, p. 151ff.

though these seem to conform to all the rules of grammatical pattern. Grammarians do not, generally speaking, much concern themselves with the rejection of such 'sentences' as these, for whatever short-comings they may have are considered to be grammatically irrelevant and more a matter for the lexicologist. There are of course marginal cases in the judgement of which the grammarian may feel doubtful whether he has or has not a claim to be involved; this is a difficult matter, to which I call attention but which I do not care to pursue.

In all this there are certain similarities between the problem of evaluating words and that of evaluating larger structural units, such as sentences. Is *histle* a word in English? Or *geed* or *plint*? The answer is that they are not, but we do not make it because we can indicate some lack of eligibility from the point of view of pattern or allowed shape. Their not being words has something to do with no referent ever having been associated with them.[4] We may say that they could be adopted as words if the need for extra words happened to arise; they have an orthographic (and implied phonological) shape which makes them eligible for such adoption, and it might be said to be a mere matter of chance whether this or that particular exponent 'exists' or not. On the other hand *brdliou* or *pdilb* are ineligible as English words because they would not be exponents with an allowed shape.

At the rank of the sentence something of the same sort occurs. *The flaming waste-paper basket snored violently* awaits only, as we might put it, a need for its use, and it would not be difficult to devise one, e.g. to construct a fairy tale to fit it into.[5] It answers in this sense to *histle* or *geed* or *plint*. But *Twenty because tomorrow the had a it* can have no use as a sentence. It therefore answers to *brdliou* or *pdilb*. Finally, we should note, we have obviously genuine sentences like *Jane has just come in* or *The old man seems to have gone out of his mind*, just as we have obviously genuine words like *basket* or *though*.

But it is worth while asking what it is that leads us to label these obviously genuine, and whether our criteria for passing judgement on words are the same as for passing judgement on sentences. When I say

[4] A formal indication of this being the case is that they would collocate no better or worse with one word than with another. And if, by the imposition of a *grammatical* restriction, we were told that *plint* was to be assessed as a noun, there would still, for example, be no adjectives which we felt to be more appropriate or less appropriate than any others to qualify it. Cf. footnote 11, p. 189.

[5] An interesting lexical study could be made of the shifts of meaning undergone by words in fairy tales. An important point would be the very limited group of words so affected, all the rest remaining more or less stable and 'normal'.

that *basket* and *though* are words, it is because I know from experience that they play some kind of role that I regard as sufficiently typical of words to justify their being so labelled; I remember having used them in this sort of way or having heard them or seen them written. But in evaluating sentences the situation is rather different, because I am usually prepared to pronounce on the genuineness of a sentence even when I cannot recall having used it or heard it or seen it written. Thus (even if these circumstances pertain) I still have no hesitation in maintaining that *Jane has just come in* is a genuine sentence.

So it would seem that there is a difference in my attitudes here. I can never say: 'Though I cannot recall ever having used it or heard it or seen it before, *basket* is certainly a word.'[6] But with something which I am evaluating as a sentence I am not worried by the question: 'Have I ever encountered this alleged sentence before?'[7] It is sufficient that I should somehow be satisfied that this sequence of words, taken as a sentence, would make perfectly good sense in some situation (or perhaps a large number of situations) which I can describe or envisage. Dictates of grammatical pattern obviously come in here, but in evaluating e.g. *Jane has just come in* I have certain additional requirements in mind. I shall return to these later.

We should note that the problems I am considering crop up only rarely in the day-to-day interchanges of accomplished users of a language. For such people use for the most part only sequences of genuine words; it is by no means usual for non-words like *histle* or *plint* to be found dotted here and there among them; similarly such people use only sentences and normally avoid non-sentences. Nevertheless these problems assert themselves in our dealings with children and other learners of the language, so that many of us do encounter them; they are not mere theoretical possibilities. And we can say that we are at once suspicious or on our guard if we encounter, posing as a word, a form which we have never encountered so doing before, whereas we are continually confronted by sentences which we willingly accept as such though we have never been confronted by them before. When we sit in judgement on sentences, we certainly require first of all to be satisfied as to grammatical pattern; this criterion is enough in itself to put *Twenty because tomorrow*

[6] I may of course encounter a hitherto unfamiliar form, e.g. in a technical work, and decide that it is a word, simply because I am persuaded that it would not otherwise occur, still less recur, in this work. But this is a different matter.

[7] As elsewhere, I am assuming here that the sentence under scrutiny consists of one or more morphemes whose status as such is not in question.

the had a it outside the pale at once. But there are some sequences of words which satisfy our demands about pattern and which nevertheless we may hesitate to call sentences; they are not (it seems to me) all acceptable, and of those that are, some are more obviously acceptable than others.

We may consider some examples. We can pronounce in favour of *Jane has just come in* without hesitation. *The flaming waste-paper basket snored violently* is perhaps less readily acceptable, at least by the man in the street; he is likely to object that the situations where it would be appropriate are so few as to be negligible. This kind of consideration has linguistic importance of a statistical kind, but it scarcely entitles anyone to deny to our example the status of sentence. In any case we should certainly not object to it in the same kind of way as to *Twenty because tomorrow the had a it*. Are we then to say simply that we have three grades: the readily acceptable, the rarely needed but acceptable, and the impossible? And that, before we can unreservedly write off a sequence of words as a non-sentence, it must have the characteristic our last example has, of being grammatically unacceptable? I do not think that we can proceed in this way; even a detailed treatment of our three examples or of any similar ones would not cover the situation adequately. For there are other problematic cases of a rather different order.

Let us take the sequence *The molten postage feather scored a weather*. Does this, like the waste-paper-basket sentence,[8] only await a need for its use, or is there some objection to it that we could not make to the other? We can hardly object to it on the grounds of pattern, in the sense I have been using this term, for it corresponds in this respect to readily acceptable sentences such as *The aged chemistry professor caused a sensation*. Nevertheless it differs from the waste-paper-basket sentence in one quite fundamental way. For we cannot easily, to put it in everyday terms, 'attach enough meaning' to *the molten postage feather* or to *scored a weather* to be able to conceive of any situation (in a fairy tale or elsewhere) where it might be appropriate.[9] This is a way of saying that words have only a certain tolerance of compatibility, only a certain *potential of*

[8] The great rarity of the collocation *waste-paper-basket sentence* must put us on our guard against a possible misconception. A very rare collocation may be perfectly clear in the appropriate context and may not involve us in any agonizing speculations about possible radical shifts of meaning of one or other of the words in it.

[9] The only situation that I can think of (other than in a paper about language) where it would be wholly appropriate would be on the lips of someone in a pathological state of mind, e.g. in a delirium, where regularity of grammatical pattern and eccentricity of collocation often go together.

collocability, quite apart from any considerations of pattern in the grammatical sense. It need hardly be said that the edges of this range of tolerance are vague and unstable, and that the question of what we mean by compatibility is a complicated one.

We can look at the matter of collocability from two different points of view. In the first we judge according to whether a word (to take the simplest sort of case, where we focus our attention on one only as being the oddity) achieves the purpose we suppose it to be intended to be carrying out in a particular context. Thus in a certain real-life situation I may object to *bitter* and demand its replacement by *sour* when someone says to me, *This lemon* (which we have just cut in two and are both sucking) *is bitter*. I am not thereby denying the possibility of lemons ever being bitter, but I am maintaining that *bitter* is certainly no adjective to use to describe this lemon: I am charging my companion with a lexical lapse. If he had said *This lemon is sweet*, I should probably not, curiously enough, have questioned his linguistic competence, but have doubted rather his gustatory judgement or even his sanity. But if he uses the word *bitter*, I may well assume that his reaction to the taste of the lemon more or less coincides with mine; so if I object I am then accusing him of the misuse of a word.

In cases like this collocation of *bitter* and *lemon* we encounter an extremely common problem of applied linguistics which tends to be pushed into the background by descriptive linguists. They handle a corpus of many possible sentences which, in varying degrees of detail, they classify according to, or use to illustrate, the characteristics of the structure and of the system of the text or the language under analysis. But what is usually quite taken for granted is that the reader (or listener) will without question accept all these sentences as such; it is more or less left to him, if he so wishes, to work out for himself a context or contexts into which they will fit. Apart from any shortcomings of this approach from the standpoint of learning a language, there is a theoretical consideration here. If one sentence differs significantly from another even though their structure is the same, this is a *linguistic* difference. And if a description merely lists them as alternative exponents of the same structure and says nothing in lexical terms about the nature of the difference, it is for no better reason than that descriptions of this kind are mostly made by grammarians and not lexicologists. A merely grammatical description is no more a complete linguistic description than is a merely lexical one.

This needs to be kept in mind more than it is by those who are primarily preoccupied with grammatical structures as such. For even in grammar, the choice of one structure rather than another or of one member of a paradigm rather than of another is significant, so critical a matter indeed that it can on occasion be a matter of life or death. Yet a great deal which follows from this is entirely taken for granted and passed over in descriptive grammars. Both from the grammatical and the collocational point of view there is for the user of a language a continual problem of decision in such matters, an incessant process of choice or selection from a number of alternatives. For him it is clearly not enough to be able to 'create' or 'generate' an unlimited number of 'good' sentences, i.e. sentences all of which would be appropriate in imaginable contexts. It should not therefore be beneath the dignity of the linguist to try to understand the strictly linguistic problems which are connected with the final selection of particular clusters of lexical items in particular grammatical patterns in a given instance of a sentence as used in a live situation.

The second way of looking at the matter of collocability is the one we have been following in the previous pages. In evaluating a collocation, we often tend to assess it without reference to a given context, and to pass judgement on it according to whether we can imagine a possible setting or settings into which we could appropriately insert it. This, of course, gives us much greater scope and allows us to toy with various possibilities of 'meaning' of one or more of the words involved in a way which would not be feasible if we were tied to a single contextualized instance. Thus, without such restriction, I can easily find numerous suitable settings for *This lemon is sweet*, e.g. where two women are discussing different fabrics for a cushion cover, or where somebody is exclaiming over a child's painting of still life.[10] I shall proceed on the assumption that this kind of scrutiny is perfectly legitimate and try to show that it has its own merits. But it is not at all the same thing as evaluating an instance of a collocation in an actual context.

We come now to a rather critical point. Do we, in judging the eligibility of collocations, use the sort of criteria we used for the eligibility of words, or those we used for the eligibility of sentences ? Since, in all these cases, it offers more scope to pronounce on their eligibility in possible contexts which we are free to excogitate, rather than in some given context, I shall adopt here the second or general rather than the first or particular

---

[10] *Additional note.* Professor Dwight Bolinger begs me not to overlook the further simple fact that *sweet* may with perfect propriety be applied literally to *ripe* lemons—at least to those grown in California.

approach. And for the sake of clarity I shall simplify the question of criteria somewhat by assuming throughout that we are working within the bounds of well defined syntactic units about whose grammatical structure we are not in doubt. In this way we shall get as little involved as possible in irrelevant syntactical complications, and there will thus be no question of this or that collocation being ineligible because it fails to satisfy the requirements of grammatical pattern.

The answer to our question must certainly be that we do not write off collocations as impossible simply because we have never encountered them before. For if we did, we could not give our blessing to any new sentence except one which was made up, by some different permutation, of old familiar phrases. And even here we should have to say that those *phrases* collocated in a new way and could not therefore be legitimately juxtaposed. Nevertheless we certainly do not give our blessing to all sequences of words or phrases, however acceptable they may be grammatically. So it is still not clear how we are able to decide in favour of one collocation and to reject another. For instance one may balk at *the molten postage feather* as a fit subject for any sentence. Yet one may have no difficulty in accepting *the aged chemistry professor* as perfectly reasonable, even though, in the experience of many of us, it may not have the advantage over the other of having been encountered before. And those to whom it is not new, did they not once encounter it for the first time, and did they not accept it there and then?

In taking different attitudes towards these two sequences we rely, I suggest, not only on the test of familiarity, but on criteria of pattern. But the underlying patterns which are relevant here are of a quite different order from the grammatical patterning of which I have spoken hitherto. Hereafter I shall therefore distinguish this new kind by speaking of *range*, using 'pattern' only in relation to grammar. There is for instance a range, however laborious it may be to define or describe, which is represented by the fairly strictly limited inventory of nouns which may without any question be qualified by the word *molten*. The set of alternative available possibilities which this inventory consists of is just as much a part of the form of the language as is a grammatical system, and a full account of this set goes a long way towards constituting the meaning of *molten*.[11] Now this meaning itself rests (though it will of

[11] Another way of saying this is that if there were no restrictions on the collocability of *molten* (or any other word we may care to select), it would then have no meaning other than 'grammatical', i.e. what it had by virtue of whatever restrictions there still were as to the places in grammatical structure it was eligible to occupy. Cf. footnote 4, p. 184.

course depend on other collocational relationships as well) to a consider-able extent on a certain similarity of meaning of all the nouns in ques-tion[12]; this, in turn, is merely another way of saying that there are marked similarities between the collocational habits of each and all of these.[13] Therefore if (ignoring *postage* for the moment) an attempt is made to collocate *molten* with a noun of a quite different 'family'[14] (that is, one with a very different set of collocational habits) such as *feather*, the only experience we can fall back on to deal with it is experience of that aspect of linguistic form which in one way or another has to do with the phenomenon of range.

Confronted with *molten feather* we are likely to attempt to draw on this experience. We shall do so both for its direct bearing on these two words and for what it can provide for us in the way of other previously encountered words and collocations which in one way or another may seem analogous. According to our personal experience and how we draw upon it, we may react in at least three different ways:

1. We may write the whole thing off as meaningless.

2. Because we recall having encountered this kind of possibility before, we may search around for some hitherto unexperienced meaning of one or other of the two words, in the hope that this single adjustment will put everything right. Thus *molten pig* would become clear to a child when (but only when) he became aware of the relevant meaning of *pig*. So we might seek to discover or postulate some similar use of *feather* with a subrange of collocability which (though it was hitherto unknown to us) would at once align it with that group of nouns which may be qualified by the word *molten*. In particular we might examine hopefully the rare use where *feather* designates a kind of iron wedge used for splitting stones.[15] Alternatively (clutching at another quite different formal characteristic of the language) we might seek to discover some connection between *molten* and *moult* which would lead to our being satisfied with the collocation.

[12] Or perhaps rather what Ludwig Wittgenstein calls 'a complicated network of similarities overlapping and criss-crossing: sometimes overall similarities, sometimes similarities of detail.' See *Philosophical Investigations*, Vol. I, Oxford, 1953, p. 66.

[13] It need not, incidentally, disturb us if some words seem to have more than one range, such as a dictionary would signalize by listing separate meanings in a succession of sub-headings. This is precisely what we must expect, and we may often find it convenient to divide our range into sub-ranges as circumstances and our intentions suggest.

[14] Wittgenstein, op. cit., Vol. I, p. 67.

[15] See the *Oxford English Dictionary* s.v. *feather* sb. 16b.

Another related approach would be to decide that no amount of adjustment of this sort with respect to one of the words would be sufficient, and to try to tackle *molten feather* in the light of such phrases as *Bloody Mary* or *black velvet* or *cat's eyes* or *red herring*, on the hypothesis that our difficulty may well spring from the fact that, as in so many other cases, the lexical item and the word are not coextensive.

3. In accordance with an intuitive understanding of 'range-extending' tendencies which are characteristic of language,[16] we may seek to read into one or the other of the words some plausible extension of a familiar meaning, i.e. an extension of collocational range which we might be ready to accept on account of analogous phenomena with which we are already familiar in connection with other words, particularly other words whose collocational habits associate them fairly closely with *molten* itself.

Thus we know that *flaming, burning, incandescent,* and others have, for whatever reason, a broader range of collocation than that which we have hitherto associated with *molten*. We might therefore seek to interpret *molten* in some such terms as 'radiant liquefaction', arguing perhaps that if Herrick can use *liquefaction* of Julia's clothes, then a hotted-up version of the same image may well be applied here to *feather*. Whatever we may do on these lines, we shall be attempting to understand our collocation by postulating an extension of range for which we can find reasonably close parallels.

In practice, of course, in coming to a conclusion on any of these lines about *molten feather* in an actual instance, we should always be guided by collocational evidence of a more varied sort. What this molten feather 'is' (if it is anything) will be decided not only on the basis of possibilities we can think of in the various ways suggested above, but also on the basis of such evidence as the kind of verb our phrase is in subject relation with, and numerous similar factors. For the assessment of a collocation in the last resort involves in one way or another all other lexical items in the context, and there is scarcely a limit to the remove at which these may affect our interpretation of the word we happen to be specially preoccupied with. Furthermore various circumstances in the situational context are likely to be relevant.

There is, fortunately, no need for us to come to a final conclusion

[16] There are of course pattern-extending tendencies also, which amounts to saying that grammar does not remain fixed either, but we are not concerned with these here; they form an ill-explored branch of the history of English. Cf. footnote 19, p. 196.

about the validity of *molten postage feather* or of *scored a weather*, each judged in isolation, but there would be few who would accept these in a subject-predicate relationship; in other words, this 'sentence' must be judged in a way quite differently from our waste-paper-basket sentence. And if (as seems likely) we reject it, it is because of departures from tolerated ranges of collocability, and neither because it violates pattern on the one hand nor because it 'only awaits a need' on the other.

It is always dangerous to assert that a short sequence of this sort could in no circumstances constitute an acceptable sentence, but longer sequences can easily be produced which would daunt the most ingenious devisers of plausible contexts. And an account of a situation where even the present example might grudgingly be given acceptance would almost certainly involve at the same time the postulating, for certain of the lexical items, of meanings for which there was nowhere any previous evidence. The fictional situation devised would have to include 'meanings' which, however plausible, were themselves also fictional. In other words no mere description of a context for our example will in itself clear up anything; we shall be asked at the same time to accept that in this context these lexical items have certain rather odd meanings. And we shall run the risk of overlooking the purely fictional nature of these alleged meanings, partly through being spellbound by the oddity of the situation described, and partly because it will have been specifically designed to make the meanings as plausible as possible.

It is typical of such cases that even though every effort is made to invent a situation which will do least violence to the use of lexical items, it is impossible to invent one in which no violence is done at all. In such a case this feature of oddity of use of lexical items must itself therefore be accepted as one of the characteristics or ingredients of the situation which has been devised. I would suggest that we do not encounter this kind of difficulty when dealing with the waste-paper-basket sentence, because we feel that there is nothing in it which is beyond our normal experience of 'range-extending' tendencies.

With these matters in mind, let us turn to the question of what goes on in the matter of collocations when language is actually being used. When we speak or write, we have to strike a rather delicate balance. If we stick entirely to familiar collocations, then, to put it mildly, we run a grave risk of being trite. Indeed we can only escape this danger by departing from the familiar at some dimension or other, phrase, clause, or whatever it may be; anything new we have to say will demand this. It is important to stress the word 'dimension'. For different users of language (and indeed different traditional styles of language) vary as to the point at which they tend to kick off into the void; below a certain dimension their collocations may be very 'ordinary', but the collocation of these collocations may be much more daring and unusual.[17]

At whatever point we kick off, if we depart too far from some sort of tolerated range we run the risk of being obscure. The balance we have to strike is therefore between triteness and obscurity. I am not concerned here with the somewhat similar way in which one can be cautious or daring about grammatical patterns. But I wish to note this similarity and to point out that collocational caution or abandon and grammatical caution or abandon may or may not march in step. For instance, my colleague Dr Halliday has made me aware of the contrast there is in many poems of W. B. Yeats between the normality of most of his grammatical patterns and the unusualness of many of his collocations. When something of this sort is going on, the possibility of a fairly precise analytical way of handling it is clearly of importance for anyone making an approach to the analysis of style.

So, to put the matter with considerable crudity, we can already say on this basis that there is the possibility of four obviously distinct stylistic modes: normal collocations and normal grammar, unusual collocations and normal grammar, normal collocations and unusual grammar, unusual collocations and unusual grammar. This of course is only a beginning. For that which is collocationally unusual may or may not involve individual words which are themselves unusual; contrast *flaming waste-paper basket* with *indesinent hebetude*. And we should make a distinction between that which is normal in the sense of 'already familiar' and in the sense of 'not hitherto encountered but normal according to criteria of range'; I shall give an example of this kind of collocation later. I do not propose to elaborate here on these stylistic modes and their variations; I merely suggest them as part of a useful basic framework with the help of which, it seems to me, one might profitably explore many fundamental stylistic problems.

[17] It is in contexts like this that it is useful to keep in mind the distinction between the general and the special approach. One might say for example that *sour lemon* is a familiar enough collocation but that if the whole phrase is used in an unfamiliar context its impact may be considerable, e.g. if I use it in reference to my uncle. Strictly speaking, then, it seems that we should distinguish between familiarity from the point of view of the forms involved and from the point of view of the referent. In practice this is not important, because (unless 'uncle' figures only in the situational context and not in the text) at the dimension where we are dealing with *uncle* and *sour lemon* as themselves a collocation, we shall already have made a distinct step towards the unusual.

The question of the limitations imposed on *choice* by the dictates of tolerated range is one of some interest. Since we are dealing with collocations, I am not primarily concerned here with the choice or use of the intrinsically rare word and the numerous different reasons there may be for such a choice. Nevertheless this is an important aspect of style and it is worth while to keep in mind the various effects intended or achieved by the use of such words. We might note likewise of different kinds of intrinsically rare grammatical patterns that the effects achieved by these too may be very diverse. For here, as with vocabulary, a given peculiarity of this sort may be one of many different kinds and the effect or 'flavour' will vary accordingly. This of course is a commonplace and would not be worth mentioning were it not that such problems, despite being familiar, are rarely if ever subjected to rigorous scrutiny within a proper analytical framework.

In pursuing a little further the question of collocations, normal and unusual, I shall take the position that the meanings a given word has (however we may define meaning) are in some direct way associated with our experience of that word in a variety of contexts, our association of that word with other words which have, in our experience, a somewhat similar range, and our association of the word with other words of similar shape, often but not always etymologically related. Such similarly shaped words may well play diverse grammatical roles, so they will not necessarily have at all the same range; the association, by thus straddling grammar, may therefore lead us to draw conclusions about a word with one such range from another with another range.

The experience and associative habits of no two people are exactly the same, though we tend to have a good deal in common with others in all this for the obvious reason that we necessarily share much of our linguistic experience with them. Even so there are notable discrepancies, as we may gather from the chastening experience of looking at a large dictionary, which tells us something of the combined lexical habits of many people. In so doing, it lists sometimes words of which I have had no previous experience, sometimes words which turn out to be capable of meaning things I did not know they could, i.e. which can stand in certain collocational relationships of which I was hitherto unaware. We should also note that the dictionary does not accept anything that falls below a certain generality of experience: it does not cover those private (e.g. family) words or collocations which are only shared within a small circle. And of course it cannot provide us, by paraphrase or definition or in any other way, with anything like all the numerous delicately discriminated shades of meaning which a word may have in (say) ten thousand different instances. All it can do is to list (and perhaps connect) different meanings in rough classes, each class representing what I call a *use*, i.e. a group of instances classed together because the meaning therein seems to require or justify a definition or paraphrase different from that of some other class.

Broadly speaking, I would regard a normal collocation as one which, when we encounter it, we can readily assign to one or another of the classes with which we, as well as the larger dictionaries in their overtly more ordered fashion, in some sense operate. By 'readily' I mean without any feeling that by so doing we are in any striking or significant way extending (as distinct from so to speak filling in) that class by admitting our instance to membership. I use the words 'normal' and 'unusual' rather than 'familiar' and 'unfamiliar' because the latter would tend to imply that we required some yardstick of previous experience of the instance itself; this, as I have suggested, is not the case. Previous experience of this sort does indeed validate some collocations which, judged purely on some rather vague criterion of normal expected range, might otherwise appear odd (e.g. *He was in a blue funk*), just as it validates instances of some rather odd grammatical patterns (e.g. *He came a cropper*).[18] But this particular kind of experience is not the crucial factor in many cases.

For, to go back to a point made earlier, absence of previous experience —for instance of *rhododendron bush* and *died* as exponents of a subject-predicate relationship—does not prevent me from saying with complete confidence in an appropriate situation: *The rhododendron bush died.* As I have suggested, there are complicated rules of range operating here which are based on a knowledge on our part of the 'kind of verb' which can serve as a predicate to what we might describe, if we spoke of it at all, as 'this sort of subject'. There is of course, for such knowledge, a basis of experience of instances. If we have not actually noted down all previously encountered examples bearing on this problem, we must still recognize the relevance here of the notebook of memory. But there is a further element in our knowledge than that implied by the mere possession of an inventory of instances; this we should not overlook any more than we should overlook, in the field of grammar, the importance of a knowledge which is more than mere crude inventory-information about paradigmatic phenomena.

[18] Examples such as these may well give us trouble the first time they are encountered; they then differ in this respect from *the aged chemistry professor.*

In what we are concerned with, this kind of knowledge has to do with the ways in which we order the information we have acquired from the observation of instances. It has to do with our understanding of *la langue*, an understanding only small fragments of which may be called into play when we produce any single appropriate sentence. We draw upon this both in such production and also in evaluating and attempting to understand what others produce. To take a very simple example, it is a fragment of this knowledge which forbids me to say (except in some kind of a whimsical register): *The rhododendron bush passed away*. And for pedagogical purposes we must necessarily sometimes isolate such a fragment and formulate it separately. We can then treat by themselves, when need arises, just such problems as that of the difference between the ranges of *die* and of *pass away*.

It is necessary to say this because there is too often a tendency for people dealing with a language to retreat from the handling of the trickier kinds of difficulty of this sort, suggesting as they do so that some difficulties are just not amenable to rigorous treatment in comparative isolation. They often speak as though only a total possession of the whole *Sprachgefühl* in all its sophistication can be of much avail in solving a person's difficulties with such things as the choice between *gehen* and *fahren* in German or *ser* and *estar* in Spanish. It is true that there are complex and far-reaching problems of range in the more complicated aspects of such cases. But it is not true to maintain that they cannot profitably be isolated, and thereafter handled in such a way, for the benefit of children or foreigners, as to make up in a large measure for the fact that such learners have not had full 'natural' opportunities to accumulate (as a mature native has) a sufficiency of ordered information relevant to a mastery of the problem in question.

We may also regard this systemic knowledge of range as crucial when we are considering certain aspects of the use of English by experienced native speakers or writers. For it is very much tied up with the generative or range-extending process whereby it is possible at all for unusual collocations to be added to those already experienced.[19] A great number of new collocations which, though new, we readily include in the category 'normal' are perhaps of merely minor interest. These are examples of the 'range-filling-in' type, where, though we have never encountered

[19] A matter quite as important as range-extending is the process whereby range is constricted through the abandoning of previously familiar uses, or the more complicated but also more common situation where the range is constricted at one point but extended at another. In all this there are parallels to what happens with grammatical patterns.

them before (and we may well not suspect this at all), the nature of the range in which they fall is virtually unmodified by the new instance. An example would be that where I merely added *rhododendron bush* to my previous experience of plant names which collocate with *die* in a subject-predicate relation.

It would not be just, I think, to classify within this 'normal' category all such cases as pass unnoticed when we first encounter them. For it is almost certainly true that a great many range-extending collocations are of a kind which also pass unnoticed in this way. If this were not so, it would hardly be possible to explain the enormous range drift, affecting so very much of the lexis, which has taken place and is at present taking place in English. If we were to make boggling or raised eyebrows the criterion for range-extending instances, it would have to be objected, I think, that these indications of something odd having happened simply do not occur often enough, in our individual experiences, to account for more than a small proportion of the drift. This amounts to saying that the dictates of range are such as to permit the admission of new exponents on the very margin of tolerability without our even feeling that these are in any way dubitable. Sometimes of course we may find that there is disagreement about what is dubitable, and it is no accident that what is not felt to be at all marginal or odd by younger speakers may well be felt by the elderly to be barely on or even well beyond the edge of acceptability.[20]

At other times we are aware of instances which seem daring and innovatory, which seem (though we may not put it so) to involve a real extension of range. Some instances of this kind may quickly affect a considerable proportion of the speakers of a language; for instance we may begin to be aware that many people are using the word *smashing* with a strange meaning or in a strange way, as perhaps in *We had a smashing time yesterday evening*. This implies that we are aware of having begun to hear the word *smashing* in environments (situational as well as linguistic) which hitherto we should certainly have considered inappropriate not only because of their being out of our previous experience but also because of being beyond what our range-sense would regard as even marginally tolerable.

Other instances of unusual collocations may be much more *occasional*,

[20] This of course applies also to lexical items as such and to grammatical patterns as well. Furthermore, in the case of lexis-range and pattern constriction, it may be the young who question the acceptability of something which is regarded as normal by the elderly.

even perhaps unique. These are the kind which tend to be of such importance in literature, and especially in poetry. They are part of the machinery whereby the prose writer or the poet strives, over a larger or smaller stretch of text, to convey something which he cannot achieve by normal means, and he thereby sets us a problem in which we can lean on no experience of directly relevant instances. It may be of course that in a given case we are in the presence of the very birth of something which thereafter passes into general use and from then on forms part of the normal inventory of collocations involving the words in question; so with various phrases adopted into the language from Shakespeare and the Bible. It would be an interesting study to attempt to determine what there was about them that led to their adoption on this scale while others often no less striking, passed virtually unnoticed. In cases of this latter sort the flavour of the collocation, unsullied by subsequent general employment, will tend to remain sharp and distinctive. But in either event we encounter the same general problem of the nature of the impact of unusual collocations at the time of their first use.

This problem is complicated by a factor which cannot be treated here, but which I mention because it is often lost sight of. If, contrary to normal practice, two words x and y are collocated, there is a common tendency to assume that the resultant phrase exemplifies a rare use of x only or of y only, i.e. that the oddity belongs somehow to one of the forms and not to both. It is true that there are often good reasons for looking at the matter in this way; very often everything in a whole sentence seems quite normal except one word which sticks out from all the others. When this happens, the reaction we have is based on attitudes about the expected or tolerated range of words and we can easily persuade ourselves that only one word is behaving in a curious way collocationally. But we must not forget that to look at the matter in this way is illusory; the collocational oddity must involve at least one other word quite intimately, and we are led astray simply by the fact that (though this is so) the meaning of this other word does not seem to be affected to anything like the same degree. This may well be, and it is part of the fascination of the whole business, but to concentrate exclusively and on the word in question is not to exhaust the interest of the collocation.

I shall conclude with one or two remarks about structurally very simple collocations in which we can most easily ask ourselves where the oddity lies, and why it should seem to be concentrated on one word in many cases. If I encounter for the first time the collocation *steel postage-stamp*, I am likely, I think, to modify my views (if I may so put the matter in everyday terms) about postage-stamps rather than about steel. And so with *rubber book* or *transparent dog* or *talking bear*. But with *hammering weekend*, in similar circumstances, I feel that it would be the adjective to which I should have to adjust, and a weekend would remain much the same thing in my mind as before. And so perhaps with *constipated river* or *witty putt*. Profitable work could be done on the factors which operate to focus our attention on particular words in this way on some occasions and to produce quite different reactions on others, such as in those cases where the oddity seems to lie in the phrase as a whole, and the somewhat eccentric implied relationship, rather than anything remarkable which seems to have happened to the meaning of either word. My own collocation *waste-paper-basket sentence* will serve as an example of something in this kind. An investigation of this problem would certainly have to pay due attention to two factors: the role which the items concerned play in the grammatical structure, and the 'power' of each item in informational terms, i.e. the relative degree of restriction of their accepted collocational range.

What I have tried to deal with is one or two aspects of the problem of the choice or decision which confronts us continually in using language, even within a prescribed framework of grammatical patterns. In particular I have tried to deal with the factor of *range*, and to suggest that the term might profitably be used in connection with lexis in a sense whereby it then answers to what, on the grammatical side, I have labelled *pattern*. Pattern has to do with the structures of the sentences we make; range has to do with the specific collocations we make in a series of particular instances. Since collocations, in larger and larger units, are the material out of which instances of sentences are made, it is these considerations of range which we must take into account, within the dictates of pattern, in dealing with the text of actual sentences. I have thus attempted to bring into the open a number of questions that tend to be overlooked by those who focus their attention on matters of grammatical pattern to the exclusion of almost everything else.